Also by Mindy Aloff
Night Lights: Poems

DANCE ANECDOTES

Stories from the Worlds of Ballet, Broadway,
the Ballroom, and Modern Dance

MINDY ALOFF

OXFORD
UNIVERSITY PRESS

2006

OXFORD

UNIVERSITY PRESS

Oxford University Press, Inc., publishes works that
further Oxford University's objective of excellence
in research, scholarship, and education.

Oxford   New York
Auckland   Cape Town   Dar es Salaam   Hong Kong   Karachi
Kuala Lumpur   Madrid   Melbourne   Mexico City   Nairobi
New Delhi   Shanghai   Taipei   Toronto

With offices in
Argentina   Austria   Brazil   Chile   Czech Republic   France   Greece
Guatemala   Hungary   Italy   Japan   Poland   Portugal   Singapore
South Korea   Switzerland   Thailand   Turkey   Ukraine   Vietnam

Published by Oxford University Press, Inc.
198 Madison Avenue, New York, NY 10016
www.oup.com

Oxford is a registered trademark of Oxford University Press

Library of Congress Cataloging-in-Publication Data
Aloff, Mindy, 1947–
Dance anecdotes : stories from the worlds of ballet, Broadway,
the ballroom, and modern dance / by Mindy Aloff.
p. cm.
Includes bibliographical references and index.
ISBN-13: 978-0-19-505411-8
ISBN-10: 0-19-505411-3
1. Dance—Anecdotes. 2. Dancers—Anecdotes. I. Title.
GV1594.A46 2006
792.8—dc22
2005024553

1 3 5 7 9 8 6 4 2
Printed in the United States of America
on acid-free paper

To my father, Jack Aloff, genius,
and to the memory of my mother, Selma Album Aloff, genius loci

Contents

Preface

This is a book of stories about dancing from all over the globe. I wanted to put together the kind of collection that one might pick up in a country inn on a rainy day and while away an hour browsing through: the group as a whole is subjective and partial. For dance fans and balletomanes, I've tried to avoid repeating many of the most famous dance anecdotes and, instead, to choose those that might be unexpected. Some of the stories are recent, and some are ancient.

Although novelty was my concern, history was my guide. Dance has inspired the sweetest, noblest, and most affecting stories of any of the arts, and in constructing this anthology I was thinking, especially, of readers whose first encounter with the variety and shadings of the dancer's world might take place in these pages. It is my hope, too, that the fragments here will prompt readers to seek out the wonderful books listed in the bibliography, from which most of the anecdotes have been drawn.

M.A.

DANCE ANECDOTES

Towering Figures

Marie Taglioni (1804–1884)

Why She Was Great

Choreographer, teacher, artistic director of several ballet companies, holder of a master's degree in arts and literature, and co-author (with Jean-Pierre Pastori) of the book, *Tradition*, Pierre Lacotte is best known internationally for his attempts to reconstruct works from the repertory of nineteenth-century ballet that were hitherto considered lost. He embarked on his first reconstruction in 1968, when he discovered documents concerning Filippo Taglioni's landmark 1832 production of *La Sylphide*, starring the choreographer's daughter and principal pupil, Marie—an encounter that led Lacotte to reconstruct the ballet for a televised production and, in 1972, for the Paris Opéra, which had first performed *La Sylphide* nearly a century and a half before and where Lacotte himself had been a premier danseur in the 1950s. He is certainly among the leading authorities on Marie Taglioni in our time. In the following account, Lacotte gives a historian's idea of *La Sylphide*'s opening night and of the ballerina's contribution:

> Until the 1820's were seen what we call "ballets d'action." The ballerinas, generally dressed "à la grecque," danced in a very realistic manner. . . ."Provocative smiles, poses bordering on the obscene," to quote Veron. The ballet master, Auguste Vestris, used to say to his dancers: "Be coquettish, give to your every movement the greatest liberty possible. Before and after each pas, you must inspire love; everyone in the parterre and the orchestra must want you in his bed." Ten years later, [Filippo] Taglioni was to say the exact opposite: "Your dancing must be imbued with austerity, delicacy, and taste. Women and young girls must be able to watch you dancing without blushing."

Everything changed on the evening of March the 12th, 1832; this was a turning point in the history of ballet. In the milky white light of the gas lamps (which had only just recently been installed in the theater), the ballerinas made their appearance; they were light, modest, dressed in white. The costume [that] Eugène Lami had designed for them was, and still is, a chef d'oeuvre: The romantic tutu—long line; bras that left the shoulders bare; the skirt, which was white and diaphanous. The proportions were perfect; they allowed free movement and brought out the best in the dancing.

And, then, these "sylphides" covered long patterns on [their] pointes. In the period just prior to the première of *La Sylphide*, certain ballerinas had been seen in Vienna, in St. Petersburg, and in Paris rising on pointe, but the result was not always a happy one. This was the first time that the entire stage was crossed with ease. One can only imagine how impressed the audience was with these aerial passages, and how unreal everything seemed when, in [the] course of this two-act ballet, unseen wires lifted the ballerinas into the air.

In addition, a certain young woman of 28, Marie Taglioni, had the main role. She was the daughter of the author-choreographer of this *Sylphide*. Marie's renown had been gaining in luster over the previous seasons; she had enchanted the Paris public a few months earlier in the divertissement of the opera *Robert le Diable*. On this particular evening, however, she demonstrated that she was an artist of genius. "Her feet seem not to touch the ground," ". . . she walks on flowers without damaging them," were the reactions of critics and poets. . . .

She never showed the beginning or the end of a pas. Her style was fluid, smooth, distinguished but never affected. When she was dancing at a fast tempo with extraordinary precision, she would suddenly slow her movements down as if she were holding her breath, and the lie would be so subtle, so delicate, that she would appear to belong no longer to the terrestrial sphere, that she would become immaterial, unreal.

Her way of using pointes, which had just recently been invented and which no one could employ with her ease, was another trump in her performance. She seemed to float on the tips of her toes, accomplishing the most difficult movements with extraordinary facility and charm.

She was the first dancer to balance on one foot. This was not an attempt to create an effect but rather a means of punctuating a movement, similar to an organ point on a note which is held for a short time. She never finished a pirouette with an accent intended to demonstrate her virtuosity; on the contrary, she made an effort to finish smoothly, so that the movement looked simple, natural. She delayed the ends of her turns and the descents from her pointes so as to finish with grace, marking an opening of the hands, just after the music, the end of the pirouette. This expression of good taste astonished and subjugated the audience.

—Lacotte, unpaginated

Endless Pleasure at the Paris Opéra

In 1860, the great nineteenth-century Danish choreographer, August Bournonville (1805–1879), published eight essays on the ballet, in French, in the form of "Letters" (*Lettres sur la danse et la choréographie*). These clearly articulated personal writings appeared in the Parisian weekly *L'Europe artiste*, and— as much fine journalistic writing often used to—evolved from conversations with an enlightened editor, in this case, the founding editor of *L'Europe artiste*, Charles Desolme. In the following paragraph from the Third Letter, an appreciation of Marie Taglioni, the leading ballerina of the Romantic period, Bournonville functions as a critic in the sense that he conveys something of what his cherished art ought to be able to achieve, even though it rarely does:

The arrival of *Mlle Marie Taglioni* (1827) heralded a new era for the dance at the Opéra. This excellent dancer had an expression of innocence, a youthful freshness that, without inspiring voluptuousness, charmed the heart with endless pleasure. She was a real sylph, a daughter of the waves, a virtuous maiden, a young lady of good family, in short everything that can be imagined as pure, gracious, and poetic, combined with a talent whose outstanding quality was an airy lightness. It gave great satisfaction, both to the professional and to the amateur, to see her appear on stage, since the former was happy that he, too, professed such a charming art, and the latter was struck by a poetry he had previously thought impossible to find in dance; finally, she represented to me the living image of Terpsichore, in spite of the imperfections that more malevolent eyes than mine took the trouble to try to find in her. The finest praise of her, and thus of her profession, was expressed by a serious old gentleman who, on his way to a performance by the famous dancer, told me in passing: "Sir, I am going to the Opéra to have a lesson in good taste."

—Bournonville, *Letters*, pp. 37–38

Not Amused

One prominent friend of the choreographer August Bournonville, the writer and fellow Dane Hans Christian Andersen (1805–1875), frequently attended the ballet; as a young man, he wanted to study it as well. Andersen first saw Taglioni when she was already middle-aged, and, like the twentieth-century dance critic Edwin Denby (who wrote of Taglioni as a wizened Victorian), he exhibits no deference to the ballerina for the effects she might have achieved in her own youth, invoking a phrase from Virgil ("We Trojans are lost!") to express the depth of his objection to her in a late-career performance he attended in London, in 1847:

She danced in *Les Pas des Déesses*. Before she appeared, I felt a throbbing of my heart, which I always have when my expectation is raised for something excellent and grand.

She appeared as an old, little, sturdy, and quite pretty woman; she would have been a nice lady in a saloon, but as a young goddess—*fuimus Troes!*
—Andersen, pp. 297–298

On Perfection and Beauty

Tamara Karsavina, trained at the Imperial Ballet School, was a ballerina of uncommon theatrical gifts, both lyrical and dramatic. A keen analyst of ballet technique and ballet pantomime, she was a principal dancer with Diaghilev's Ballets Russes and a favorite of Diaghilev's and his circle for her keen intelligence and devotion to ballet as an art.

In pursuit of contemporary ideals, our stage lost sight of what may seem a paradox but is a truth—that the ends of choreographic beauty are not always best served by perfect physical harmony. Some of Taglioni's most exquisite poses had their origin in the fact that her arms were disproportionately long.

—Karsavina, p. 70

Foot

6/25/83: Leningrad—Petrodvorets [Peterhof palace]
In a small building on the palace grounds, in the section marked "Mon plaisir," an exhibition of "Ballet Relics," probably from the Leningrad Theater Museum says Tania, our guide.

A carving of Taglioni's naked foot on ¾ pointe—first two toes quite long, then third + fourth toes recede. The fifth is a stub. The arch is high, as in Greek sculpture.

—Aloff, unpaginated

Diamond Pinpoint

Taglioni's physical qualities as a ballerina and her ethereal effects were to some extent captured by artists of her time in engravings and lithographs that showed her in aspects of her various roles while she was at the height of her powers. Prized by collectors and frequently reprinted in books for generations after her death, the best of them serve as both factual reports on her art and also interpretive appreciations of it, and they have certainly inspired many dancers. One of those was the dancer Tamara Geva, who, as a child in St. Petersburg at the turn of the twentieth century, was introduced to some pictures of Taglioni by her father, a sophisticated art collector with sufficient resources to pursue his tastes, which usually ran to cutting-edge work, although not in this instance:

Every Saturday, he changed all the paintings on our living room walls. I used to sit and watch him take down the old paintings and replace them with a new crop. . . . One day, Father hung six pictures everybody understood. They were large engravings of Maria [*sic*] Taglioni, caught in quite improbable dancing attitudes—floating on a cloud, balancing on one toe on the tip of a flower, or leaping high over a brook. In her diaphanous tutu, with her swanlike neck and spiraling curls, she transcended anything that my imagination had concocted thus far, and she promptly entered my private world of dreams. . . . Father explained to me that she had gained fame by being the first dancer to get up on her toes, and that information was nearly fatal. I almost broke my ankles trying to imitate her. She became a diamond pinpoint on the horizon— a goal.

Next Saturday Taglioni was gone, and paintings of clouds took her place, but her ghost was to remain with me for years and years to come.

—Geva, pp. 20–21

Taglioni's Jewel Casket

On a moonlight night in the winter of 1835 / the carriage of Marie Taglioni was halted by a Russian highwayman, and that enchanting creature was commanded to dance for this audience of one / upon a panther's skin spread over the snow beneath the stars. From this actuality arose the legend that, to keep alive the memory / of this adventure so precious to her, Taglioni formed the habit of placing a piece of artificial ice in her jewel casket or dressing table / melting among the sparkling stones, there was evoked a hint of the atmosphere of the starlit heavens over the ice-covered landscape.

From Joseph Cornell's box construction *Homage to the Romantic Ballet* (1942). The anecdote is based on one related in *An Englishman in Paris* (1892) by Albert D. Vandam, who had met with Taglioni in 1844, when she told him the story, adding, "I have never had such an appreciative audience either before or afterwards."

—Starr, pp. 13–14

Marie Taglioni: Good Vibrations

"Je ne sentais presque point la terre. Réellement je vibrais dans l'air."

—Lacotte, unpaginated

("I scarcely felt the earth at all. In truth, I quivered in the air.")

—(Christopher Caines, trans.)

Anna Pavlova (1881–1931)

She Might Catch Us by the Throat

During the Victorian era of her childhood and adolescence, Pavlova's magnificently proportioned physique was considered uncommonly delicate for a ballet dancer. The ballerina Tamara Karsavina, another student at the Imperial School in St. Petersburg, remembered in her memoirs, *Theatre Street*, that Pavlova was considered so unbecomingly and unhealthily thin that she was administered regular doses of cod liver oil. It didn't help in a period that prized buxomness and muscular virtuosity: her famously slender body, despite its preternatural fluency and expressiveness, was disparagingly reviewed in the early years of her career.

Pavlova was a different breed of cat from the whirlwind turners and athletic jumpers who provided the models of virtuosity when she began to perform. Not until her 1910 Paris season with Diaghilev's Ballets Russes did her genius for rendering a choreographer's particular style while connecting intimately with an audience begin to be celebrated on its own terms. By the time she formed her own company, World War I also had radically changed cultural expectations of feminine beauty. Pavlova scorned jazz; however, it was in the era of the boyish flapper that her body could be fully appreciated as a feminine ideal. And yet, unlike the ballerina (and sometime rival) Olga Spessivtzeva, another delicately built dancer, Pavlova is not remembered for her classical purity as much as for her spontaneity and charisma. Her face and her abandon within her roles are what seemed to move audiences most. One of Pavlova's students and dancers in her company, Muriel Stuart, who went on to dance for George Balanchine in America and later to become a revered teacher at his School of American Ballet, gives a sense of those elements. When Stuart told Pavlova that she was leaving the company to marry, Pavlova said, "If you insist upon marriage, please have a child . . . because I never did."

Oh, she was extraordinary looking. She had an ivory complexion. I wouldn't say she was a beautiful woman, but she transcended beauty. She had those dark, piercing eyes. She was the sort of person who could, as they say, see from the back of her head. And, she had the uncanny ability of sensing what was right and what was wrong. . . . In performance, I've never seen anything greater in my life. When she danced Giselle, we were almost terrified of her in the first act, because we used to so *believe* her madness, that she might catch us by the throat, that we were lucky if we got away. It was extraordinary! I would say that, basically, Pavlova was a lyrical poetess in her movements. Of course, today, dancers are much more prepared technically. Pavlova never did *fouettés*—she didn't have the strength for them. She was simply an artist.

—Gruen, pp. 41, 42

Antique Epigraph

Although Pavlova was showered with costly and precious gifts during her career, and—as her erstwhile American impresario Sol Hurok noted, she left an estate of a half million dollars (Otto H. Kahn had managed her securities)—she was also known throughout her life for living with comparative modesty, storing her jewels and furs in a vault and spending most of her earnings on her company. One of her dancers, Sylvia Kirkwhite, remembered that "her company was better paid than any other ballet company of the day," and several of her dancers have testified to her efforts to teach the young English dancers she employed to dress well yet without ostentation. In our age, it is very difficult to believe, or even to understand fully, the principles by which Pavlova conducted her life and career; however, principles they were, as the following passage by the writer A.H. Franks explains:

> She appeared in New York for the first time in 1910. Here, the touch of her foot and the flutter of her arms turned everything into dollars. Yet, in spite of the vast sums she earned in the U.S.A., no taint of vulgarity marked any of her activities, either on stage or off stage. It was the custom then, almost as much as it is today, for famous personalities to lend the luster of their names, for enviable sums of course, toward the promotion of the sale of breakfast foods and patent medicines; but although she was constantly besieged by tempting offers, Pavlova never permitted her name to be used in this way. Her agents and impresarios obtained publicity for her by far more judicious and dignified but nevertheless extremely successful methods. Sol Hurok, too, the famous American impresario who promoted her tours in the U.S.A., although he kept her name continuously in bright lights, illumined only her fame, and never employed sensational stunts.
>
> Throughout her life, Pavlova shrank from any kind of scandal. From what little evidence remains available today I do not doubt that this warm and passionate creature had her affairs of the heart, but far from flaunting them she regarded them as essentially of a private and even sacred nature. Any tinge of scandal would have cheapened her to herself, and throughout her life her own opinion of herself remained far more important to her than the opinion of others.
>
> —Franks, pp. 19–20, 83

To See Her Dance

Diwan Chamanlall, ambassador from India to Turkey, in a 1949 interview with the dancer Ram Gopal:

> It was to me, a Hindu, a religious experience to see her dance. Her spirit and her expression reached out and touched me, carried me away, uplifted me and filled my eyes with tears, for in her art was great tragedy, a great veil of sorrow. In the dance she seemed to create an image of all

classical music and drama and all the pathetic helplessness of the striving
of the human spirit imprisoned within its mortal frame, seeking to burst
forth and escape. . . . I have seen the great ballerinas of today, French,
English, and American, and I have no doubt they have attempted to turn
faster, jump higher, and balance according to the rigid standards required
today; but, much as I admire their industry, they seem to lack that spirit
with which Pavlova imbued every movement. When Pavlova danced there
were no strained neck muscles, no hurried movements, no conscious "timing"; it was the whole effect of the spirit of her dances that enraptured
and intoxicated one. It was indescribable, and in the world of Western
ballet I have not seen her like.

—Franks, p. 99

Pigeonholed

In 1915, Pavlova saw the Nebraska-born aspiring dancer and painter Hubert
Stowitts (1892–1953) performing in San Francisco and invited him to join
her company. Canceling his plans to attend graduate school at Harvard, he
toured with her for several years before leaving to pursue a solo career, eventually landing in the Folies-Bergère, costumed by Erté:

According to many of her colleagues, Pavlova constantly desired to create certain modern works but felt that her public would not favor such
works. From time to time she discussed the possibilities of such projects
with whatever partner she happened to have at the time. Stowitts, for
instance, wrote the following:
"On the way to South America, we walked the decks together for hours
discussing ballets we wanted to do. Sometimes she would cry because
she was not permitted to experiment, to be modern, to do the new things
that she wanted to do . . . she wanted to do modern ballets that we outlined together. She realized that most people thought she could only do
the conventional—the traditional dances—and that hurt her."

—Franks, p. 39

In the last year of her life, Pavlova was planning to commission a ballet from
the young Frederick Ashton.

A Philosophy of Life

The dancers in Pavlova's company have gone on record with their memories of her unparalleled dedication to the ballet; her self-discipline and energy, which surpassed that of dancers half her age; her combination of
generosity offstage and severity in the classroom if she thought the dancers
were slacking off; her insistence that they dress and conduct themselves according to a high standard of style and understatement. But the strongest

memories one finds are of her demand that they be compleat artists—that, on tour, they visit museums in their off hours or read classic or enlightening books rather than "lurid" magazines, potboilers, or bodice-rippers; that they waste no time in an effort to feed their intellects and their senses. Perhaps the most penetrating remembrance of Pavlova's effect on young dancers is the following one by Muriel Stuart, who, as a child, studied with the ballerina and later performed in her company:

> What she imparted to us was a philosophy of life. She would give us a class in the morning, and then, afterward, she would gather us around her chair. She would say, "Look, you're going to take a bus or a train to get home. You'll see lots of people when you're in this bus or train. Well, I want you to look at all the faces around you, and you'll see someone who is sad or angry. You must feed yourself through your eyes as well as your ears. If you're going to be an artist, you must do this. This is just as important as the exercises you did with me this morning. You must try to understand people. You must try to understand *why* they behave as they do. One day you *will* dance on the stage, and you must think that if you can make one sad person in the audience happy, even for a moment, you'll begin to be a little bit of an artist." She said these things to us very often. Of course, we didn't really understand all this at the time. I mean, we used to think how strange she was.
>
> —Gruen, p. 39

Ballerina to Ballerina-to-Be

As a ballet student of the Russian émigrée Serafima Astafieva, in London, the ballerina Alicia Markova (1910–2004) proved to be a child prodigy. Serge Diaghilev saw her in Astafieva's class when she was ten years old and invited her to join his Ballets Russes when she was fourteen. However, before there was Diaghilev, there was Pavlova, as Markova remembers:

> I don't think it entered my head that I wanted to be a dancer. Even when my parents took me to see Pavlova, it never entered my head. Of course, I was deeply impressed. I thought Pavlova was absolutely out of this world! I thought she was *so* beautiful, but I was merely an admirer, and I was only nine years old. . . . After the performance I was brought backstage to meet her. I was already spinning like a top, having been enrolled in Astafieva's class. Well, Pavlova told my father that I might come and visit her the following morning. Naturally, I was thrilled. And, so, I went to Ivy House. She started putting me to work in her studio by giving me a barre. . . .
>
> After the barre, Pavlova told me something amazing. She said that the most important thing for me to remember was to take very good care of my teeth. I've never forgotten that. She was so right, because bad teeth

can affect your whole body. After she told me that, she asked me to get out of my work clothes and rub myself down with alcohol or eau de cologne. Well, I hadn't brought anything like that along. I said to her, "But I had my bath this morning, Madame Pavlova." She disappeared, and in two minutes came back with a beautiful towel and a flask with cologne, which had her initials on it, painted in gold. "Here," she said. "Rub yourself down, because after working, your pores are open, and it is dangerous to rush out without first having a thorough rubdown." I did as she told me. All the while, I was eyeing the cologne flask she had left with me with the initials "A.P." on it. But I didn't. She might never have asked me back.

—Gruen, p. 45

"PAVLOVA MUFFS FIRST DATE IN THIRTY YEARS"

As her American impresario, admirer, and friend, Sol Hurok, remembered, this was the cable to the New York newspapers on January 20, 1931, that signaled the ballerina's imminent death at the age of fifty. (Embarking on a final world tour, she had arrived at The Hague on a train from Paris, suffering from what had started as a cold, and could not perform.) "Her death was tragically unnecessary," Hurok went on. "She should not have been making those killing tours, travelling in the bad winter months, sitting in ill-heated trains on long, jolting rides, suffering fatigue, courting illness." Hurok noted that she didn't need the money. "Why then did she work until she died of it?" he asked and offered one answer:

I have my own theory of course, as everyone who knew her had. I believe she could not live without working, because she had emptied her life of everything but work, and it was by then too late to turn back and taste the kind of living she had missed. In another world, under another system, she would have been cherished as a jewel. She would have worked perhaps a few months of the year, would have danced perhaps once or twice a week. She would have had time and leisure, both for working and for living, for love and children and the exquisite art of being happy.

—Franks, pp. 61–62

Anna Pavlova: A True Artist

In my opinion a true artist must devote herself wholly to her art. She has no right to lead the life that most women long for.

The wind rustles through the branches of the fir trees in the forest opposite the veranda, the forest through which, as a child, I longed to rove. The stars shine in the evening gloom. I have come to the end of these few recollections. While writing them down I began to realize more fully the purpose of my life and its unity. To tend, unfailingly, unflinchingly, towards a goal, is the secret of success. But success? What exactly is success? For me it is to be found not in applause but in the satisfaction of feeling that one is realizing one's ideal. When, a small child, I was rambling over there by the fir trees, I thought that success spelled happiness.

I was wrong. Happiness is like a butterfly which appears and delights us for one brief moment, but soon flits away.

—Franks, pp. 123–124

Vaslav Nijinsky (1890–1950)

Le Spectre de la rose

Everyone who saw Nijinsky in this ballet will recall that wonderful leap by which he entered from the rose garden, through the open French window, to alight beside the young girl asleep in her chair. There was a rose-colored flash, and he was seen to describe a graceful parabola with the ease of a grasshopper leaping from one blade of grass to another. There was no flurry, no strained features, no thud as the feet came to the ground; it was just as though a rose petal had been caught up by a night breeze and wafted through the open window.

Le Spectre de la rose achieved a furor wherever it was given. On one occasion, when it was danced at an official charity performance held at the Grand Opéra, Paris, it achieved so overwhelming a success that, in response to the clamors of the audience for an encore, the whole was repeated—an unprecedented event for Paris.

—Beaumont, p. 586

The Rose Backstage

After kissing the young girl, the ghost of the rose leaps out the window . . . and drops down among the attendants, who spit water in his face and rub him down with Turkish towels, like a boxer. What a combination of grace and brutality! I will always hear the thunder of the applause; I will always see that young man smeared with rouge, gasping, sweating, pressing one hand to his heart and holding onto a prop with the other, or even collapsed in a chair. Then, after being slapped, sprayed, and shaken, he went back before the curtain to bow and smile. (Jean Cocteau)

—Steegmuller, p. 84

Near the Stars

Polish-born dancer Marie Rambert, sometimes called "the mother of British ballet," is known for her fostering of the early choreography of Frederick

Ashton and Antony Tudor. However, before she moved to England at the outbreak of World War I, she was employed by Serge Diaghilev as a kind of dance translator for Nijinsky—drawing on her training in eurhythmics to communicate the complex counts and iconoclastic movement ideas of his choreography to the dancers of the Ballets Russes. Rambert seems truly to have loved Nijinsky, and she paid him the supreme compliment in her memoirs of describing him carefully:

He had such a high arch and such strength and suppleness of foot that the sole of one foot could clasp the back of the ankle of the other, as though it were a hand (in the position *sur le cou de pied*). . . . One is often asked whether his jump was really as high as it is always described. To that I answer: 'I don't know how far from the ground it was, but I know it was near the stars.' . . .

The most absurd theories were put forward about his anatomy. People said that the bones in his feet were like a bird's—as though a bird flew because of its feet! But, in fact, he *did* have an exceptionally long Achilles tendon, which allowed him with his heels firmly on the ground and the back upright to bend the knees to the utmost before taking a spring, and he had powerful thighs. As to his famous poising in the air, he indeed created the illusion of it by the ecstasy of his expression at the apex of the leap, so that *this* unique moment penetrated into every spectator's consciousness, and seemed to last. His landing, from whatever height he jumped, was like a cat's. He had that unique touch of the foot on the ground. . . .

—Rambert, p. 60

Disappearing Act

There was a definite puppet-like quality about Nijinsky's Petrouchka. He seemed to have limbs of wood and a face made of plaster, in which his eyes resembled nothing so much as two boot buttons. Only now and then did he make you aware that beneath this façade there was a tiny spark of human life, which you caught sight of by accident, as though it were something you were not meant to see. Gone were those fascinating features with the slanting eyes, that marvelous elevation—all had vanished, to be replaced by this wretched puppet—beaten, humiliated, and the sport of its fellows—a victim of cruel injustice, which moved by jerks and starts and hardly left the ground. Nijinsky's Petrouchka was a puppet that sometimes aped a human being; all the other interpreters of the role that I have seen suggested a dancer who was imitating a puppet.

—Beaumont, p. 590

America Weighs In

In 1916, Diaghilev's Ballets Russes made its first and only tour of the United States—without Diaghilev. The tour was something of a disaster. Nijinsky, who was running the company as well as dancing, couldn't cope well with the stress; and U.S. audiences and newspapers had no context for some of the company's repertory. Even *Le Spectre de la rose*, which enjoyed a ten-minute ovation in the theater, prompted *Musical America* to speak of Nijinsky's "unprepossessing effeminacy." The dancer's account of the title role in Michel Fokine's *Narcisse* prompted one headline that read:

> "NIJINSKY DANCES: AUDIENCE LAUGHS . . . MYTHOLOGICAL POEM EFFEMINATE EXHIBIT. STORY OF NARCISSUS AND THE SPRING, TOLD TERPSICHOREAN FASHION, GREETED BY GIGGLES."

Nijinsky, himself, however, spoke eloquently to his critics in an interview at the time:

> One must be as a changing chameleon in the varying roles one enacts. . . . One must be prepared with shades to enhance one's meaning—in the morning, perhaps a boy, at noon a creature sans sex, at night a full-grown man. . . . For instance in *Narcisse*, there is no virility, only boyish pureness. Effeminate it is not—for even in adolescence a boy is not like a girl. True, he is not yet a man, any more than she is a woman, but there the resemblance ends. His thoughts and desires are different, therefore his movements are different.
>
> —Parker, pp. 163–164

"Manifold Nijinsky"

Henry Taylor Parker—music, theater, and dance critic for *The Boston Evening Transcript* between 1905 and 1934—interviewed Nijinsky when the Ballets Russes performed in Boston in 1916. The profile from which the lead has been excerpted below ran in the paper on November 9, 1916. The "vote" to which Parker refers was the close presidential election of 1916, which Woodrow Wilson finally won after some suspense during the counting.

> Seen on the stage in the illusion of personation, costume, action, Mr. Nijinsky seems a tall, even substantial figure. Seen in his own person in the quiet of his rooms or across a dinner table, he is actually of no more than medium height and of slender contours. A Slav unmistakable in the smallness of his head, the fineness of his features, the brightness of his narrow eyes, the mobility of sensitive mouth and chin. A dancer, or at least a personage of the theater in a flowing ease of carriage that has become a second nature. A man of the cultivated world, not only in the intonations of his speech, which is French, when it is not Russian, but also in the plasticity of his mind and manner—all three mirrors, as it were, of a quick sensibility to many varied interests. (Mr. Nijinsky may dwell and work apart, except when he is before his audiences, but he follows nonetheless the ways and the concerns of the immediate mankind about him, even to the conditions that make slow the counting of

the vote of California and Minnesota.) A man, finally, who is no mere dancer and mime by natural aptitudes, arduous training, assiduous application, and the general applause, but who kindles his artistries, faiths, and ambitions out of a keen and meditative mind and a finely touched and unquenchable spirit.

—Holmes, p. 125

On Nijinsky's Greater Gift

Dame Ninette de Valois, the formidable founder of what became Britain's Royal Ballet, performed as a soloist for Diaghilev, but not until the 1920s, some years after Nijinsky had disappeared into madness and left the stage:

I only saw Nijinsky dance once. . . .

I was very young when I went to Covent Garden to see *Les Sylphides*. I had been used to seeing Mikhail Mordkin, Pavlova's partner, a more august type of Russian male dancer. Suddenly, here was this very small boy, with hair down to his shoulders and wearing a strange costume; I am afraid I turned to my mother and said, "I don't like that man."

If we saw him dance now, he would perhaps not make the impression he did in his day. When you look at the photographs of him, so small and with those extraordinarily muscular legs and rather overdeveloped figure, I think today he would be regarded as a wonderful virtuoso dancer and kept for such roles as the Bluebird. I can't see him in the great *classical* roles—indeed, Diaghilev didn't use him a great deal in them, but kept him in virtuoso and distinguished *demi-caractère* parts.

He must have been wonderful and also a fine actor. . . . We must remember that we had never seen a male dancer with such a fantastic jump until he leapt into our midst, and his elevation was his greatest sensation as a dancer. But I do think he was perhaps an even greater choreographer. There seems to me to be no doubt that if he were alive today, it would be his choreographic ideas we would be chasing, rather than his great leaps.

—Parker, pp. 9, 11

Reality

When Nijinsky was on the point of leaving his theatrical career forever, he began to keep a diary. The three notebooks that comprise this diary are in Russian, and the story of their full publication in English is long and complicated. To sum it up: the diary was translated into English in 1978, yet the translation wasn't published until 1999. If you're interested in what Nijinsky actually wrote, and in what his horrific medical condition and treatment actually were, this is the edition to consult.

An earlier version of the diary, first published in 1936 and still available, turns out to have been a fragmentary and distorted representation of the original, made by Nijinsky's wife, Romola, with the assistance of Lincoln Kirstein, in order to cement Nijinsky's public reputation the way she thought it should be.

In a landmark essay to introduce the unexpurgated version, Nijinsky scholar Joan Acocella throws buckets of cold water on any sentimental idea about the ineluctable relationship between Nijinsky's genius and his insanity, or, indeed, on such a relationship in the matter of any artist. Acocella also gives a persuasive account of Nijinsky's tortured career as a choreographer for Serge Diaghilev. ("I worked like an ox, and I lived like a martyr," Nijinsky wrote.) She notes that most of the remembrances of him by his colleagues depict him as "remarkably introverted. At parties he would sit silently and pick his fingers. Even his wife, so protective of his reputation, reports that the dancers called him 'Dumb-bell' behind his back." And yet, she explains, he was also widely read in Russian literature and a creative artist of original ideas for his time. One of the tragedies of Nijinsky's life is that Igor Stravinsky, whose *Le Sacre du printemps* Nijinsky choreographed to legendary opprobrium in 1913, dismissed the choreographer's endeavor as unworthy of the music and maintained this point of view publicly until nearly the end of his life, when he changed his mind, conceding that the choreography was actually better than he had claimed. Stravinsky had tremendous influence, and the revision of his attitude toward Nijinsky seems to have freed such individuals as Kirstein to applaud Nijinsky's staging in print. The paragraph from Acocella's essay below—an outstanding example of dance scholarship as well as dance writing—is a summary of hundreds of pages of memoirs, histories, and newspaper ephemera; it also shows the writer's underlying compassion for the subject, which makes the writing sing:

These social difficulties made his choreographic career a nightmare at many points. The Ballets Russes dancers had been trained in the academic style. To induce them to forget all that and move like figures in an antique frieze or aborigines around a campfire required tact, patience, and excellent communication skills: precisely what he lacked. Sokolova says that when, in rehearsing *Faun*, he told her to move through rather than to the music, she burst into tears and ran out of the theater. Others stayed but loathed his work and let him know it. *Faun*, an eleven-minute ballet, is said to have required over a hundred hours of rehearsal. And Nijinsky had to deal with opposition not just from the dancers but also from his collaborators—Debussy, the composer for *Faun* and *Jeux*, disliked both ballets and said so—not to speak of critics and audiences. During the première of *The Rite of Spring* the uproar in the theater was so great that the dancers could not hear the music. Nijinsky stood in the wings, sweat coursing down his face, screaming the musical counts to the performers—a terrible image. Whatever the stresses of his career as a dancer, those of his choreographic career were probably greater.

—Acocella, *The Diary*, p. xiii

Nijinsky on Nijinsky

I did not want money. I wanted a simple life. I loved the theater and wanted to work. I worked hard, but later I lost heart because I noticed I was not liked. I withdrew into myself. I withdrew so deep into myself that I could not understand people. I wept and wept. . . . (Kyril FitzLyon, trans.)
—Acocella, *The Diary*, p. 145

Isadora Duncan (1877–1927)

The Parthenon: 1903 or 1904

Anyone who, arriving at the foot of the Acropolis, has mounted with prayerful feet toward the Parthenon, and at length standing before this monument of the one immortal Beauty, feeling his soul lifting towards this glorious form, realizing that he has gained that secret middle place from which radiate in vast circles all knowledge and all Beauty—and that he has arrived at the core and root of this beauty—who, lifting his eyes to the rhythmical succession of Doric columns, has felt "form" in its finest and noblest sense fulfill the spirit's highest want of form, that one will understand for what I am striving in my first dance tonight. It is my effort to express the feeling of the human body in relation to the Doric column.

For the last four months, each day I have stood before this miracle of perfection wrought of human hands. I have seen around it sloping the Hills, in many forms, but in direct contrast to them the Parthenon, expressing their fundamental idea. Not in imitation of the outside forms of nature, but in understanding of nature's great secret rules, rise the Doric columns.

The first days as I stood there my body was as nothing and my soul was scattered; but gradually called by the great inner voice of the Temple, came back the parts of my self to worship it: first came my soul and looked upon the Doric columns, and then came my body and looked—but in both were silence and stillness, and I did not dare to move, for I realized that of all the movements my body had made, none was worthy to be made before a Doric Temple. And, as I stood thus, I realized that I must find a dance whose effort was to be worthy of the Temple—or never dance again.

Neither Satyr nor Nymph had entered here, neither Shadows nor Bacchantes. All that I had danced was forbidden this Temple—neither love nor hate nor fear, nor joy nor sorrow—only a rhythmic cadence, those Doric columns—only in perfect harmony this glorious Temple, calm through all the ages.

For many days no movement came to me. And then one day came the thought: These columns which seem so straight and still are not really straight, each one is curving gently from the base to the height, each one is in flowing movement, never resting, and the movement of each is in harmony with the others. And, as I thought this, my arms rose slowly toward the Temple, and I leaned forward—and then I knew I had found my dance, and it was a Prayer.

—Isadora Duncan, *The Art*, pp. 64–65

The Spring of a Cat, the Wiggle of a Water Moccasin

Isadora Duncan was the first dancer in the West to intuit a kinesiological truth: that human movement starts in the spine and pelvis, not in the extremities—the legs and arms. That is: human movement, when it obeys the nature of its functioning, when it is not distorted by erroneous concepts of the mind, starts in the body's center of gravity and then—in correct sequence—flows into the extremities.

Photographs and drawings of Isadora Duncan indicate—and her writings try to say this, too—that she conceived the essence of movement to lie in transition, not in position. When she says "Study Nature," she means "flow organically," in arcs, like the spring of a cat, the wiggle of a water moccasin, the gallop of a horse, the wave on a beach, the toss of a ball, the bellying of a sail—not like a man's mind-contrived, inorganic machine, which essentially cannot move but only take position. (Erick Hawkins)

—Cohen, p. 41

"To Nijinsky she was 'the great inspiration.'"

The American journalist Mary Fanton Roberts, who provides this cameo, was one of Duncan's most perceptive friends, as well as one of the most loyal:

I recall one memorable time when a little party of us were together at a studio luncheon in New York, and both Isadora and Nijinsky were there. After the table had been cleared away, someone played the piano. I cannot recall who it was, but it was one of the great men playing divinely. And Isadora and Nijinsky danced together—Isadora creating the dance as the music flowed from the piano, and Nijinsky dancing with her as though he had rehearsed each entirely new measure for weeks. It was an amazing performance—Isadora's extraordinary power of instantaneous creation and Nijinsky's sensitive response to her mood and to the music.

—Isadora Duncan, *The Art*, p. 27

No Sex Appeal

Edward Craig, a son of the stage designer and theatrical visionary Gordon Craig, served as his father's assistant, collaborator, and confidant. In his biography of his father, he discusses Craig's liaison with Duncan, which had dimensions both personal (Craig fathered their daughter, Deirdre) and artistic. The British musician Martin Shaw (1875–1958), referred to below, was a close friend of Gordon Craig's.

> The names of Isadora Duncan and Gordon Craig have been coupled as "lovers" for so long that their real significance to each other has been lost under the fast-growing weeds of sentimentality and sensationalism.
>
> It was not Isadora's physical appearance that particularly attracted Craig (Martin Shaw even said that she was lacking in sex appeal). But she had the plump prettiness of a Colleen, "the tip-tilted nose and the firm little chin, and the dream in her heart of the Irish, who are so sweet to know"; most important of all, she was "full of natural genius which defies description."
>
> —Craig, p. 189

Isadora Duncan on Gordon Craig

> I do not know how other women remember their lovers. I suppose it is the correct thing to stop always at a man's head, shoulders, hands, etc., and then describe his clothes, but I always see him, as that first night in the studio, when his white, lithe, gleaming body emerged from the chrysalis of clothes and shone upon my dazzled eyes in all his splendor.
>
> So must Endymion, when first discovered by the glistening eyes of Diana, in tall, slender whiteness, so must Hyacinthus, Narcissus, and the brave, bright Perseus have looked. More like an angel of Blake than a mortal youth he appeared. Hardly were my eyes ravished by his beauty than I was drawn toward him, entwined, melted. As flame meets flame, we burned in one bright fire. Here, at last, was my mate; my love; my self—for we were not two, but one, that one amazing being of whom Plato tells in the Phaedrus, two halves of the same soul.
>
> This was not a young man making love to a girl. This was the meeting of twin souls. The light covering of flesh was so transmuted with ecstasy that earthly passion became a heavenly embrace of white, fiery flame. . . .
>
> When two weeks had passed, we returned to my mother's house; and, to tell the truth, in spite of my mad passion, I was a bit tired of sleeping on a hard floor, and having nothing to eat except what he could get from the delicatessen, or when we sallied out after dark.
>
> —Isadora Duncan, *My Life*, pp. 132–133

Storm

Irma Duncan, one of Isadora's adopted daughters and protégées (nicknamed "the Isadorables"), was the author of a memoir, *Duncan Dancer*, that is full of persuasively authentic remembrances:

> The future seemed bright for me and my schoolmates, too. Our dream had come true at last—to be studying once more with Isadora. . . .

The nineteenth of April [1913], that tragic turning point in Isadora Duncan's life, dawned wet and cold. We girls went as usual from our pension around the corner from the Rue Chauveau for our morning workout at the studio. A pleasant surprise awaited us. We found Deirdre and her little brother Patrick there playing games. They had come in that morning from Versailles, where they had spent the winter months. At the age of three, Patrick could not yet talk except for a few words, but he understood quite well when his nanny coaxed him to show us how his mama bowed to the audience at the end of a performance. Deirdre always acted bashful when asked to do something, but not Patrick. Like a real actor, he gave a cunning imitation of his famous mother acknowledging the applause. As we laughed and asked him to do it again, Isadora came in. She joined in the laughter and told us that we would all have luncheon at an Italian restaurant in town as the guests of Paris Singer [Patrick's father]. It was the last time we would all be so happily together.

We girls returned to our pension after lunch for our daily music lesson. Professor Edlinger, our teacher, had a nice baritone voice and loved to sing entire scores of operas, doing all the parts. That particular afternoon, while the rain continued unabated, he chose the stirring music of Wagner's *Die Walküre* for our lesson. All devout music lovers, we could sit and listen to him for hours.

While he sang Sigmund's impassioned "Winterstürme wichen dem Wonnemond," I watched the heavy rainstorm bending the budding trees outside on the lawn, tearing off the tender green shoots and scattering them about in its fury. With branches wildly waving, the trees seemed to be dancing grotesquely to Wagner's music.

The room felt cold and damp. I shivered and drew my woolen jacket closer about me. The hours passed. Twilight was descending when we reached that state of repleteness which beautiful music engenders and which is accompanied by a mild state of drowsiness. Then, suddenly, like one of the great composer's own leitmotifs, we were all roused from our lethargy by a frantic knocking at the front door. We heard a door slam and rapid footsteps approached our room.

Temple's father appeared pale and haggard-looking, like a phantom in the twilight. In a frantic state, his clothes dripping wet, he rushed to his daughter and held her tight. Frightened, she cried out in alarm, "What is the matter, father, what has happened?"

In a broken voice that sounded hollow in the gloom, he announced the dreadful news: "Isadora's children are dead."

—Irma Duncan, pp. 130–131

"Woolcot [*sic*] Hotel," New York City: 1917

Being temporarily deprived of the services of a personal maid, she was sitting on the bed sewing on a button when I happened to come in one day. Seeing her occupied with such a domestic chore gave me quite a start. It struck me for some reason as being very funny, and I started to laugh. "Why do you laugh?" she asked. "Do you think I am incapable of doing this sort of thing? I want you to know that I can also bake a very good peach pie. I bet that is more than you can do!"

She was right. We had been taught housekeeping at school, but not cooking. Our hands had to be beautiful for dancing. . . . She did not generally take life too seriously—only her art. She had a nice sense of humor and liked to tell amusing anecdotes that had happened to her.

—Irma Duncan, pp. 158–159

There Are Days

Just as there are days when my life seems to have been a Golden Legend studded with precious jewels, a flowery field with multitudes of blossoms, a radiant morn with love and happiness crowning every hour; when I have found no words to express my ecstasy and joy of life; when the idea of my school seems a ray of genius, or when I actually believe that, although not tangible, my school is a great success; when my Art is a resurrection; so there are other days when, trying to recollect my life, I am filled only with a great disgust and a feeling of utter emptiness. The past seems but a series of catastrophes and the future a certain calamity from the brain of a lunatic.

—Isadora Duncan, *My Life*, p. 245

"Isadora Duncan Is Dead."

Like her two children—who were killed, along with their governess, when their driverless car rolled down an embankment into the Seine—Duncan met her death in a bizarre auto accident, when the trailing scarf she was wearing as a passenger in a sportscar got caught in the spokes of one of the wheels, instantly breaking her neck when the car began to advance. Among the many published memorials to her is this touching remembrance by the journalist Max Eastman, originally published in *The Nation*:

Isadora Duncan was the last friend I saw when I left Europe this spring. She stood in the little crowd on the platform at the Gare Saint Lazare. I was standing at the car window, laughing and half crying at the sadly funny excitement of people parting with their friends, and suddenly I heard her voice calling my name and "Goodbye!" She raised her hand when I caught sight of her, and stood still with it raised in the air and moving slowly in a serene and strong benediction. A great beam of that energetic and perfectly idealistic light shone out of her eyes to me. She looked very great. She looked like a statue of real liberty.

—Isadora Duncan, *The Art*, p. 37

But, Why Was It Called *Diana*?

Late in 1929, the actor and writer Robert Benchley began reviewing theater
for *The New Yorker*. His first column, from December 21, included a notice
of a play called *Diana*, by Irving Kaye Davis, based on the life of Isadora
Duncan, who had died just two years before. *Diana* was a play in which stage
and silent screen star Jeanne Eagels, who died of complications from drug
and alcohol addiction in October 1929, was thinking of making a comeback.
Benchley doesn't say who actually took on the title role, although, consider-
ing his critique, that omission was probably a kindness:

> Probably eight out of ten people who read the autobiography of Isadora
> Duncan remarked to themselves: "There is a great play there! Someone
> ought to write it." And probably five out of each eight started to write it
> themselves. Out of all these starts, Irving Kaye Davis was the first to fin-
> ish and reach Broadway with his product. This was too bad, for some of
> the others must have been better. I was not so upset at the outrage to
> Isadora Duncan's memory as were many of the reviewers, but I was dis-
> appointed that it wasn't a better play. There should be a great play in that
> vivid, madcap career, and I hope that I do not further affront Isadora
> Duncan's admirers when I suggest that it be written by Edna Ferber and
> George Kaufman in much the same spirit as that in which they wrote *The
> Royal Family*. Maybe such tragic-comedy should be postponed for a few
> years and even then should eschew such a complete adherence to the
> facts as Mr. Davis blundered into, but there, I think, lies the real play. The
> tragic ending would lose nothing by the preceding chaotic comedy, in
> fact, it would be doubly effective—always provided, of course, that it was
> well done. There lay the greatest fault of Mr. Davis's play: it was not well
> done. Let the others who follow take warning.
>
> —Benchley, pp. 103–104

A Biographer: I

Isadora Duncan and I lived under one roof in Moscow for several years.
I accompanied her on her tours to Petrograd, the Ukraine, the Crimea,
the Northern Caucasus and Transcaucasia. I worked with her as an orga-
nizer of her school, was responsible for all her public performances, created the librettos for her new productions, and was in charge of the lighting
effects which she insisted on as an important element of her performances.
I had literally hundreds of conversations with her, remember her ideas
and the manner in which she expressed them, and was familiar with her
creative plans and aspirations. Finally, I was the witness of her great love
affair with Sergei Esenin, one of the outstanding Soviet poets. During the
last years of her life, she wrote to me constantly from Paris. For more
than two decades after her death in 1927 I was in charge, first of her school,
later of her studio, and, finally, of the studio-theater bearing her name.

The reader will perhaps reproach me for indulging in some prosaic details. For me, Isadora Duncan was a great woman as well as a great artist. Once, talking to a biographer, Isadora said: "You cannot write only half the truth about a great man. A good biography must tell of all the sides of his character, the bad and the good. That is absolutely necessary if we are to achieve a complete picture of the man. Even his thoughts and emotions, provided you can vouch for them, must be described with absolute clarity. I hope that everything written about me will be true, regardless of any feelings for me. . . .

—Schneider, pp. 7–8

A Biographer: II

Why does she appeal to us?

Fernand Divoire describes a dance which she once improvised as an encore at the end of a concert at the Théâtre Lyrique de la Gaité. She said, "I am going to dance the philosophy of my life." To Divoire, she seemed to be standing before an invisible bronze door. Again and again she hurled herself against the door, and again and again the unyielding door felled her. Finally, bruised and shaken, with a tremendous effort of will, she gathered up all her strength and flung herself against the invisible door. And the heavy door, unhinged, at last fell open.

The tragedy of Isadora is that she was broken by the effort of opening the door—nevertheless she forced it open.

—Blair, p. xii

A Dance

The following passage, which describes the first time that Gordon Craig saw his Isadora dance, in 1904, comes from the typescript of a radio talk that Craig gave on May 31, 1952, for the BBC:

She came through some small curtains which were not much taller than herself; she came through them and walked down to where a musician, his back turned to us, was seated at a grand piano; he had just finished playing a prelude by Chopin when in she came, and in some five or six steps was standing by the piano, quite still and, as it were, listening to the hum of the last notes. . . . You might have counted five, or even eight, and then there sounded the voice of Chopin again, in a second prelude or etude; it was played through gently and came to an end and she had not moved at all. Then one step back or sideways, and the music began again as she went moving on before or after it. Only just moving. . . . She was speaking in her own language, not echoing any ballet master, and so she came to move as no one had ever seen anyone move before. The dance ended, and again she stood quite still. No bowing, no smiling—nothing at all. Then again the music is off, and she runs from it—it runs after her then, for she has gone ahead of it.

How is it that we know she is speaking her own language? We know it, for we see her head, her hands, gently active, as are her feet, her whole person. And if she is speaking, what is it she is saying? No one would ever be able to report truly, yet no one present had a moment's doubt. Only this can we say—that she was telling to the air the very things we longed to hear and until she came we had never dreamed we should hear; and now we heard them, and this sent us all into an unusual state of joy, and I sat still and speechless.

I remember that when it was over I went rapidly round to her dressing-room to see her, and there, too, I sat still and speechless in front of her for a while. She understood my silence very well, all talk being unnecessary.

His son Edward Craig adds: "His silence was induced by a mixture of overwhelming admiration and furious resentment—admiration of what had been, to him, the greatest artistic experience in his life, resentment that this revelation should come from a woman."

—Craig, pp. 191–192

Dancing at 31

Some of the most perceptive dance reviews in the United States of the past one hundred years have been those of H. T. Parker. Most of them, apparently, were written on a tight deadline; however, his insights into such artists as Adeline Genée, Anna Pavlova, Ruth St. Denis, La Argentina, Uday Shankar, and Angna Enters—and his gift for recreating the effect of a dancer in motion—don't seem to have been compromised by the newsroom stresses. Parker reviewed Duncan herself in 1908, 1911, and 1922, and he also reviewed the separate performances of her six pupils, the Isadorables (whom he calls the "Duncanettes") in 1920 and 1929. Below is a passage from his first, intoxicated 1908 review of Duncan, followed by a passage from one of his last, sobering 1922 reviews. In the fourteen-year interval, of course, not only did Duncan's body change but she also underwent some profoundly damaging life experiences, beginning with the deaths in an automobile accident of her two children, Deirdre and Patrick. Among the elements that make Parker's criticism valuable are that he is never so drunk with pleasure or so softened by sympathy that he omits to note his instances of resistance. Although I have chosen passages that give the essence of his perceptions on the given occasions, it would be misrepresenting his criticism not to add that in 1908 he took Duncan to task for her moments of conventional pantomime, and that in 1922 he reported her difficulties in rising "with grace from a crouched or recumbent position."

It is these clear-sighted and honestly spoken moments of "No," however, that lead the reader to trust his "Yes."

> She moves often in long and lovely sinuous lines across the whole breadth, or down the whole depth of the stage. Or she circles it in curves of no less jointless beauty. As she moves, her body is steadily and delicately undulating. One motion flows or ripples, or sweeps, into another, and the two are edgeless. No deliberate crescendo and climax ordered her movements; rather, they come and go in endless flow as though each were creating the next. And those movements have no less plastic beauty. They change, they fall together, so to say, like the colored glasses in the kaleidoscope, and Miss Duncan seems a figure off a Greek vase. They flow and fall again, and she is like to a dancing figure upon a Roman wall. Again, and she plays at ball like Nausicaa by the sea in the *Odyssey*, and each movement turns the game—an imaginary game in which there is only one player—into an idealizing beauty. She plays at knucklebones—the ancient jackstones—upon the shore at Colchis with Iphigenia's train, and it is as if she were the lovely essence of their sport. . . . It is the custom to speak of absolute music—of music that exists in itself and by itself, that imparts nothing but itself, that makes its own beauty and emotion and thereby persuades and stirs its hearers. Of such, for example, is a symphony by Mozart. Miss Duncan's dancing is absolute dancing in a still fuller sense. It is peculiar to itself; it knows no rule, and it has no customs except those that she imposes. . . . Everywhere it cultivates fineness, in its rhythm, its harmonies, its shading and suggestions. Everywhere it cultivates a chastity of motion and expression that give it a spiritual quality, a disembodied and poetic sensuousness—the sensuousness of Shelley's poetry. . . . It accomplishes its ends in seeming spontaneity and innocence, as though it were of childhood. It really achieves them—it is easy to suspect—by calculated, practiced, and reflective artistry.
>
> —Holmes, pp. 59–61

Dancing at 45

> Nowadays, Miss Duncan most engrosses the eye and quickens the imagination when she is semi-static; most achieves beauty when she seeks it, so to say, in sculptured pose and gesture, in surface and plane, rather than in movement. . . . Isadora is ceasing, inevitably, to be a dancer in the sense of vivid motion. Instead, she is becoming sculptress, while the medium upon which she works is her own body, her own mantling raiment. For Miss Duncan no longer arrays herself in a few scarves of flying chiffon. Oftener than not last evening, she was clothed from head to foot in far-flung veils and mantles that she might set them flowing in curves and lay plane against or on plane. Becoming sculptural, she becomes also more independent of the music. More than once yesterday, it was hard to dis-

cover its office, except as glamour to listening ears, while she, herself, held watching eyes.

—Holmes, p. 69

Lynn Seymour in Frederick Ashton's
Five Brahms Waltzes in the Manner of Isadora Duncan

This passage by Arlene Croce was first published in *The New Yorker*, July 26, 1976:

> Seymour's rightness for the part isn't measured only by her magnetism. If there had been a poll in the dance world on the question of whom to cast in the movie of Duncan's life that was made a few years ago, the choice would have been Lynn Seymour—Seymour the actress, the performer of epic daring, but most of all Seymour the dancer. She has always possessed the roundness and fullness of contour, the plastic vigor, and the coherent rhythm to express the sculptural depth that Isadora's dancing must have had. Beautiful in classical effacé positions, Seymour is heroic in Duncan plastique. The back yields, the chest lifts, the arms expand and float, and then from this open aspect the figure suddenly withdraws in a crouch or a stance braced and turned in on itself. The reversal seems miraculous each time because Seymour is so securely centered. She doesn't have to stop and relocate, and she doesn't tighten up or rigidify or signal ahead; she simply arrives in one piece, loosely disposed, the arms coiled about the head, the hips angled, the turned-in knee relaxed. The whole scroll-like motion is carelessly light and free, yet it's indelible. Ashton's and Seymour's Isadora is a virtuoso.

—Croce, p. 174

Isadora Duncan: Dancing
in Relation to Nature and Love

> Often when people have questioned my morals, I have answered that I consider myself extremely moral, because in all my relations I have only made movements which seem beautiful to me.
> —Isadora Duncan, *The Art*, p. 127

Martha Graham (1894–1991)

Many remembrances of this genius, including her own, concern her lightning-bolt displays of passion toward her dancers and other colleagues and her clashes with well-known figures. However, there were many sides to Graham, and in the second half of her career especially she could display tremendous sympathy and sometimes even look back at herself with amusement. Regardless of who writes about her, she makes for engaging stories. Below are some that are less well known. More stories about Graham are distributed among other categories of this collection.

Lecture-Demonstration, 1930s, The New School for Social Research, New York City

A bald man in a dark business suit stood up and aggressively questioned Martha about the "improvisation" at the beginning of the evening, and he mimicked the way we lifted our arm in the Greek greeting. Martha tried to brush him off, but he persisted. Why couldn't we simply lift the arm up? Why all the fuss about the breathing and the shoulder? I felt he was pressing her, and I thought Martha was trying hard to control her temper. She explained patiently, in terms that any layman might understand, that when lifting the arm to reach a book on a high shelf it is necessary to press down the shoulder muscles in back to cause the arm to rise in front. She compared the motion to that of a seesaw and added that, in the process, the lungs fill with breath. She seemed almost triumphant for having broken it down so clearly for him.

The man burlesqued what she had shown him, moving his arm this way and that, as if he were trying to crank up an old Model T Ford. People laughed. Martha was livid. He baited Martha maliciously, retorting, "If I go to a high shelf to pick up a book, I most certainly do not lift MY shoulder and then drop it," and he lifted his shoulder in a very bizarre way, then jerked it down. Throughout this exchange, the dancers, including me, were seated on the curved steps that led down to the studio floor. John Martin [dance critic for *The New York Times*] was behind us. He whispered urgently for someone to tell Martha that the man was the great Russian choreographer Michel Fokine. I reached out and tugged gingerly on Martha's skirt, but she was so wildly angry by now that she paid no attention to me.

Finally, John stood up to fulfill his duty as moderator, deftly closed the subject, and moved on. When Martha finally learned that the man in the audience was Michel Fokine, she was shocked and upset. She protested, "But he was wearing a suit! He looked like a Wall Street banker to me." Years later, Michel Fokine wrote about the incident. He described Martha's work, and all of us, as grotesque. He even used the words "the Graham girls were like barking dogs." . . . When Agnes de Mille read this manuscript shortly before her death, she told me that she recalled that Martha Graham went so far as to order Michel Fokine to leave the auditorium.

—Bird, pp. 84–85, note p. 253

Gutsy Goddess

Martha Graham was introduced to Lincoln Kirstein—dance historian, polemicist, and eventual co-founder of the New York City Ballet—by a mutual friend in 1937 after a performance of the Federal Theatre's production *The Cradle Will Rock*. Kirstein, who published essays and tirades, had already written about Graham in several forums.

> I admire your dance," Graham remembered in her memoirs as his opening line upon being introduced.
>
> "Well, that isn't what you recently wrote," Graham remembered replying. "You called me the goddess who belched and I have never forgotten that."
>
> "But that was before I knew you," Kirstein protested, to which she recalled responding,
>
> "You don't know me now." Then she walked away. "And that was that."
> —Graham, p. 113

"Why Don't You Work on It?"

Choreographers have individual methods of working, and sometimes they make dances differently at different points in their careers. When Martha Graham assigned a first-rate dancer to a solo, she often invited the person to develop the actual movement along the lines of her own initial concept for the role, as was the case with Merce Cunningham, who created the part of The Revivalist in her 1944 masterpiece, *Appalachian Spring*:

> Graham said, as I remember it, "I don't know whether you are a preacher, a farmer or the devil" (I think there were four categories and don't remember the last). She shortly said, "Why don't you work on it?" She left the room, and I began to try out movements with the pianist obligingly playing short sequences over and over. I worked that afternoon and part of the next, and later on the second afternoon asked Graham to come and see what I had made. "I don't know if this is what you want," I said. I did the dance, and afterward Graham said, "Oh, it's fine. Now I know what to do with the rest of the piece." (Merce Cunningham)
> —Copland, p. 41

On Vagina Envy

> I know my dances and technique are considered deeply sexual, but I pride myself in placing onstage what most people hide in their deepest thoughts. . . . It bemuses me that my school in New York has been called "The House of the Pelvic Truth," because so much of the movement comes from a pelvic thrust, or because I tell a student "you are simply not moving your vagina." . . .
>
> Not that my frank descriptions haven't gotten me into more than a little trouble. On our first tour of Asia, in Tokyo, one of my chorus girls had wandered off with several American sailors and was nowhere to be

found for the matinee performance. After we left the theater, I turned to a friend in the taxi we hailed and said, "She never would have been a great dancer, and doesn't understand how to move from her vagina." The taxi driver nearly swerved off the road. "You understand English?" I asked. He turned and smiled, "Yes, ma'am. I was raised in Brooklyn."

—Graham, p. 127

On Graham's Collaboration with the Sculptor Isamu Noguchi

It was always agitated, never peaceful. She always wanted something more, and he always thought she should have something less.

—Francis Mason, chairman of the board
of the Martha Graham Dance Company,
speaking at the press preview of
"Noguchi-Graham: Selected Works for Dance"
(a show of Noguchi's set designs for Graham),
Queens, New York: The Noguchi Museum, 2004

The Difference between East and West

Beate Sirota Gordon, the daughter of the pianist Leo Sirota, grew up in Japan during the 1920s and 1930s. Her experience during the Occupation—when, fresh out of college, she was assigned by a member of General MacArthur's staff to write the clause of the Japanese Constitution according women basic human rights—occasioned the title of her memoirs, *The Only Woman in the Room*. However, not until the memoir was published in 1997 did most people in the dance world international know about that. What they were acquainted with were Gordon's activities as a New York impresario who traveled to remote corners of the globe in search of the finest and most authentic practitioners of traditional performing arts. The following story concerns a trip she made to the Southeast Asian country that now calls itself Myanmar:

When I told people I wanted to see traditional Asian arts, I was often shown new arrangements of them, either because they thought I would prefer them that way or because they were trying to conform to what they considered Western standards. On such occasions, I would use Japan as a model to explain what I wanted. In Japan, I told them, Kabuki and No theater are preserved strictly according to the old style of doing them, and they are flourishing, alongside other, modern forms of entertainment. What is important, I pointed out, is to avoid mixing old and new haphazardly, spoiling both of them.

In Burma one year, after making laborious arrangements to attend a national festival, I was confronted with versions of classical Burmese dances that had obviously been influenced by a popular all-girl Japanese revue, which is notorious for the level of flashy kitsch it manages to attain. As a producer, I felt let down, and wandered disconsolately through the streets of Rangoon that night. Cities in the tropics come alive at night, and Rangoon throbbed to the sound of American pop music performed by local groups. It didn't bode well. But then, walking again the next morning, I suddenly heard the rhythmic sound of wooden clappers. When I asked my interpreter what it was, he said it came from a school of dancing nearby. I asked to see the school. We entered a ramshackle building. To the beat of the clappers worked by an old woman, a group of ten girls was going through some of the 104 time-honored exercises of classical dance (boys do 103). Watching their fluid, intricate movements, I thought: this is it. They reminded me of Martha Graham's famous exercises in their formal presentation.

After overcoming the objections of Burmese officials, who could not understand why I wanted to present mere "exercises" to American audiences, and after adding a few actual dances to the program, I left them to prepare for their visit to New York.

Several months later I flew back to see rehearsals and, in particular, costumes. It was a shock. Instead of the unobtrusive movements and plain cotton sarongs I'd seen before, it was all velvet and silk and pearls, and girls dancing with boys. I put my foot down. "But the choreography's classical," I was told, "—from 1942."

Persuaded to resurrect the original costumes and format, they went on to an enthusiastic reception in New York. Martha Graham saw them and invited them to perform at a party in her studio. The elite of the dance world was there. The Burmese in their simple earth-colored sarongs gave an impression simultaneously of great suppleness and great dignity as they changed position seamlessly, one movement flowing into the next, never seeming to strain or lose breath, however demanding the move. They were followed by the large and powerful Graham dancers in flesh-colored leotards. Although they performed their exercises expertly, you could hear them breathing, and their bodies ran with sweat. It was a display of aggressive physicality.

One of the spectators came over to me afterward and said: "You know what the difference is between East and West?"

"No."

"It's sweat."

—Gordon, pp. 163–164

Spectator

David Zellmer, who died in 2004 at the age of 88 after a long career as a producer with CBS News, was among the first group of male dancers to be taken into Martha Graham's company in the early 1940s. He was also one of several of them to be drafted into military service. After training stateside, he became a flier in the Pacific theater, and during his time there, Graham wrote him long, meditative letters that, among other things, discussed the works she was making and the people she saw in New York. (Although Zellmer's letters to Graham are now lost, her letters to him—which he kept close to his person and frequently reread during his years in the service—have been deposited in the Dance Division of The New York Public Library for the Performing Arts.)

In 1999, Zellmer published a memoir of his combat experiences during World War II, in which he frequently touches on his brief time as a Graham dancer. The excerpt below describes his visit to New York on furlough in May of 1944, when he visited Graham and her dancers in her studio and also got to see, in performance, dances he'd once appeared in or about whose gestation Graham had written him: *Deaths and Entrances*, *Salem Shore*, *Herodiade*, *Appalachian Spring*. The "Yuriko" of whom he provides a cameo is the great Graham dancer, stager, choreographer, and California native of Japanese descent, Yuriko Kikuchi, sometimes known as Yuriko I, to distinguish her from the excellent Yuriko who danced with the company in the 1960s, Yuriko Kimura (Yuriko II):

I also got to meet a stunning new member of the company known simply as "Yuriko," who, unbeknownst to me, had joined while I was overseas. I was told she had come to New York directly from a relocation center out west for Japanese aliens, having been interned with her parents, even though she was born in the United States and was an American citizen. Unexplainably, Yuriko had never been mentioned by Martha in letters to me. I could only guess that Martha had, naively, been fearful of my reaction to meeting the "enemy," albeit in the guise of a beautiful young dancer. But, as Martha had intended, and hoped, Yuriko and I became friends.

On the second night of the performances, *Letter to the World* was presented, evoking bittersweet memories of the last time I had danced my small part so long ago, wondering if I would ever again know the thrill and excitement I felt then. What I had come to learn was that only the threat of death—the attack of a Zeke fighter, exploding anti-aircraft shells under the wing, being lost a thousand miles from our island home in a starless night sky—could bring the same intensity of feeling.

Later that week in May, a telegram from Fort Logan informed me that I was eligible for discharge from the Air Force and should return there immediately.

Martha's last letter to me, dated June 5, 1945, told me she had received a card the Air Force sent former employers of servicemen being discharged. She said there was an initialed postscript at the bottom of the card reading:

"Plié inspected and O.K."

—Zellmer, pp. 123–124

Real Characters and Ingrid Bergman's Pliés

For decades at The Neighborhood Playhouse in New York, Graham worked with a roster of very famous actors. Among them was Tony Randall, who studied Graham technique daily with Graham company member Jane Dudley and who also studied acting there.

> I wasn't terribly good at her work, but I loved it. I was only 18 and re-fused to wear a jockstrap under my one-piece leotard. Jane Dudley, who was a wonderful teacher, asked me if I would please wear one. I hated jockstraps and wouldn't wear one.
>
> The school did a play by Ibsen that was not to be seen by anyone except the class and teachers. Martha saw it and stopped me in the hall afterward. "You were too much in character," she said. And I, being a pompous young ass, replied, "Yes, that was what I was *trying* to do."
>
> "No," she said, "you must always do something out of character. Human beings do things out of character. Your best friend does things that you would never dream he or she would do. It's part of the human condition and makes a character real. To develop a character fully, you must look at the other side of them and find the secrets that are there, contradictory things that are not obvious the first time you read the role. You have to do something out of character." I remembered that advice all my life.
>
> At that time Martha was giving private lessons to Ingrid Bergman, who would come up to the studio for her class, and some of us peeked through the door at this famous movie star. One day, Martha caught us and chewed us out with: "And you should see Ingrid Bergman's pliés. They are diabolically good!"
>
> —Horosko, pp. 98–99

Martha Graham: The Absolute Dancer

> I am certain that movement never lies. The inner quality of the dancer is inherent in all that he does. I am not saying that a good person makes a good dancer or that a bad person makes a bad dancer. The motivation, the cause of the movement, establishes a center of gravity. This center of gravity induces the co-ordination that is body-spirit, and this Spirit-of-body is the state of innocence that is the secret of the absolute dancer.
>
> —Morgan, p. 11

Margot Fonteyn (1919–1991)

Pointes (or Toes?) of Steel

In a full-length production of *The Sleeping Beauty*, the title role requires a number of lengthy—and, for the ballerina, traditionally anxiety-provoking—unpartnered balances on full pointe, especially in "The Rose Adagio," the

scene where (in most productions) the sixteen-year-old Princess Aurora
celebrates her birthday and is presented with four suitors from around the
world, who partner her between those balances. Fonteyn, perhaps the most
beloved Aurora on record, was also famous for having "soft" feet ("pats of
butter," is how her principal choreographer, Frederick Ashton, characterized them early in her career); and she often spoke of her anxieties at the
prospect of dancing Aurora, as well as other leading roles in the big classical ballets. Nevertheless, she gave celebrated accounts of all those roles
and many more demanding ones over the course of her long career, as she
not only persevered to dance all the steps, no matter how difficult, but also
to dance them soundlessly—something only possible if the blocks of her
pointe shoes (i.e., the tips of the toes, stiffened with glue) had been ham-
mered into a semi-pulpy state. Observers have often wondered about this
paradox: if her feet were so soft, how was she able to do all that she did?
One answer is that although she started out her career with truly soft feet,
her eventual training with the esteemed teacher Vera Volkova helped
Fonteyn to strengthen them. However, the following story, in which
Fonteyn coaches a younger dancer in the role of Aurora, is something of
an additional revelation, since it suggests that although Fonteyn's feet may
have *looked* soft in performance, they were, in fact, supporting her without
much help from her pointe shoes:

Maria Almeida spoke at the Fonteyn conference about being coached
by Fonteyn as Aurora. Fonteyn watched her dance and then said, "Maria,
do you get nervous about dancing this role?" Almeida, who said that
she was terrified of it, thought, "Is this a trick question? What should I
say?" She said, "Yes." Fonteyn said, "Well, so was I. *Use* your nerves.
Turn it all into the role, to give it energy," or words to that effect. Then,
a little later, after Almeida had done "The Rose Adagio," Fonteyn asked
to see Almeida's blocks. Almeida, telling the story, admitted that she had
wide and solid blocks. Fonteyn looked them over and then said to her:
"But, Maria, with blocks like these, why are you nervous?"
—Anecdote related to M. A. by Alastair Macaulay,
who conceived and co-directed "The Fonteyn Phenomenon,"
the 1999 Royal Academy of Dance conference, in London

On Fonteyn's Musicality

Dancer, choreographer, and teacher Pauline Koner, the author of the penetrating tribute that follows, enjoyed one of the most critically distinguished
careers in American modern dance of the past half century, beginning, perhaps, when Michel Fokine said of her, at the age of thirteen, "In her, the soul
dances":

Margot Fonteyn dances with her inner ear because she is listening to
how she feels, because she experiences the moment of doing as a mo-

ment of living. Therefore, she phrases. When she dances with a man, you feel she relates to the man. She "is" with the other person.

—Cohen, p. 78

In the Dark

Arts manager Maxim Gershunoff, who worked with Hurok Concerts, remembers an unchoreographed moment during a Boston appearance by Margot Fonteyn and Rudolf Nureyev in The Royal Ballet's production of Kenneth MacMillan's *Romeo and Juliet*:

The performance had been going well, but at the scene where Romeo discovers the body of Juliet after she has taken the sleeping potion, the lights in the orchestra pit blacked out completely. The orchestra's musicians attempted to keep on playing whatever they could remember of the score. However, one by one each instrument gave up until it was practically like a performance of the Haydn "Farewell" Symphony. All that was missing were the candles. From the stage, Margot could be heard from Juliet's funeral bier saying, in full voice, "Rudy, either I am growing deaf or I really am dead." The curtain had to be lowered until the audience stopped laughing and the theater's electricians could restore power to the orchestra pit.

—Gershunoff, p. 165

Shocked into Laughter

In the 1970s, Martha Graham began to invite stars of the ballet to perform in her works. For Margot Fonteyn and Rudolf Nureyev, she made a new dance, *Lucifer*, for which she had to argue with Fonteyn to wear ballet slippers. (The ballerina, wanting to do everything properly, protested that she ought to dance barefoot.) "A great and beautiful figure. . . ," is how Graham remembered Fonteyn in her memoirs, adding, however, that "no one could be a more severe critic of Margot than Margot." As an example, Graham recounted a performance by Fonteyn, with Nureyev, in *La Bayadère*, for which Graham stood in the wings. "When the curtain came down for good," Graham went on, "she threw herself on the floor in tears because she felt that she had danced it so badly. She had not met her own standard, no matter how high the praise." The only person capable of bringing Fonteyn back from this state was Nureyev, who, Graham observed, went over to his Nikiya and whispered something that made her laugh, "that wonderful laugh that is only Margot's, a reluctant laugh," as Graham characterized it. Later, Nureyev told Graham that what he had whispered "was every shocking obscenity he could think of." Graham added, "I believed him."

—Graham, p. 150

Uncontrollable

The dance historian and British native David Vaughan, who began to watch Margot Fonteyn dance with the Sadler's Wells Ballet in the 1930s, forgets where he heard this anecdote:

> The story is that when John Cranko was choreographing *Poème de l'ecstase*, in which Fonteyn appeared as a diva surrounded by young men, he asked her if she would mind if they were nude. She said, "I don't really mind, but of course your eye always goes to that one place, and it's always behind the music."
>
> —Macaulay, unpaginated

A Miracle

The ballerina Lynn Seymour was an admirer of Fonteyn from the time Seymour was a young teenager in Canada. When she joined the touring company of The Royal Ballet and danced the lead in *Swan Lake* at the age of nineteen, Fonteyn did try to coach her in the role, but the session was unsatisfactory for both dancers. As the years passed, however, they developed a warm collegiality, and at the 1999 Royal Academy of Dance conference, "The Fonteyn Phenomenon," in London, Seymour read an eloquent testament to Fonteyn's powers both onstage and off, from which this passage has been excerpted:

> The area in which I did not question or ignore Margot's example or advice was in the classroom. Here, her influence was profound, and most particularly in the latter stages of her career. It was here that I avidly sought to emulate her approach.
>
> Firstly, she never missed class. And never left before the end. She never shirked exercises that caused her difficulty or discomfort—most especially in the jumping department, which was her bête noire. And in pirouetting, which had to be done in equal measure, both to the left and to the right. Each exercise was instantly analyzed, and she would include épaulement, head movement, eye focus, and appropriate ports de bras—and whilst working like a navvy, rendered the whole with grace and ease, so that it was a perfectly finished product. Nothing was omitted, and all this without any excess. It was riveting to behold, and a miracle of very complex coordination. Her attention to detail seemed as natural as a heartbeat, or as drawing breath. But it was, of course, the result of intense concentration and agility of mind.
>
> Her approach never altered. And even when her physical powers were on the wane, she focused on this completeness and finish. So that you did not notice that she was minimizing some movements and prudently saving energy in others. She perfected ways of making you see her strengths—drawing your eye from what she didn't wish you to observe.
>
> —Macaulay, unpaginated

Super

Valda Setterfield, the dancer and actress, is cherished for her performances with Merce Cunningham's company and later in productions by her husband, the postmodern choreographer David Gordon, and by their son, Ain, a playwright.

Born in England, she studied ballet in London with Marie Rambert during the 1950s, when she saw Fonteyn dance "countless times, . . . especially in *The Sleeping Beauty*." Setterfield adds: "Her technique was modest, but her musicality and the fullness of her acting were magical."

After such riches, it seemed preposterous but absolutely necessary to wait outside the stage door to meet this princess in person. Fonteyn emerged radiant, beautifully groomed, and spoke with each one of us, including us in her success. (Years later, she told me she had learned this from Markova, who had learned it from Pavlova.)

In New York in the 1960s, I "super-ed" with The Royal Ballet and was onstage with Princess Aurora. I swear she smiled at every member of her court as she ran around the stage before the difficult balances that end "The Rose Adagio." She showed no signs of nervousness, but sweat poured down my torso. The excitement in the house was electric. There was nothing to fear. We saw a sixteen-year-old princess dancing with her suitors; and technical difficulties or successes became a part of her struggle with the beginnings of adult responsibilities. The applause broke like a storm.

During that season, she had trouble with specific passages, which she matter-of-factly acknowledged in rehearsal and practiced in the intermission. When the moments came in performance, she neither shirked them nor rushed them; simply *did* them. Her capacity to be so completely in the moment led us to the next moment, and the next. . . .

This is the greatest lesson she taught me, and I think of it whenever I walk onstage.

—Macaulay, p. 21

The Language of Dance

Mikhail Baryshnikov first met Fonteyn in 1970, when he danced in London with the Kirov. Some years later, the two performed together in Fokine ballets, which were filmed for Fonteyn's television series, *The Magic of Dance*. He remembers her as personally generous ("quite wonderful and immensely kind") and professionally helpful, generous, and precise.

My impression of her is that she was always thinking of other people—of Tito [her husband's nickname], for example, or of "BQ" [nickname for her mother]. And her thoughts were practical. How to deal with this or with that? She had a tough life, and her mind was tough when it came to sorting out problems. Yet she was also very light and amusing. When we first met in 1970, I spoke no English. So we conversed in French, which she spoke fluently. But she had learnt from Rudolf Nureyev several Russian "four-letter" words, which she would drop occasionally into conversation, to impress me. They took me completely by surprise! And she knew exactly what they meant. I, hearing them, would blush bright red from the neck up; she would just laugh, in that bright, elegant, and musical laugh of hers.

—Macaulay, pp. 32–33

As Author: A Report from Her Editor

When my publishing house, Alfred A. Knopf, acquired the American rights to Margot's *Autobiography*, the manuscript was already written, but I had the chance to work with her on it—and she did her best to allow me to feel that I was being useful. But whenever I proposed some change of substance, she was . . . elusive. "Perhaps there might be more about certain individual roles—Giselle, for instance." "Well, you know, Bob, I never really thought about it. I stood behind my cottage door and when I heard the music for my first entrance, I just came through the door and did it." That insight did not make it into the book. Only on the subject of photographs was she ruffled, since she seemed to hate every performance photo ever taken of her. She was in obvious distress as we went through great piles of images, and only after some tough negotiating did we finally dwindle into a modest picture selection.

Some years later, we worked together from scratch on the text for the book that accompanied her BBC series, *The Magic of Dance*. She was eager and determined, I was obsessed, and wonderful Catherine Ashmore, who had been sent over by the BBC to do picture research, rounded our jolly team. But everything was desperately late. Margot was now writing in our offices, turning over pencil drafts for typing as we stood by to start laying out the next chapter. It was a close-run thing, and certain topics were loaded; we had, for instance, spent years jokily dueling over the relative merits of Ashton and Balanchine (not that she failed to admire Mr. B., or I Ashton). One day, she handed me some pages with a suspicious gleam in her eye. She had written something like "Frederick Ashton, the greatest choreographer of our time." By now, I had come to understand her maddening but adorable combination of loyalty, stubbornness, provocativeness, and professionalism. I took the pages, read them in front of her, and with no comment handed them to my assistant for typing. The next day, with another gleam in her eye, she gave me a revised version: this time, it was "Frederick Ashton, with George Balanchine, one of the two greatest choreographers of our time." We had both had our fun. (Robert A. Gottlieb)

—Macaulay, pp. 35–36

Simplicity I

I think Margot was a mystery to herself in a number of ways, and although her "simplicity" of style and nature was widely remarked, it always seemed to me that she was an extremely complex—indeed almost split—personality. It is doubtful if she could have survived some of the extremes of pressure, which frequently descended upon her, had she been otherwise, and it surely requires a great complexity of resource to suggest simplicity, without appearing merely simplistic; a rare art, in fact. (Keith Money, biographer)

—Daneman, p. 578

Simplicity II

Margot Fonteyn Arias

The entire legend on the bronze plaque in the cemetery outside Panama City, where the ballerina's ashes are interred at the foot of the tomb of her husband, Tito Arias.

—Daneman, p. 578

Simplicity III

Give the audience what it wants to see.

—Fonteyn in conversation with Joy Williams Brown, in a dance studio following a class both had taken with Valentina Pereyaslavec, ca. 1970s

Sir Frederick Ashton (1904–1988)

Sir Frederick Ashton, the choreographer whose classical eloquence and exquisite theatricality shaped much of the style of England's Royal Ballet from its earliest years, is considered by many dance fans to be one of the twentieth century's two greatest choreographers for the ballet, the other being George Balanchine. Offstage, Ashton could also be a raconteur of tremendous wit and charm. That gift was on display full strength in his 1981 interview with Dick Cavett in New York for Cavett's television show on PBS. In the course of the conversation, Cavett led Ashton to touch on highlights of his choreographic career and to discuss dancers such as Vaslav Nijinsky, Mikhail Baryshnikov, Rudolf Nureyev, Anna Pavlova, Tamara Karsavina, Lydia Lopukhova, Dame Ninette de Valois, Isadora Duncan, Martha Graham, and, of course, Dame Margot Fonteyn—the ballerina for whom Ashton made so many beautiful and sensitive roles. Cavett's show hasn't been on television for a while, and since his interview with Ashton gives so much of the choreographer's career and permits him so many amusing observations on outstanding figures in the world of ballet, the section on him here will be devoted to excerpts from the transcript.

CAVETT: If someone were to ask, where was Sir Frederick Ashton in his earliest years, I doubt if I would have guessed Peru. How did that happen?

ASHTON: Well, it happened because my father was a constable. I was born actually in Ecuador, but I never lived there, and he was moved then to Peru, so that's how it came about.

CAVETT: In looking up things about you, I found that your—I think it's your first ballet—was *A Tragedy of Fashion.*

ASHTON: *Fashion,* yes.

CAVETT: . . . *Or Scarlet Scissors.*

ASHTON: Yes, that's it.

CAVETT: That sounds wonderfully intriguing. Can you tell me?

ASHTON: Well, I tell you it was done in a revue, in a rather sort of high-brow revue that there was in those days. It was very, very short, and it was rather sad, because after I got this opportunity I thought, "Well, here I am a star," and I thought all the offers were going to come pouring in, and nothing happened at all.

CAVETT: The phone didn't ring?

ASHTON: The phone didn't ring, not a single offer or anything. So I had to start all over again, so to speak.

CAVETT: That ballet is not in the repertory?

ASHTON: Oh, no, no, no, good gracious. Much too trivial. It was a sort of number in a revue, really, but still it was the beginning.

CAVETT: What was it about? I imagine it as being something in which a model murders the—someone with some scissors.

ASHTON: No, I was the couturier, who tried to launch a model which nobody liked, and then in despair I cut myself with scissors. It was rather based on the story of the chef of Louis Quatorze or something, who made a dish that was bad, and so he killed himself because it wasn't right.

CAVETT: With one of the kitchen tools?

ASHTON: Probably; yes, exactly.

CAVETT: They knew how to go in those days.

You turned, Sir Frederick, to choreography rather early, you might say. Does this mean that you were not the great dancer you thought you were, or had hoped to be?

ASHTON: Precisely. Well, I started very late, you see. I became quite adequate but I was no—you'd never say that I would set the dance on fire, by no means.

CAVETT: What would it have taken for you to be another Nijinsky?

ASHTON: Well, I'd had to have started at the right age, instead of which I was wasting time being educated, because with education I always put up a resistance to learning. I could only learn what interested me. It was useless to try and teach me mathematics or anything like that. I couldn't.

CAVETT: Were you limited by your size?

ASHTON: No, no, no, no. Size was all right. Because, I mean, the dancers, all the dancers of that day weren't giants like they are now. They were all rather small.

CAVETT: How tall was Nijinsky?

ASHTON: Very small. Much smaller than me.

CAVETT: Baryshnikov's size rather than Nureyev's?

ASHTON: A tiny bit smaller than him, I would say.

CAVETT: Really!

ASHTON: And you see, all the people like Pavlova and Karsavina and Lopukhova were quite small. . . .

CAVETT: . . .When you left as director [of The Royal Ballet, in 1970], that wasn't a full retirement, was it? You didn't feel you were turning your back on—

ASHTON: Well, I thought that I was, but I mean, it hasn't turned out that way, you see. I thought that I would do something, be on call, and I'm always delighted to help dancers, and I'm delighted to take, you know, Swan Queens through [the role of] Swan Queen and Beauties through *Beauty*. . . . but . . . I didn't want to have to attend every performance, and when I actually did retire, I said, "Well, thank God I never have to sit through *Swan Lake* or *Sleeping Beauty* ever again."

CAVETT: Have you made good on that?

ASHTON: Unfortunately not, unfortunately not.

CAVETT: As we sit here now, Prince Charles was just here and attended *The Sleeping Beauty*. Were you at that performance?

ASHTON: Yes I was.

CAVETT: Was it shocking when it was disturbed by—

[On June 17, 1981—a month-and-a-half before his wedding to Lady Diana Spencer—the Prince of Wales attended a performance of The Royal Ballet at the Metropolitan Opera House while 2,000 pro-Irish demonstrators protested outside Lincoln Center. Several protesters apparently gained entrance to the Met during the performance.]

ASHTON: Well, it was, sort of . . . but I didn't think it was that bad. I mean, if they'd been shooting or something—

CAVETT: —demonstrators?

ASHTON: —that would have been one thing, but it wasn't bad . . . they shouted, you couldn't hear what they were saying anyway; they were hustled out very quickly.

CAVETT: Did the dancers freeze in position?

ASHTON: Oh no. The dancers never—they just went on. They're well trained for that sort of thing. I mean, during—in the War [WWII], when there were air raids, we just went on the same, without stopping.

CAVETT: You mean even when the signal went to take cover?

ASHTON: Yes, when the shooting was going on and everything, we still went on.

CAVETT: Really?

ASHTON: Yes.

CAVETT: That isn't foolhardy?

ASHTON: Well, possibly, but I mean, what are you to do? If a bomb falls, it falls and could fall anywhere. You might as well go on; you might as well die doing *The Dying Swan* or something.

CAVETT: You'd call it *The Really Dying Swan* . . .

ASHTON: Yes. . . .

CAVETT: . . .Why, in sports—and I was talking to Dame Ninette de Valois about that on another program—so many advances have been made in preventing injury, and ballet is so rife with injury? I don't know what could be developed, unless they wore ankle supports and knee braces and things basketball players wear.

ASHTON: No, I think why, the reason is that modern choreography demands much more than, say, they were in the nineteenth century. I mean, there was more classical form which people performed to; but now they're asked to do such incredible things that they can injure themselves much more easily, and the strain on certain muscles can end in disaster.

CAVETT: What if a dancer said to you, "I don't want to do that; it's too risky"?

ASHTON: Well, then, I would respect it. I would respect it. . . .

CAVETT: They would tend not to do that, though, wouldn't they?

ASHTON: Oh, yes, they would tend not to. I mean, sometimes with Fonteyn, I'd give her something to do, and she'd say, "Do you mind if I do it this way?" And I said, "Well, try it," and I said, "No, I like it the way that I did it," and she'd say, "Well, you're always right," so she went back to it. But no, I'm perfectly amenable. I don't think one should be . . . I mean, my choreography isn't sacred; I don't feel that way. Some people feel that way, you know, like musicians feel every bar is sacred. I don't feel like that at all. There are always ways of doing the same thing differently. And why not? The whole point is, a dancer should be happy and not be worried by difficulties and ought to be able to interpret, to move an audience . . . that's what matters, isn't it?

CAVETT: When Dame Ninette was here, we talked about the fact that you and she had known each other for many years and not always agreed. And one of the things you didn't agree on was whether Isadora Duncan was a great artist or an old bag. . . . I'm not being irreverent on my own, but Elsa Lanchester was on the show, and she studied with Isadora, and I said, "How was she?" expecting to hear that reverent outpouring of, "This is the greatest . . ." And she said, "This untalented old bag of beans."

ASHTON: No, not to me. I mean, admittedly I saw her when I was about fifteen or sixteen, and I hadn't seen a great deal of dancing then, but I went—she gave a series of matinees in some theater in London, and I went to three of them, and I was tremendously impressed by her, tremendously taken by her, and, of course, there was a lot of galumphing, and she was getting quite stout in a way, but nevertheless there was some extraordinary force of personality, and a system of dancing which was to me absolutely fascinating. She had a wonderful sense of repose and stillness, which was, you know, incredible, and I mean, really, she'd stand still for a very long time, and you thought, "Well, when on earth is she going to move?" and suddenly she would just put out a hand and it was magic. And she had beautiful feet and grace, you see. People forget that; people think with modern dancing people have to be all like that [shaking his fists in the air]. Not at all, she had enormous grace.

CAVETT: It is surprising, the two polarities, really, of how she impressed people. I know George Balanchine said it was a fat lady rolling around on the stage.

ASHTON: But there you are, you see. But not to me. . . .

CAVETT: . . . In England, are choreographers as scandalously underpaid and unrewarded as they apparently have been in America?

ASHTON: Absolutely. Of course. When I first came to do *Four Saints in Three Acts*, I got five dollars a week, which paid my fares up to Harlem to do it. Of course, I stayed with friends, but that's all I got.

CAVETT: You didn't say five dollars a week?

ASHTON: Five dollars a week, which in 1933 was perhaps 20 dollars. . . . In those days, we used to come to America thinking this is the land where we'll go back enormously rich. But not a bit of it. I was writing home for money.

CAVETT: Gold in the streets.

ASHTON: Yes. But they didn't have—. . . I mean it was done by a society called Friends and Enemies of Modern Music, and they didn't have any capital, and so we didn't mind. It was interesting to do.

CAVETT: The work was interesting.

ASHTON: Yes, and if the work is interesting to me, I don't care all that much about the money. It's when it's not interesting, then I want to be paid a lot.

CAVETT: Make them pay you.

ASHTON: When I did musical comedies and revues, in those days I used to try and get as much as I could, because I didn't really like doing them, but I had to do them to pay the rent.

CAVETT: Financed your other work perhaps?

ASHTON: Yes, absolutely.

CAVETT: Pavlova: there's no way any of us who didn't see her dance I suppose will ever get an impression of what the magic was.

ASHTON: I doubt it. It's rather difficult to describe. I mean she, again, was a woman of enormous personality, and it wasn't just the technical thing about her, but it was an incredible plasticity, incredible mobility that she had, the incredible grace also. . . . She came out and she just took the audience, dancing to rather indifferent music and everything. I mean, that was understandable: she toured the world in those days, probably, you know; the orchestras didn't amount to anything, and so she had rather tea-shop music.

CAVETT: Tea-shop?

ASHTON: Yes. Palm Court, as we call it in England.

CAVETT: What was it like to talk to Pavlova?

ASHTON: Well, rather fascinating. I didn't know her all that much, but she was tremendously prejudiced. She hated modern choreography and all that sort of thing. She thought it was ugly. She couldn't stand anything that she thought was ugly, what she called ugly. She had her theories of what was beauty and what wasn't beauty. But she was fascinating, really; and when I once went round to her dressing room, I said, "Now, notice everything; notice how she's made up, notice the whole thing." And the only thing I noticed is that she had a hole here [gestures to the space between breasts]. There was a sort of hole here, and I was riveted by this, and so I never noticed what the make-up was, and so I came out after that and said, "What was that hole?" And they said, "Oh, that's when she was doing *Bayadère*, and she stabbed herself." So it left a hole here.

CAVETT: I thought you meant a hole in the costume.

ASHTON: No, no, no, on her person. And I was riveted by this and didn't notice anything. However, she then took my hand, and she said, "You have a great future. It will come slowly, but it will come."

CAVETT: Can you give an impression of how she actually spoke?

ASHTON: She took the hand: [With a Russian accent] "You have a great future; it will come slowly, but it will come." Rather like that.

CAVETT: Now, how would Isadora have spoken?

ASHTON: Ah, that I don't know. But she used to speak to the audience quite a lot. But it wasn't, if I may say so, a strong American accent. It was rather sort of "Englishified" in a way. . . . At the end of performances, she would talk to the audience quite a lot, and she was always rather like a nightclub queen. She would say, "And today in the audience is Bernard Shaw, would you mind standing up?" . . . . And I remember there was a famous tenor at the time, called Vladimir Rosen, who you, of course, don't know. Anyway, he was in the audience. She got him up, she brought him on stage, and he sang the "Death of Isolde," and she danced it. She did that sort of thing.

CAVETT: Just on the spot.

ASHTON: Just on the spot.

CAVETT: Without any—. . .

ASHTON: Absolutely. Because, I imagine, she was the great improviser. I don't imagine that her dances were all that set, you know.

CAVETT: You wouldn't care to give us an impression of how she moved on stage?

ASHTON: Me??

[At this point, Ashton gets up and moves about the seats in a circle, waving his arms, and then sits down.]

ASHTON: Always ready to make a fool of myself.

CAVETT: That's the best impression I've ever seen a knight give of Isadora.

ASHTON: Well, funny enough, when I met Martha Graham . . . I said, "Did you ever see Isadora?" And she said no, and she said, "I can't imagine what she's like." So I said, "Well, I'll show you." And she said to me, "Well, this is the first time that I've got an impression of what she was like," so that was nice. . . .

CAVETT: . . .We have a lot of balletomanes and also people who love ballet in the studio audience today who knew you were going to be here.

ASHTON: Well, I don't want to offend them.

CAVETT: Would you care if I asked them for a question or two in the minutes that we have left?

ASHTON: Certainly.

CAVETT: Does anyone have something they would like to ask Sir Frederick before he slips back across the sea? Gentleman in front?

AUDIENCE MEMBER: Yes, I was wondering, Sir Frederick, if you could please comment on any works that The Royal Ballet has had commissioned and perhaps any work that you have done with composers?

ASHTON: Well, I've done commissioned work with Sir William Walton, Benjamin Britten, [Heinz Werne] Henze—I did *Ondine* with him. Dame Ninette de Valois did commissioned works with Bliss, with *The Rake's Progress*, I've forgotten his name—[gestures to audience]. Come on—. . . .

AUDIENCE: Gavin Gordon.

CAVETT: You have a group of prompters!

ASHTON: I need them.

CAVETT: Yes, the lady there? Stand up: maybe they'll catch you on mike there.

AUDIENCE MEMBER: Many of your ballets have been enriched by the presence of Margot Fonteyn in lead roles. Were you a perfect team from the beginning?

ASHTON: . . . Not from the beginning, not at all from the beginning. When I first made contact with her, I didn't respond to her at all. I found her stubborn. I found her difficult to mold, and we had quite a sort of altercation after one tour. She went back to her mother and said, "That man's mad." But after, I was doing a ballet, *Baiser de la Fée* of Stravinsky, and she did the variation, and I said, "That's no good at all, work much harder," I said. And she was trying very hard, and she did it once more, and then she came and burst into tears on my shoulder, and then I knew that I'd won. And then from then onwards it was perfect. We had this wonderful collaboration together, and the glorious years of working with such a wonderful person. . . .

CAVETT: . . .Why should it be so that The Royal Ballet is said to dance better away from home than they do at home? One hears this.

ASHTON: The audience here is so incredibly electric, and they respond so much more, and they urge them on, and that's why. I mean, an artist is perfectly human; if they're dancing against an indifferent, polite audience, and it's a very different matter from dancing with an audience who's electric, who's giving out—of course, it's easy to respond.

—Cavett

George Balanchine (1904–1983)

Youth

The dancer and Broadway star Tamara Geva, Balanchine's first wife, married him in Petrograd when she was fifteen and he was eighteen. In her memoirs, she gives two physical descriptions of him that are unusual among all the remembrances on the Balanchine bookshelf—in the first case, because she gives his height and a sense of his physique and, in the second case, because her word portrait is clearly that of someone who studied his features and expressions:

> He was about five feet ten, slight of build, yet possessing a quiet force. His hair was long, and a lock of it fell over one eye, like Father's. His movements were smooth and graceful, and although his voice was soft and his manner polite, his whole presence projected the confidence of a leader. With his aquiline features and Byronic hair, he seemed a combination of poet and general. . . .
>
> George had an impregnable face. His eyes, alert, vaguely suspicious and full of wonder, guarded his emotions and the endless images in his mind like two little animals protecting their hideaway. Even excitement could not alter that façade; it exhilarated his speech and widened the pupils of his eyes, but his countenance kept its enigmatic mold.
>
> —Geva, pp. 272, 295

Bicycle Ballet

The following story, originally published in *Dance News*, by one of Balanchine's classmates at the Imperial Ballet School, exemplifies Balanchine's devotion to duty, even at the expense of his personal well-being. The "dire food shortages" referred to had occurred a few years before, during the Revolution and the Civil War. The school itself was closed for a time, and Balanchine, like many St. Petersburgians, roamed the streets looking for food and, accounts have it, was reduced to eating stray cats. Eventually, he would spend time in a sanitorium from tuberculosis, one of his lungs having collapsed, a medical condition probably traceable to the ravages of those difficult years.

There can be little doubt that his concentration on both dance and music—the foundation of his later excellence in choreography—coming as it did at a time of dire food shortage, damaged his health for life. By this time he had already begun to show symptoms of tuberculosis and to spit blood, but he never spared himself. His friend Mikhail Mikhailov, a student one class behind him in the school, remembers that during the first or second summer recess after his entry into the corps de ballet of the State Theater, Georgi was chosen by Elizaveta Gerdt, whose usual partner was suddenly indisposed, to support her in an afternoon performance at the outdoor theater at Pavlovsk, the country palace, 16 miles south of Leningrad, built by Catherine the Great for her son Paul. They were to dance a pas de deux from *Swan Lake.* The flattering summons arrived on the morning of the matinee itself, and Georgi went off in search of a costume. The first half of the performance was over, and the bells for the second had rung, and there was still no sign of him. At the very last moment, the reassembling audience parted to let through a frantic cyclist, and Georgi arrived at the stage door clasping a parcel. He apologized to his partner. "I am late. Please forgive me. It took a long time to find a costume, and when I got to the railroad station I could see only the end of the train vanishing into the distance. There was nothing for it but to borrow a bicycle from some people I know." After his 16-mile bicycle ride, he partnered Gerdt in the *Swan Lake* pas de deux.

—Buckle, *Balanchine,* pp. 16–17

"Will She Dance?"

The first studios of the School of American Ballet, when the school opened on January 2, 1934, were located at 59th Street and Madison Avenue on the East Side of Manhattan—"a space that, some 30 years before, Paris Singer had leased for Isadora Duncan," is how Lincoln Kirstein, whose imagination was intoxicated with layers of history, remembered it. The now-classic anecdote below, from the same essay, is quintessential Kirstein:

Odd parents, a few very odd, commenced bringing children—mostly girls, too tall, short, or plump—to be auditioned by this young master, who, not yet known to America, had already been interviewed by the dance critic of *The New York Times.* One woman asked him, after he'd inspected her daughter in a practice class, "Will she dance?" What she meant was, "Do you think she is beautiful and talented, as a child, and will she be a star?" A middle-class American mother was seeking a prognosis, as from an allergist about her child's rash. The putative ballerina clung to Mummy's skirt, exhibiting filial attachment worthy of a Shirley Temple. Balanchine was unassertive, slim, no longer boyish, and, with his grave, alert mannerliness, the more daunting in his authority, instinctive and absolute. He hesitated, perhaps to make sure he would be understood; she repeated her question, "Will my daughter dance?" A Delphic response was the reply she received, sounding more oracular couched in French, although the sound of its meaning was plain enough through its four transparent cognates: *"La Danse, Madame, c'est une question morale."*

— Kirstein, *Portrait*, pp. 15–16

The Ideal Balanchine Dancer

Lacking stars, or refusing to project given dancers into an unwarranted prominence, Balanchine began by distributing virtuosity itself more evenly over his entire corps. But if one were to analyze this corps with attention, one would soon see that there was very little uniformity, except in a capacity to move fast. There would be tall girls and short ones and those between. His notion of a working company was a kind of visual organ with many stops; one needed blonde notes as well as brunette, with an occasional redhead. There would be approximate giantesses and token dwarfs; acrid and piquant notes were valuable and needed. The essential, without which no Balanchine-dancer could be imagined, was one whose motion was unconstricted, who did not resist his often extraordinary convolutions that deformed or denied the ordinary habit of how a dancer saw herself as beautiful, plus a capacity for ever-accelerating quickness. If one could imagine a slim arrow with the resilience of a snake of toughened steel, headed by a thinking dart, this would symbolize the ideal Balanchine dancer. (Lincoln Kirstein)

— Reynolds, pp. 5–6

Imprisoned in a Cage, Guarded by Enormous Birds

In 2004, to celebrate the centenary of George Balanchine's birth, the Harvard Theatre Collection mounted a ranging and detailed exhibition of its collection of Balanchine's personal papers and possessions such as theater designs, photographs, and paintings. The materials contained a number of surprises, such as an application for a Vespa franchise, from the early 1950s, made out by Balanchine and dancer Frank Hobi. One could also read a heartbreakingly affectionate, handwritten letter, complete with drawings, that Balanchine wrote to his paralyzed wife Tanaquil Le Clercq in 1965, by which time, memoirists tell us, the couple were essentially separated. (It was unclear from the exhibition whether, in fact, the letter was ever sent to Le Clercq.)

Perhaps most unexpected of all was the typescript of what seems to be a mystical narrative for *Le Palais de cristal*, the apparently storyless 1947 ballet— set to the symphony that Georges Bizet wrote when he was seventeen—that Balanchine made for the Paris Opéra, transforming it the next year into the unquestionably storyless *Symphony in C* for the newly founded New York City Ballet. *Le Palais de cristal*, a reconstruction of which the Paris Opéra Ballet performed in New York in the 1990s, has costumes by the Surrealist Léonor Fini that are differently colored for each of the ballet's four movements.

(In the program of the Paris production, Balanchine identified each color as that of a different jewel.) Not until the Harvard exhibition, however, could most Balanchine fans have ever guessed that the colors may have represented what was once an ornate, quasi-narrative vision. The actual typing of the libretto was probably done by someone other than Balanchine, who may have also performed copyediting on his writing. Even so, according to Barbara Horgan, his personal assistant of long-standing, the ideas are indisputably Mr. B's. Below is the script's first page, which was all that was visible in the exhibition vitrine:

The Crystal Palace
Libretto, Choreography, and Production by George Balanchine

Score Mark	Scenario
Part	Part I—The House of Rubies
1st mvt.: allegro vivo	Tableux [*sic*]. Lights brighten slowly upon the façade of an Indian Temple, encrusted with rubies, set in heavy gold.
10 bars after /1/	Dancers appear, in short tutus, bearing gifts to the Ruby Priestess.
12 bars after /5/	Each lays her present on a low table in front of the center of the doorway.
/7/	The Ruby Priestess appears and greets dancers bearing gifts.
/9/	Ruby Priestess reappears, describing an episode from the Ramayana. Pas de deux with Ruby Priest.
7 bars after /15/	Gift bearers express amazement at her beauty and pay homage.
/18/	Priestess chooses most beautiful stone and exits.
/20/	Recapitulation. Priestess reappears, wearing the chosen stone and leads celebration.
	Part II—The Sapphire Gate
2nd mvt.: adagio	The Sapphire Spirit, imprisoned in a cage guarded by enormous birds.
/3/	She tries in vain to open the gate.
/5/	The birds lull her to sleep.
7 bars after /7/	In a dream the Sapphire Sultan seems to open the gate and in a languorous dance they celebrate their passion.

/19/   At the end the cage vanishes and the birds turn
                              into beautiful girls and handsome men.

Rehearsing *Concerto Barocco* with The Royal Ballet, 1950

Moira Shearer:

A passage in the extremely taxing piano score was not quite as he wanted
it. After some discussion with the pianist, he asked her to move from the
piano stool. Taking her place, he played the entire section with the exact
variations of tempo that he required. I already knew that he was the most
musical of choreographers, but this mastery of the piano was a revelation.
I was hopelessly in love with him for a full ten minutes.

—Shearer, p. x

Trouper

In 1951, Jerome Robbins, then dancing with and choreographing for the
young New York City Ballet, made a work for the company called *The Pied
Piper*, to the *Clarinet Concerto* of Aaron Copland.

The Piper is the clarinetist and his part calls for wandering around on
stage, and then parking himself on a high stool. At the end of the ballet, a
large group of dancers participate in a kind of conga line behind the Piper.
I am told that once, when the ballet was performed on tour, a clarinetist
simply refused to be onstage, and George Balanchine had to go up and
pantomime the part while the clarinetist played it from the pit!

—Copland, p. 97

A Cup of Coffee

In 1953, the critic Edwin Denby—one of the most sensitive observers of
George Balanchine's art ever to commit his impressions to print—had a few
questions to ask the choreographer, whose company, the New York City
Ballet, was then performing at City Center, on West 55th Street in Manhattan. "One evening," Denby wrote, "after watching an excellent performance
of *Four Temperaments*, I found him backstage and we went across 56th Street
together to the luncheonette for a cup of coffee." They talked for a while of
such subjects as the ballet tradition in Balanchine's native St. Petersburg
("He spoke as a quiet man does of something he knows entirely and knows
he loves," Denby wrote), and then "Balanchine noticed that Steve wanted to
close his luncheonette," so the two men returned to the theater, whose stage
door fronts 56th Street, and they continued their conversation in the backstage corridor.

We got on the subject of notation. He emphasized the continuity of movement it could reproduce. I asked if *Four Temperaments* had been notated, adding that I felt sure the public in 40 years time would enjoy seeing it as we do, and would want to see it danced in the form it has now. "Oh, in 40 years," he said, "ballet will be all different." After a momentary pause, he said firmly, as if returning to facts, that he believed ballet was entertainment. I realized he meant the word in its large sense of both a social and an attractive public occasion. But he looked at me and added, in a more personal tone, that when one makes a ballet, there is of course something or other one wants to say—one says what one says. He looked away, as if shrugging his shoulders, as one does after mentioning something one can't help but that one doesn't make an issue of in public.

—Denby, *Dance Writings*, pp. 433–434

Drills

Later rehearsals were moved to the theater building [City Center], to a gloomy echoing room upstairs modeled on a chapter-room in a castle of the Knights Templar. Here, Balanchine took the dancers by shifts and choreographed from 10:30 to six. "I work like a dentist," he remarked.

—Denby, *Dance Writings*, p. 477

Early Experiments

Ballerina Yvonne Mounsey danced for Balanchine in the 1940s at the Ballet Russe de Monte Carlo and in the 1950s at the New York City Ballet:

Sometimes, backstage, during *Serenade* or something when we were all in costume, Mr. B. would decide to switch people's roles, roles they'd rehearsed. "You do that, you do that part." He would switch at the last minute to see what people looked like in different combinations.

—Hite interview

From Russia, with Love

During an interview with a group of American dance critics who traveled to the Soviet Union in 1983, the late Russian dance historian Vera Krasovskaya recalled the first night of the New York City Ballet's first appearance in St. Petersburg, in 1962:

Balanchine] opened in *Serenade*. And I thought how sorry I was that I had to stay for more ballets. I just wanted to walk along the Neva and think about all the beautiful things I'd seen.

—Aloff, unpaginated

Ballet Is Woman

Man is a better cook, a better painter, a better musician, composer. Everything is man—sports—everything. Man is stronger, faster. Why? Because we have muscles, and we're made that way. And woman accepts this. It is her business to accept. She knows what's beautiful. Men are great poets, because men have to write beautiful poetry for woman—odes to a beautiful woman. Woman accepts the beautiful poetry. You see, man is the servant—a good servant. In ballet, however, woman is first. Everywhere else man is first. But in ballet, it's the woman. All my life I have dedicated my art to her. (George Balanchine)

—Gruen, p. 284

Secretariat?

Bernard Taper, Balanchine's biographer, remembers an instance when Balanchine gave him some advice:

I was complaining to Balanchine one day about the scarcity of documentary materials pertaining to his life, particularly his inner life. I had been reading some biographies of literary figures—abounding in quotations from the subjects' diaries, letters, journals, and memoirs—and, as a biographer, I was feeling deprived. Balanchine had never journalized and in his lifetime had written perhaps fewer letters than the number of ballets he had choreographed. Balanchine listened to my complaint and then replied, "You should think of your task as if you were writing the biography of a racehorse. A racehorse doesn't keep a diary."

—Taper, p. x

To Be of Use

Robert A. Gottlieb, the editor and dance critic, is a native New Yorker who has followed the New York City Ballet from its founding in 1948. He was once a member of its board of directors, and for ten years in the 1970s and '80s he worked for the company as a volunteer, drawing up the programs and serving as a consultant on publicity. In his recent memoir-biography of Balanchine, Gottlieb makes the point that the choreographer was, by nature, a fatalist and, for the most part, an unflappable one. In times of crisis, he husbanded his energy to focus on tasks that he knew he could accomplish and left the tasks he wasn't good at to others. As examples, Gottlieb relates two anecdotes of moments that he personally observed:

During the 1976 orchestra strike the dispute had been submitted to arbitration and been moved to the World Trade Center. (We had been in discussions for almost six months.) One morning, after hours of sitting around waiting to meet with the orchestra committee, all of us on the management team ran out of dimes to use in the public telephones—this was before cell phones, of course—but were afraid to leave the building to get more, in case we were suddenly summoned to the bargaining table. Eddie Bigelow used his last dime to leave a message for George Michelmore, the company's orchestra contractor, to bring dimes, and plenty of them. An hour later Balanchine burst into the room with a bag of dimes, asking, "Am I in time?" They had given the message to the wrong George, and he had assumed that the dimes were somehow crucial to the negotiations. He was so grateful to have been given a useful job to do that no one had the heart to disillusion him.

Another scene: The Tschaikovsky Festival of 1981 was notable for an amazing backdrop that had been commissioned from Philip Johnson for the entire celebration. It was a gigantic assemblage of translucent plastic tubes strung together and hung from the top of the stage, and it was very beautiful when properly lit. But on the day it was being installed—which was the day the festival was to begin—all was chaos. One of the very large, heavy tubes crashed to the stage, narrowly missing a stagehand, who would have been seriously injured if it had struck him. And then, as the tubes were exposed to the heat of the powerful stage lights, they began to smell (actually, they began to stink). No one knew whether the stage would be ready in time or whether the theater would be habitable. Balanchine sat in the middle of the theater, ignoring the hysteria surrounding him, totally focused on the way Merrill Ashley's *Swan Lake* tiara sat on her head. That was the one thing he could do something about, and he was doing it.

—Gottlieb, pp. 189–190

An Irony Curtain

Among the many saddening stories that the thrilling Bolshoi ballerina Maya Plisetskaya tells of her thwarted career under Soviet rule, one of the saddest is a little moment with Balanchine, whom she met at a party, given in her honor by Jacqueline Kennedy, during Plisetskaya's tour of the United States with the Bolshoi, in 1966. One can hardly imagine which was more painful—Balanchine's stinging assessment of her technique or her inability to speak to him openly of her situation, for fear the KGB might overhear:

At the party, I had an interesting chance to talk with Balanchine. He came with Lucia Davidova, his close friend and awed fan. In the aristocratic tones of the first wave of émigrés from revolutionary Russia, Lucia called Balanchine *bozhenka*, the diminutive form of "God." He responded to her unearthly nickname without a murmur.

"Maya, who is your teacher?" Balanchine asked unexpectedly.

"On this trip?"

"No, always. Who keeps an eye on you?"

I hesitated. The KGB kept an eye on me. Mikhail Vladimirovich had brought me from the theater to the door of Jacqueline's apartment. He didn't have the nerve to go in himself, without an invitation: she was the President's widow, after all. Even though he was dying to do it. He might have still been out there, stamping his feet. Who knew?

"I can't name just one teacher. I go to Asaf Messerer's class. I rehearse with Ilyushchenko and Semyonova. But to tell you the truth, I'm my own boss."

"Being your own boss isn't bad. But, don't be angry, Maya, you need a good teacher."

—Plisetskaya, p. 263

Last Easter Feast

Many stories about Balanchine have been published by Francis Mason, both in *Ballet Review*, the quarterly he now edits, and in his anthology of memoirs, *I Remember Balanchine*. The following remembrance is contained in the last of a four-part *Ballet Review* memoir about Balanchine's love of cooking by Karin von Aroldingen, former ballerina with the New York City Ballet and a person with whom Balanchine was very close in the last years of his life, to the extent that he would join her, her husband, and their daughter for holidays— on the occasion of at least one Christmas Eve, arriving fully costumed as Santa Claus. In his will, Balanchine bequeathed von Aroldingen the rights to six of his ballets, among them his hour-long choreographic essay about love and spirit, *Liebeslieder Walzer*.

Balanchine was deeply religious, and he had great affection and reverence for the traditions of the Russian Orthodox Church. In old Russia, these traditions included the celebration of many holidays with parades, puppet theater, fairs, circuses, fireworks, and grand displays of every kind. Anniversaries, weddings, and the more important saints' name-days were celebrated lavishly. Balanchine did not celebrate his own birthday; instead, he celebrated the name-day of his patron saint: St. George. What a nice custom.

Easter is the most important Orthodox holiday and is celebrated by Russian émigrés all over the world. Mr. B became thoughtful and solitary during this sacred time, observing the religious rites quietly in his own home. He adorned a small altar with candles, photographs, and precious icons, of which he had a treasured collection. I noticed one photograph in particular; it was of one of Balanchine's uncles, a bishop. I was mesmerized as Mr. B described to me his sacramental clothing and mitre; it sounded so theatrical.

Easter was also the rare occasion on which Balanchine visited the Orthodox church—Our Lady of the Sign, at Park Avenue and 92nd Street. The mass ended long after midnight on Saturday night, with the priest announcing *"Christos voskres!"* ("Christ is risen") and the congregation answering *"Voistinu voskres!"* ("Truly, He is risen"). Then the priest led a procession out into the night. The worshippers followed him with lit candles for a time, then spread out, gathering in the streets for a while to exchange greetings and wishes before heading home.

In Russia the symbol of the home is the table, and preparations for the Easter feast begin weeks ahead of time. In 1982, Orthodox Easter fell on April 18. Despite his failing strength, Balanchine had done all his work to perfection and joined his friends in church for mass, as usual, late on Saturday night. Most of his dinner guests attended the Easter mass with him, and most had attended Balanchine's Easter feast many times before; still, when we finally arrived at his home and he opened the door for us all, we were overwhelmed by the sight of the decorated tables, the fragrance of fresh flower arrangements with lilies and hyacinths, the sound of a choir coming through the radio. It was like a spring tide of life-force.

—Aroldingen, pp. 48–49

Last Illness

Balanchine died at Roosevelt Hospital in 1983, at the age of seventy-nine. The following account is based on ballerina Moira Shearer's interview with Barbara Horgan, his devoted assistant, who, after his death, went on to found The George Balanchine Trust, which oversees the leasing and teaching of many of his ballets. The ballerinas referred to by first name are, in order of mention, Vera Zorina, Tamara Toumanova, Maria Tallchief, and Alexandra Danilova:

He lay in his hospital bed for five months. At first he talked frequently about coming home and resuming work, then less, and then, if he mentioned this at all, it was always "next week" or "next month." He was very ill much of the time, his memory and power of speech often deserting him completely, but his room was always filled with visitors. Barbara Horgan speaks of the generosity of the hospital authorities, who waived almost every rule and regulation at this time; she was continually involved with the staff as she had to arrange for day and night nurses during this long period. Dancers and wives all came to see him—Brigitta, Tamara, Maria, Choura Danilova and, of course, the company. Karin von Aroldingen was perhaps his greatest comfort: she attended him devotedly and even at his lowest moments he always recognized her step in the corridor before she entered his room. Barbara Horgan speaks particularly of Maria and Choura. Maria was more outwardly upset than anyone, "near hysteria" each time she left his room and always in tears when she telephoned from Chicago. But Danilova was the most affecting of all. She came only once to the hospital, and when she left his room she said, "I won't come here again—I have said goodbye to him." Watching her walk slowly away, Barbara Horgan felt a great sorrow for Choura, realizing that she was losing her oldest and dearest friend.

—Shearer, p. 172

A Butterfly's Account

Susan Pilarre, née Susan Pillersdorf, danced for Balanchine at the New York City Ballet for seventeen years, primarily in solo roles. Since 1986, she has been a member of the faculty of the School of American Ballet:

Mr. B used to call me "PillersDORF, dear." And he was very nasal, and the accent on the "dorf," it just bothered me. He liked how it sounded, he just liked to say it. But it made me upset, and at one point I said to him, "Mr. B, can't you just call me Suzy?" And he said, "You don't call me Georgy." So I decided to change it, because the heavy accent on the "dorf" just didn't befit the ethereal creature I was trying to be. Everybody called me Suzy Pill, so if I changed my name to Montgomery or something, it would have been really odd. So I decided I would make it two r's and an e, because I liked the French. So I changed my name, and that was fine, and eventually he did call me Suzy. But one night we were down on stage before the performance, and he used to dress up, and he had on his blazer and his western tie. I noticed on his lapel he had a pin, and it was a butterfly. It was very pretty, and he liked jewelry. So I said, "Oh, Mr. B, I love your pin. Is it a new pin?" And he said, "Oh, no, dear, it's a very old pin." I was trying to be very clever, so I said, "Oh, did you have it when it was a caterpillar?" And he said, without taking a beat, "CaterpillarsDORF, dear." He was unbelievable!

—Phillips, p. 23

Of Steps and
Their Authorship

The Dying Swan (Le Cygne)

This famous ballet solo, created in St. Petersburg in 1905 by Michel Fokine for the young Anna Pavlova, has been danced by many ballerinas around the world, each of whom has changed or adjusted the choreography to her technique and temperament. Indeed, as early as the mid-1920s, Fokine, by then permanently transplanted to the West, published an official version of the choreography, a "detailed description of the dance," accompanied by thirty-six photographs of Vera Fokina demonstrating the ballet's key sequential poses (J. Fischer and Brother, New York, ca. 1925). This document would not have been available to the Soviet ballet companies that preserved the solo as a ballerina vehicle, which would account for Kirov-trained Natalia Makarova's assertion below that Fokine had really provided only a sketch of the steps for Pavlova, when, as his description makes clear, he had also set specific poses and a dramatic throughline—elements from which Pavlova herself may have departed over time. Still, Makarova's account of learning the dance (which she performed beautifully on her own terms) and of its tradition in Soviet Russia conveys an excellent example of how choreography is transmuted—and, sometimes, radically altered—in order to serve the varying gifts of individual performers:

> It is another matter with Fokine's *The Dying Swan*, which has celebrated its 70th anniversary by now. Of Fokine's original choreography, however, only scattered fragments remain; as is well known, he created only the bourrées for Pavlova. Subsequently, every performer, be she Ulanova or Plisetskaya or Chauviré, has used the piece to her own taste and at her own risk. In Russia I had danced Dudinskaya's version and never felt

myself at home in it. Moreover, I experienced a certain discomfort in front of the audience, from all the sentimental stuff—the rushing around the stage, the flailing of arms, the direct imitation of a dying bird. To the contemporary eye, its conventions look almost ludicrous. . . .

The Dying Swan has certain specific difficulties: the expressive character of the arms-wings and the free plasticity of the body are combined with continuous bourrées suggesting the movement of a swan gliding on the water. These bourrées look as if the dancer's feet were moving independently from the rest of the body, and at the same time the dance needs total emotional abandon, conveying the image of a struggle with death or a surrender to it. Without this emotional content there can be no drama. What is difficult is that, as I say, the chest and the legs are "divorced" in this dance: the continuous bourrées must be perfectly coordinated with the plasticity of the body thrown into the element of free motion. Otherwise, *The Dying Swan* is not very difficult technically; it is necessary only to rehearse with the arms a lot, and to overcome the tension of the bourrées, which should not exhaust you but come almost mechanically. As for the emotional content, I was helped by Pavlova, whose film of the work I saw. Even today her *Swan* is striking—the flawless feeling for style, the animated face—although certain melodramatic details seem superfluous.

—Makarova, p. 119

Practically a Joke

The following story was related—with much more literary style than this paraphrase—by the late David Daniel in conversation. (Daniel, a critic of ballet and classical music and a great admirer of Suzanne Farrell, interviewed her for publication several times.)

The ongoing tension in ballet between virtuosity and vulgarity—exemplified by Anna Pavlova's observation that more than two continuous pirouettes from a single preparation would be vulgar, because more than two cannot be appreciated individually as turns but rather only perceived as undifferentiated spinning—is summed up in the following anecdote about Farrell, a dancer who could turn like a top yet who characteristically observed Balanchine's preference, like Pavlova's, for two pristine, sculptural revolutions, rather than a whirling sequence.

At some point in the life of *The Nutcracker* that George Balanchine staged for the New York City Ballet, it became a company ritual to play insider practical jokes during the New Year's Eve performance. Farrell, who was reserved, did not take easily to this practice. The first time she danced in the production on New Year's Eve, she stood alone, in costume, in the wings, a formidable creature who didn't talk to anyone. Another dancer ran up to her, however, and said, "It's New Year's Eve. What are you going to do?"

"Do?" Farrell said.

"Well," the dancer said, "like So-and-So, who comes out of the box in Chinese ["Tea"] and does Violette Verdy's variation from "Emeralds."

According to one report, Farrell's eyeballs rolled back in her head. She couldn't bring herself to make a travesty of Balanchine's choreography, even to welcome in the New Year. On the other hand, she didn't want to be thought a stick-in-the-mud.

"Okay," she said. "I'll do four pirouettes in the pas de deux."

—Aloff, interview

The Hornpipe on Tap

Theatergoers could see a considerable amount of dancing by visiting professionals from Europe in the Thirteen Colonies and, later, the United States during the eighteenth century. However, the first celebrated American-born dancer was John Durang (1768–1822), who is remembered today most especially for his hornpipe dance, which he popularized in the 1780s. Julian Mates, a historian of early American musical theater, explains that to see the contribution of the hornpipe to the art of tap dancing, all one needs to do is to look at the directions for Durang's "A Sailor's Hornpipe—Old Style"; John Durang taught it to his son Charles, who reproduced it in a study of theatrical dancing, published in 1855. Mates notes that "each step takes up one strain of the tune":

1. Glissade round (first part of tune)
2. Double shuffle down, do.
3. Heel and toe back, finish with back shuffle.
4. Cut the buckle down, finish the shuffle.
5. Side shuffle right and left, finishing with beats.
6. Pigeon wing going round.
7. Heel and toe haul back in.
8. Steady toes down.
9. Changes back, finish with back shuffle and beats.
10. Wave step down.
11. Heel and toe shuffle obliquely back.
12. Whirligig, with beats down.
13. Sissonne and entrechats back.
14. Running forward on the heels.
15. Double Scotch step, with a heel Brand in Plase. [sic: "Place"]
16. Single Scotch step back.
17. Parried toes round, or feet *in* and *out*.
18. The Cooper shuffle right and left back.
19. Grasshopper step down.
20. *Terre-a-terre* [sic] or beating on toes back.
21. Jockey crotch down.
22. Traverse round, with hornpipe glissade.

Bow and finish.

—Mates, p. 167

Jump Cut

Moira Shearer, the star of the 1948 movie *The Red Shoes*, had an idea about the tragic ending, which she relayed to the director, Michael Powell:

> Mr Powell! I can jump over the balustrade onto a mattress, if you have one."
>
> A mattress was found.
>
> "Mr Powell! Shall I jump like a girl committing suicide, or like a ballerina?"
>
> I thought. "Like a ballerina."
>
> She is only in the air for about eight frames, but it is one of the most beautiful cuts in the film.
>
> —Powell, p. 653

Policing the Language

Breakdancing, now practiced internationally, began in the Bronx as a competition dance among kids, who performed its maneuvers on cement and macadam, using pieces of discarded cardboard boxes as their only cushioning. The first dance critic to write about them was Sally Banes, in a story called "To the Beat Y'All: Breaking Is Hard to Do," published in the *Village Voice*, April 10, 1981:

> Chico and Tee and their friends from 175th Street in the High Times crew were breaking in the subway, and the cops busted them for fighting.
>
> "We're not fighting. We're dancing!" At the precinct station, one kid demonstrated certain moves: a head spin, ass spin, swipe, chin freeze, the "Helicopter," "the Baby."
>
> An officer called in the other members of the crew, one by one. "Do a head spin," he would command as he consulted a clipboard full of notes. "Do 'the Baby.'" As each kid complied, performing on cue as unhesitatingly as a ballet dancer might toss off an enchaînement, the cops scratched their heads in bewildered defeat.
>
> Or so the story goes. But then, like ballet and like great battles (it shares elements of both), breaking is wreathed in legends. . . .
>
> Some people claim that breaking is played out. Freddy Love disagrees. "The younger kids keep developing it, doing more wild things and more new stuff. We never used to spin or do acrobatics. The people who started it just laid down the foundations. Just like in graffiti—you make a new style. That's what life on the street is all about, just being you, being who you are around your friends. What's at stake is a guy's honor and his position in the street. Which is all you have. That's what makes it so important, that's what makes it feel so good—that pressure on you to be the best. Or to try to be the best. To develop a new style nobody can deal with. If it's true that this stuff reflects life, it's a fast life."
>
> —Banes, pp. 121, 125

Music Makes Me . . .

Fred Astaire on George Gershwin

"He wrote for feet."

—Behrman, p. 256

Hot Needles

Eudora Welty:

Our Victrola stood in the dining room. I was allowed to climb onto the seat of a diningroom chair to wind it, start the record turning, and set the needle playing. In a second I'd jumped to the floor, to spin or march around the table as the music called for—now there were all the other records I could play too. I skinned back onto the chair just in time to lift the needle at the end, stop the record and turn it over, then change the needle. That brass receptacle with a hole in the lid gave off a metallic smell like human sweat, from all the hot needles that were fed it. Winding up, dancing, being cocked to start and stop the record, was of course all in one the act of *listening*—to "Overture to *Daughter of the Regiment*," "Selections from *The Fortune Teller*," "Kiss Me Again," "Gypsy Dance from *Carmen*," "Stars and Stripes Forever," "When the Midnight Choo-Choo Leaves for Alabam," or whatever came next. Movement must be at the very heart of listening.

—Welty, p. 851

Finding Something Else

I had a marionette theater of my own, and I used to make my own marionettes. My father gave me pocket money to buy a record a week. I bought

practically the entire repertoire of Gilbert and Sullivan. Finally, my father hinted that it might be a good idea if I found something else. So I tried ballet music. I bought *Schéhérazade* and *Firebird*, rather because of their names . . . especially *Firebird*. I started to try and imagine what they could possibly be doing. I think it was these imaginings and wonderings to music—that sort of fantasizing to music—that started me off to wish to be a choreographer. I never actually wanted to be a dancer. (John Cranko)
—Gruen, p. 171

A Basic Unobscured State of Clarity and Emptiness

In 1977, Ellen Pearlman, a practitioner of Buddhism, traveled to Dharamsala, in India, to visit the Buddhist population that had migrated there from Tibet, following the devastation wreaked on their country by China, then in the grip of the Cultural Revolution. In Dharamsala, Pearlman visited the Namgyal Monastery, "the monastic compound of His Holiness, the Dalai Lama," where she was permitted to wander rather freely, "watching in awe as monks in rough crimson robes—studying for their degree of Geshe, or Ph.D. in philosophy—smacked their malas (rosaries) together as they made a particularly invigorating point in their logical debates." It was there that she was deeply affected by Tibetan sacred dance and its powerful music:

> One overcast and soft gray afternoon I noticed Tibetans hanging around the complex speaking excitedly. Out of the corner of my eye I saw a group of dancers *whoosh* by in colorful and ornamented brocade costumes. Fortunately, I happened to be carrying a crude box camera and instinctively reached for it, clicking as they rushed by on their way to perform a sacred ceremony. Intrigued, I followed. Although I wasn't allowed to enter the shrine room, I was able to watch through the open door.
>
> Monks pursed their lips and blew through enormous long horns, followed by blasts from other monks playing shorter trumpets. The hair on my arms stood on end, and I felt something no music had ever stirred in me before, a sense of coming back into myself. Dancing slowly and deliberately, in measured, synchronized steps, the dancers turned while the cymbals clashed and a bass drum beat out a slow, continuous rhythm.
>
> I don't remember how long this went on, but I do remember that my mind, literally, stopped. All concepts drained away, and I could focus only on the spectacle in front of me. I didn't know then that I was experiencing *bodhicitta*, a basic unobscured state of clarity and emptiness. I didn't understand what I was seeing, nor did I know what it meant. I was clueless about what the monks were practicing—a special kind of meditation that used body, speech, and mind. I just knew I felt at peace, and returned to an inner tranquility I knew was there but didn't know how to find.
>
> —Pearlman, pp. 2–4

Three Meals a Day an' Jelly at Night

In 1927, the aspiring writer Carl Carmer (1893–1976)—graduate of Hamilton College, possessor of a master's degree in English literature from Harvard, and a veteran of World War I—left his position as full professor at the University of Rochester to take a job teaching at the University of Alabama, at Tuscaloosa. It was the era of the Scottsboro Boys and the heyday of the Ku Klux Klan; it was also a moment when oral folktales (such as Br'er Rabbit stories) were actively retold, when superstitions and magic spells among the black population were frequently discussed, and when people from all corners of society loved to dance. Over the next six years, Carmer traveled around the state, meeting both white and black citizens, observing behavior both public and private, hearing about a lynching that was happening as the messenger was delivering the news, and taking lots of notes. His experiences resulted in a best-selling, and controversial, book, published in 1934, called *Stars Fell on Alabama*; the title refers to a legend among black Alabamians that the state's fearsomely cruel history of race relations began back in the mists of time, when an ill-omened shower of stars poured down on the land.

Somewhere this side of fact and that side of New Journalism ("All of the events related in this book happened substantially as I recorded them," Carmer wrote in an author's note, adding that some identities had been disguised "to avoid causing them serious embarrassment" and that, in some places, time had been "telescoped"), *Stars Fell on Alabama* is filled with anecdotes about social dancing and dancelike ceremonies. In Tuscaloosa, the author attended spring dances for university students, who paid "fabulous prices running into the thousands of dollars to bring second-rate Northern bands" to the city. "The dancing itself is extraordinary," Carmer continued:

It is violent and full of strange and fanciful variations. An Eastern collegian, sedately accustomed to dignified stepping to the music of New York hotel orchestras is completely baffled here. I said something like that to a Tuscaloosa girl once. She replied that Alabama stepping was tame compared to that of Mississippi, and offered to pick out by their dancing from the mass of whirling, strutting couples, the girls who came from the neighboring state. She was right in every instance.

In Springville, Carmer watched a square-dance evening, filled with "moving squares" of four couples each, accompanied by country fiddlers who played a fantastic array of fantastically titled tunes. In the township of Nokomis, in Escambia County, he witnessed black Alabamians in a yearly "parade to make the crops grow": the participating men and women, dressed in their Sunday best, were preceded by a "tall man in front [who] led the procession in a series of wide concentric circles" around the town spring ("the best water anywhere in the county"). Some carried crosses made from twigs and others carried bits of broken glass: these items were tied to the branches of a nearby sycamore tree, to dangle down as offerings.

By contrast, in urban Mobile, Carmer attended the annual New Year's Eve ball of the Strikers, a mystic society ("a revelatory example of the quality that makes the survivals of social rituals in American life so charming"), where post-debutantes and wives were invited for a dance with a masked Striker (a "Masker") through a "call-out card." The Maskers would attend the ball dressed in costume as Louis XIV courtiers, the "regimentals" of American Revolutionaries, or other historical styles. The Captain of the Ball chose his lady and solemnly paraded her, under spotlights, down the center of the floor, followed by the other Maskers in single file. "At the end of the hall, while the Captain and his lady wait, they find their partners for the grand march—the first call-out. The Strikers' Ball has begun."

Perhaps the most detailed dance scene in the book is an account of a ring-shout dance among black teenagers, which took place in a small cabin on the grounds of the Tuscaloosa Country Club. The words of their song (an excerpt is reprinted below) anticipate "Satisfaction (I Can't Get No)" of the Rolling Stones by some thirty years:

In the middle of the narrow room, four black boys and four black girls pranced to the sensuous rhythm. A boy with gleaming teeth and protruding black eyes stepped lithely about, twisting his hips sharply within a ring the others had formed by joining hands. As he danced, he chanted in a monotone to his companions who circled about him, and they replied in an answering chorus:

See more, babe, satisfy,
(*All*) Satisfy!

See more, babe, satisfy,
(*All*) Satisfy!

Got my woman by my side
Ise satisfied, Ise satisfied
(*All*) Satisfied, Lor', satisfied.

See Corrinna tell her I say hurry home
Ain't had my rice since she been gone
What I mean when I say my rice
Three meals a day an' jelly at night.
(*All*) Satisfy, Satisfy.

—Carmer, p. 20 and passim

Music and Dance in Lockstep

The term "music visualization," sometimes rudely referred to as "Mickey-Mousing the music," is not a compliment to a choreographer these days: it suggests that the dance really has no creative independence from its score—that it does no more than translate its score into living bodies. Although

George Balanchine was sometimes accused of making music visualizations,
close analyses of his choreography (such as those recently published by the
dance historian and musician Stephanie Jordan in her study *Moving Music:
Dialogues with Music in Twentieth-Century Ballet*) unequivocally demonstrate
that he conducted highly sophisticated conversations with his scores—that
he did not simply mirror them.

On the other hand, Ruth St. Denis did truly want to produce music visualizations, a term that she may, in fact, have inspired. In her account of her
idea for them, below, she also suggests in passing that Isadora Duncan, another figure sometimes accused of visualizing the music, did not. St. Denis
interprets Duncan's spontaneous freedom from the music as a flaw, and that
interpretation stimulated St. Denis (encouraged, she writes, by her partner,
Ted Shawn, and by Denishawn pianist and composer Louis Horst) to provide an elaborate correction in her new "abstract" approach:

Two or three years before, I had seen Isadora Duncan dance again. As
usual she had stimulated me, but this time I also noticed her weaknesses.
As I watched her dancing Schubert's *Unfinished Symphony*, I noticed that
she stopped when the music became too complicated for the dance and
compromised by making one of her unforgettably noble gestures in complete disregard of the music.

The audience was enraptured, and I am sure most of the unthinking
ones felt they had witnessed a wonderful piece of musical visualization,
but that was exactly what they had not seen. She had interpreted and
reacted to the strains of this exquisite symphony, but she had in no way
maintained a consistent visualization of its structure or rhythm.

I sensed this vaguely at the time, but not until this afternoon in the
hotel at Edmonton did the solution dawn upon me—an orchestra of dancers which visualized an orchestra of music.

Ted replied to my letter most enthusiastically and said that when I returned home he would have 60 of his students waiting for me to experiment on. I was naturally very impatient to reach Los Angeles, and when I
got there I immediately went to work in Ted's studio, with his pupils and
Louis Horst.

We worked four hours a day for two months, and the time flew by.
Louis and the pupils responded enthusiastically to the new idea. Its ex-
planation sounded simple and basic: in order faithfully to visualize a symphony, the same multiple values in movement must be received by the
eye as tonal values are by the ear, and the dancers, in orchestrated embodiment, must parallel the instruments of the symphony orchestra. The
execution of this fine theory was another matter. To listen patiently to
the symphony, selecting and comprehending the themes, and after that
to listen to the individual notes played by each instrument; to correlate
the various groups and solo parts into a logical and beautiful identifica-
tion with the separate instruments, proved a gigantic task. But it grew
more fascinating as we went on. My fear that the girls would become

bored with this abstract approach to music and form was happily dissi-
pated. Their intense interest carried them from one day to the next, and
there was no longer one person with a vision, but several individual
choreographers.

—St. Denis, p. 215

Derailed

Lev Ivanov (1834–1901) was a dancer, teacher, and ballet master at the
Maryinsky. Always overshadowed by Marius Petipa, Ivanov is cherished today mainly for his haunting lakeside scenes in the 1895 production of *Swan
Lake* (his choreography is still alive in some stage productions). Ivanov was
also the choreographer of the first, 1892, production of *The Nutcracker*, and,
although that choreography as such has vanished, something of its spirit has
been preserved in the evening-length production by George Balanchine,
who danced in the Ivanov *Nutcracker* as a student.

The following excerpt from an Ivanov biography by M. Borisoglebsky
was translated and edited by Anatole Chujoy:

> During his first years in the [Imperial Theatre] School, Ivanov revealed
> an outstanding aptitude for music. Instead of being encouraged by the
> school authorities, however, he was often reprimanded and punished for
> his extraordinary love of music. His musical memory was so great that,
> after hearing a melody only once, he could play it from memory almost
> without mistakes. . . .
>
> Felix Kschessinski [a much-admired character dancer and the father
> of the ballerina Mathilde Kschessinska] relates in his memoirs the fol-
> lowing episode about Ivanov's musical talent:
>
> "Our rehearsals were very seldom conducted to piano accompaniment.
> Usually there was scraping on two fiddles by [theater musicians] Etikson
> and Rosenfeld. Etikson played only the second fiddle. Once Rosenfeld
> did not come to a rehearsal. Lev Ivanov calmly sat down to the piano and
> played the entire ballet from the beginning to the end, as if he had the
> music before him."
>
> Stubbornly and with ill will, the school authorities tried to cure Ivanov
> of his musical habit. Fedorov (head of the ballet school) threatened to "let
> him rot for his uncontrollable inclination toward music."

—Slonimsky, p. 5

High Anxiety

The Viennese ballerina Fanny Elssler (1810–1884), contemporary of Marie
Taglioni and her rival at the Paris Opéra, was the object of enthusiasm, even
frenzy, among balletomanes wherever she toured. In contrast to the spiritual
and aerial Taglioni, Elssler was admired for her terre-à-terre dancing, her
warm presence, her extraordinary gift for dance-acting, and her legendary

generosity. In 1839 she was finally persuaded to tour the United States (a country that she initially thought was too rough to appreciate the refinements of her art) and Cuba; she made her U.S. debut in New York in 1840. Henry Wikoff, a Philadelphian residing in Paris and a fan of Elssler's, offered to serve as her promoter during her American tour, and he set to work writing publicity of various kinds, including an anonymous *Memoir of Fanny Elssler: With Anecdotes of Her Public and Private Life! From Her Childhood to the Present Time.* Wikoff clearly had an imagination, possibly based on scenes he'd witnessed in London or Parisian theaters, as demonstrated by the following riff, drawn from the "memoir":

> The production of a new ballet in Europe is an event that follows months of incessant preparation—outlays, of which we have no conception here—practice, drilling, and exercise among the corps, the severity of which would exhaust a military martinet. The distribution of the characters is a duty assumed by the critics instead of the manager—the progress of the rehearsal is watched by the public with an anxiety that would surprise us phlegmatic Yankees—the *training* and *condition* of the heroine are attended to, like those of a race horse—and when, at last the momentous night arrives, the people go to the theater as to some solemn festival. Hope or fear pervades every bosom; spectators as well as actors are in a state of nervous excitement. The immense crowds that throng box, pit, and gallery are speculating on the coming performance when the ominous tap of the leader is heard through the house, and the confused hum subsides into the silence of the grave. The overture is begun—finished—and the applause perchance is long and loud. Observe that man standing in a box near the stage. His hair is long, or, rather, tall, for each individual of the shock seems endowed with the same rigidity that contracts his thin features and points to every angle, from zenith to the horizon. His brows are drawn down, and his eyes are bent on the orchestra with an intensity painful to see. His nostril is dilated, because his violent suspiration is carried on through that organ alone. His lips are pressed so firmly together that his sharply cut mouth looks like a mere line. He grasps the cushions of the box so tightly that the blood under his nails has been forced back and left the fingers as hueless as his face. He is the Composer of the ballet. During the overture just finished, that man has lived an age. Each bar of the music was an era in his life. Once or twice, either himself or the band had slightly lost time, and the throes of death seemed to be shaking him. You could not perceive by any motion of his body that he was noting the time, and in instrumentation so complex 'twould be difficult to detect discord among so many skillful professors as those before us, without some sort of bodily demonstration—but the maestro *was beating time with his soul!*
>
> —Delarue, pp. 19–20

Taking the Fifth

The Spanish composer Manuel de Falla, who wrote the score for the 1919 ballet *Le Tricorne* ("The Three-Cornered Hat": choreography by Léonide Massine)—music that is celebrated for its essential "Spanishness"—is the subject of the story here, related by the late dance historian, patron, and collector Parmenia Migel:

> To Vittorio Rieti, who composed two ballets for Diaghilev, we owe the following anecdote. Falla was late in bringing the completed score, and Diaghilev was listening to it for the first time. Suddenly he held up his hand. "Stop," he said. "Those opening bars of Beethoven's Fifth Symphony: you simply cannot include them in the score for our ballet." Without hesitating, Falla replied: "Of course they are Beethoven; but I have made a vow to the Virgin that I will definitely include them, so you must accept my score as it is or not at all."

Migel adds: "Actually, two different themes from Beethoven can be discovered in the music for *Le Tricorne*; to Falla they were a sentimental evocation of music he had first heard as a child, with his mother."

—Migel, pp. viii–ix

"Vive le son du canon"

The term "Carmagnole" is indelibly associated with the French Revolution, although it didn't originate there. As E. Cobham Brewer explains in his *Dictionary of Phrase and Fable* (1898), it was "a red Republican song and dance . . . so called from Carmag'nola, in Piedmont, the great nest of the Savoyards, noted for street music and dancing." Apparently, says the 1911 edition of the *Encyclopaedia Britannica*, the Savoyards imported it to the revolutionaries of Marseilles, who brought it up to Paris. "Dansons la Carmagnole—vive le son du canon!" went its refrain ("Let us dance the Carmagnole—long live the sound of the cannon!"). Brewer adds that "Carmagnole" came to refer as well to other revolutionary songs, such as "Ça ira" and "La Marseillaise" and that, furthermore, "the word is applied to the dress worn by the Jacobins, consisting of a blouse, red cap, and tri-colored girdle; to the wearer of this dress or any violent revolutionist; to the speeches in favor of the execution of Louis XVI, called by M. Barrière *des Carmagnoles*; and, last, to the dance performed by the mob round the guillotine, or down the streets of Paris."

Of the many passages on dance in the novels of Charles Dickens, among the very finest is the following one from *A Tale of Two Cities* (1859), describing the Carmagnole sung and danced by a mob. The point of view is that of the young, gentle Lucie Manette. One knows, too, from earlier in the book that "the wood-sawyer was a little man with a redundancy of gesture (he had once been a mender of roads)" and that "The Vengeance" was "the short, rather plump wife of a starved grocer, and the mother of two children withal," who also serves as an enthusiastic lieutenant to the revolution's bloodthirsty knitter, Madame Defarge:

> . . . Presently she heard a troubled movement and a shouting coming along, which filled her with fear. A moment afterwards, and a throng of people came pouring round the corner by the prison wall, in the midst of whom was the wood-sawyer hand in hand with The Vengeance. There could not be fewer than five hundred people, and they were dancing like five thousand demons. There was no other music than their own singing. They danced to the popular Revolution song, keeping a ferocious time that was like the gnashing of teeth in unison. Men and women danced together, women danced together, men danced together, as hazard had brought them together. At first they were a mere storm of coarse red caps and coarse woollen rags; but, as they filled the place, and stopped to dance about Lucie, some ghastly apparition of a dance-figure gone raving mad arose among them. They advanced, retreated, struck at one another's hands, clutched at one another's heads, spun round alone, caught one another and spun round in pairs, until many of them dropped. While those were down, the rest linked hand in hand, and all spun round together: then the ring broke, and in separate rings of two and four they turned and turned until they all stopped at once, began again, struck, clutched, and tore, and then reversed the spin, and all spun round another way. Suddenly they stopped again, paused, struck out the time afresh, formed into lines the width of the public way, and, with their heads low down and their hands high up, swooped screaming off. No fight could have been half so terrible as this dance. It was so emphatically a fallen sport—a something, once innocent, delivered over to all devilry—a healthy pastime changed into a means of angering the blood, bewildering the senses and steeling the heart. Such grace as was visible in it, made it the uglier, showing how warped and perverted all things good by nature were become. The maidenly bosom bared to this, the pretty almost-child's head thus distracted, the delicate foot mincing in this slough of blood and dirt, were types of the disjointed time.
>
> This was the Carmagnole. As it passed, leaving Lucie frightened and bewildered in the doorway of the wood-sawyer's house, the feathery snow fell as quietly and lay as white and soft, as if it had never been.
>
> —Dickens, *A Tale*, pp. 251, 305, 307–308;
> Brewer; *Encyclopaedia Britannica*, p. 355

The Phrases of Chopin

Many readers of Marcel Proust's epic novel, *A la recherche du temps perdu*— written between 1910 and Proust's death in 1922 and the title of which is variously translated as "Remembrance of Things Past" or "In Search of Lost Time"—have noticed that although ballet doesn't serve the novel as much of a subject directly, certain aspects of the story seem to be permeated with a balletic sensibility in a subliminal way: the linking of the characters "Swann" and "Odette," for example, which, for a balletgoer, ineluctably recalls *Swan Lake*. In one virtuoso display of such subliminal references, Proust seems to inject himself inside the consciousness of a woman listening nostalgically to a piano recital and, in doing so, to articulate her ephemeral associations between the moment of the concert and her remembered youth. Through fragmentary references to birds and to dancers, to an onstage prince and an offstage memory, perhaps even to famous photographs of Anna Pavlova cradling her pet swan, Proust animates the movement of the character's layered thoughts without pinning down what she is actually thinking:

> When he had finished the Liszt Intermezzo and had begun a Prelude by Chopin, Mme. de Cambremer turned to Mme. de Franquetot with a tender smile, full of intimate reminiscence, as well as of satisfaction (that of a competent judge) with the performance. She had been taught in her girlhood to fondle and cherish those long-necked, sinuous creatures, the phrases of Chopin, so free, so flexible, so tactile, which begin by seeking their ultimate resting-place somewhere beyond and far wide of the direction in which they started, the point which one might have expected them to reach, phrases which divert themselves in those fantastic bypaths only to return more deliberately—with a more premeditated reaction, with more precision, as on a crystal bowl which, if you strike it, will ring and throb until you cry aloud in anguish—to clutch at one's heart.
>
> Brought up in a provincial household with few friends or visitors, hardly ever invited to a ball, she had fuddled her mind, in the solitude of her old manor house, over setting the pace, now crawling-slow, now passionate, whirling, breathless, for all those imaginary waltzing couples, gathering them like flowers, leaving the ball-room for a moment to listen, where the wind sighed among the pine trees, on the shore of the lake, and seeing of a sudden advancing towards her, more different from anything one had ever dreamed of than earthly lovers are, a slender young man, whose voice was resonant and strange and false, in white gloves. . . .
>
> —Proust, p. 254

I.D.

Several decades ago, a leading U.S. weekly, perhaps *Time*, conducted an interview with the singer-songwriter Bob Dylan. At one point, the interviewer, noting that Dylan wrote the haunting lyrics for his own songs, asked him if he considered himself a poet.

"Nope," Dylan said.

Well, then, the interviewer went on, he must consider himself a composer, since he wrote all his own music, too.

"Nope," Dylan said.

But, the perplexed interviewer wondered, if Dylan didn't consider himself a poet or a songwriter, then what was he?

And Dylan said, "I'm a dancer."

> —Overheard in line while waiting to be seated for a performance
> at the Brooklyn Arts Exchange, January 7, 2004

Shipwrecked in a Field of Air

Federico García Lorca:

> In the art of dance, the body struggles against the invisible mist that envelops it and tries to bring to light the dominant profile demanded by the architecture of the music. Ardent struggle, endless vigil, like all art. While the poet wrestles with the horses in his brain and the sculptor wounds his eyes on the hard spark of alabaster, the dancer battles the air around her, air that threatens at any moment to destroy her harmony or to open huge empty spaces where her rhythm will be annihilated.
>
> The dancer's trembling heart must bring everything into harmony, from the tips of her shoes to the flutter of her eyelashes, from the ruffles of her dress to the incessant play of her fingers. Shipwrecked in a field of air, she must measure lines, silences, zigzags, and rapid curves, with a sixth sense of aroma and geometry, without ever mistaking her terrain. In this she resembles the torero, whose heart must keep to the neck of the bull. Both of them face the same danger—he, death; and she, darkness.
>
> —García Lorca, p. 63

Balanchine and Stravinsky

After he finished the scores, he gave them to me. I would visit his home in California, and we'd talk. "What do you want to do?" he'd ask, and I'd say, "Supposing we do *Orpheus*." "How do you think *Orpheus* should be done?" "Well," I'd say, "a little bit like opera. Orpheus is alone, Eurydice is dead, he cries, an angel comes and takes him to the underworld, and then Orpheus returns to earth. But he looks back, and she disappears forever."

Well, we tried to do that. And Stravinsky said, "I'll write the end first; I sometimes have an appetite to write the end first." And that's what he did, with the two horns—it's a beautiful thing, sad, hair flowing. We couldn't have a river on the stage, but it suggests something like that.

Then he asked, "Now, how to begin?" And I said, "Eurydice is in the ground, she's already buried, Orpheus is sad and cries—friends come to visit him, and then he sings and plays." "Well," Stravinsky asked, "how long does he play?" And I started to count [*snaps fingers*], the curtain goes up. "How long would you like him to stand without dancing, without moving? A sad person stands for a while, you know." "Well," I said, "maybe at least a minute." So he wrote down "minute." "And then," I said, "his friends come in and bring something and leave." "How long?" asked Stravinsky. I calculated it by walking. "That will take about two minutes." He wrote it down.

And it went on like that. He'd say, "I want to know how *long* it should be." "It could be a little longer," I'd tell him, "but at least it's not forever!" And later he played one section for me, and I said, "It's a little bit too short." "Oh, oh," he'd sigh, "I already orchestrated it, and it's all finished. ...Well, I'll do something, I know what to do." "Ah, thank you!" I replied. Things like that, you see: "How long?" he'd say. "One minute and twenty seconds," I'd tell him. "Twenty-*one*," he'd say, and smile. And I'd agree, "Fine, twenty-one!"

Stravinsky is more complicated than I am, because the body doesn't have the possibilities that music has in terms of speed. A pianist can play fast, but the body can't go that quickly. The body's different from music. Supposing you start moving fast, like sixty-fourth notes. But you can't, you can't see it. Eyes can't really see peripherally, the movement passes and is gone. So we have to calculate movements. To hear and to see isn't the same thing. You have to have fantastic eyes to see everything. (George Balanchine)

—Kirstein, *Portrait*, pp. 144–145

The Rehearsal Room

In the Skin

What you must do with dancers is to strip them of their superficialities. Strip them of their own conception of themselves, until you find something underneath. This takes time, patience, and occasional bullying. When you choreograph, there are two of you creating a dance. You've got to get the dancer to climb into the skin of the dance with you. For a while, there are two of you in the same skin. Then, happily, *you* get out of it, and leave the skin to the dancer—and she has to stay with it. If she goes back to herself, the performance won't be any good. (Antony Tudor)

—Gruen, p. 262

Permanently Impermanent

Dancers are preservationists, and choreographers are innovators. We were constantly in rehearsal, bringing a piece back into the repertoire, and the dancers were saying, "That was on count six, and I was over here. . . ." And Paul was saying, "Let's change it."

—Carolyn Adams, member of the Paul Taylor Dance Company 1965–1982, during the panel discussion "Working with Paul Taylor," City Center, New York, March 20, 2005

Dancing for Jerry

Benjamin Bowman, who relates the anecdote below, danced for Jerome Robbins during the 1980s, when Bowman was a member of New York City Ballet's corps de ballet. Robbins's rages at dancers could be unpredictable and intense. Bowman notes that "this one is rather tame":

I was sitting in the main studio in the New York State Theater, waiting for a rehearsal of *Watermill* to begin, when Jerry stomped in. He scanned the room for a moment, and his eyes settled on me. "You!" he screamed. "What the Hell are you doing? You're not doing my ballet anymore." I spent a very confused half-second trying to figure out if he meant that he was taking me out of *Watermill* (But I was never in it!) or just which of his ballets—I was performing three at the time—I was no longer welcome to be a part of, when Jerry continued: "That step, you're not doing my step anymore." This was accompanied by a miming of "AHA!" [a signal that he wanted to see] a phrase from his *West Side Story Suite.* "Get off your ass and show me that step." At which point, I did.

Several corrections followed, and I repeated the phrase . . . and again, and again, and again, and again. Chassé, step, step, battement, step, double barrel turn, POW! "Like you just got punched, POW! Jesus, do I have to punch you?" Chassé, step, step, battement, step, double barrel turn, POW. "Go." Chassé, step, step, battement, step, double barrel turn, POW! Over and over until Jerry finally looks at me and says, "OK."

Then he turned to the room, said, "Dancers, let's begin," and started the rehearsal.

Fifteen minutes late.

—Hite, interview

Bob Fosse Developing *Chicago*

The stronger he got and the more debauched he got, the better his work got. (Tony Stevens)

—Gottfried, p. 345

A Drum Set on the Hoof

I know my feet, all about them. It's like my feet are the drums, and my shoes [size 12 ½ EE] are the sticks. So if I'm hearing a bass sound in my head, where is that bass? Well, I have different tones. My left heel is stronger, for some reason, than my right; it's my bass drum. My right heel is like the floor tom-tom. I can get a snare out of my right toe, a whip sound, not putting it down on the floor hard, but kind of whipping the floor with it. I get the sounds of a top tom-tom from the balls of my feet. The hi-hat is a sneaky one. I do it with a slight toe lift, either foot, so, like a drummer, I can slip in there anytime. And if I want cymbals, crash, crash, that's landing flat, both feet, full strength on the floor, full weight on both feet. That's the cymbals.

So I've got a whole drum set down there. And knowing where all those sounds are, knowing where I'm trying to get them from, that's how I go about creating the step.

I don't worry about the look of it so much. Choreography comes later, when I'm putting together a whole piece. I'm into the sound; for me, when I'm hittin', layin' it down, it's all about the sound.

—Glover, pp. 22–23

Rhythm Is Everything

Ralph Lemon, a postmodern choreographer, whose inspiration comes from a variety of sources and whose method of composition does not refer to a traditional dance technique, dissolved his performing company of ten years in 1995 and embarked on independent projects. Most notable is *Geography Trilogy*: three evening-length performance works, based on the *Oresteia* trilogy of Aeschylus, which incorporate dancing, music, speaking, and other theatrical elements. Their theme, according to Lemon's published diaries about the project, is an investigation of "an apparent collision of cultures and a search for personal and artistic identity within the broader world arena." The anecdote below concerns one part of the "collision of cultures"— Lemon's first rehearsal, in 1997, in New York, with the African musician and dancer Moussa, originally from Guinea. One can see in it the difficulties that any choreographer has in translating his or her vision of movement to a dancer and in being open to altering that vision in order to accommodate the idiosyncracies of a given individual—not to speak of one whose background and training are quite divergent from those of the choreographer:

Day 1

Moussa came in with drum but no dance clothes. He wore a white T-shirt backward over a beige African protection tunic and French jeans with a Senegalese beaded belt that reminded me of the beadwork of South African artists. He is missing his first or second molar on the right or left side of his mouth. His hair is short and groomed in small, naturally manicured brushes. His irises are the same glowing brown of the scleras and pupils. His skin is the color born of dun and purple. At one point we take our shirts off and the structure below his skin seems perfect, I have more mass. He shows me his feet, the scars, calluses, and broken bones. They match his hands in how the flesh below the nails is tinted ochre. His wife says that he looks like me. I don't know how that is possible. Moussa moves like a deer.

I demonstrated an arbitrary series of movements, the way in which I happened to be moving that day. He imitated the first movement and seamlessly transformed it into one of the things that he masters, teaching traditional Guinean steps. I followed along. Occasionally he would smile, but it became clear that this expression was cast not out of happiness but only to demonstrate a freedom in the movement of the head. At the end of three hours he began to see me "let go"—I would say, begin to expire.

Moussa is a Malinke griot, from a family of griots. When he was a baby, he was placed underneath a balafon to sleep with his father's rhythms. Rhythm is everything to him. I must use it. There is no collaboration without it. That is shocking. . . .

Notes:

1. Try to communicate more of my expectations.
2. Can he be directed?

—Lemon, p. 76

Putting It Together I

Harvey Fierstein—the Broadway writer, Tony Award–winning star, and, as reporter Jesse McKinley of *The New York Times* puts it, "the famously, jubilantly gay actor"—was invited to take over for Alfred Molina in the central role of Tevye ("the ultimate Jewish father") in the twenty-first-century Broadway revival of *Fiddler on the Roof.* Since the original 1969 production of this show was both directed and choreographed by Jerome Robbins, Tevye has to do a fair amount of dancing. In a *Times* interview with Fierstein prior to his debut, McKinley asked the actor, fresh from his stint in drag as *Hairspray*'s 600-pound mother Edna, what apprehensions Fierstein had in taking on the character of Tevye.

Well, you may not have noticed, but I'm not really a dancer. So, I'm learning all these dances, and I learned them all in the rehearsal room, right? So today, for the first time, we're doing them on the set, with the full cast, and we're doing the wedding scene with all the wedding guests and—I've never done it except for me and a couple of stage managers. So, I'm like, "O.K., I'm going to do it," and I'm doing, with one of the guests, and I do the step, I do the step, I do the step, and I turn, and he goes away, and another person comes up. And I'm like, "What are you doing here?" And by then you've missed the step! Who are all these people? If you're a dancer, it's fine, but look at me!

—McKinley

Putting It Together II

You have to put things together like a gefilte fish. That's how I do it. (George Balanchine)

—Kirstein, *Portrait*, p. 134

Getting Down by Getting Up

Nobody cares if you can't dance well. Just get up and dance.

—Attributed to columnist Dave Barry,
from "16 Things That Took Me over 50 Years to Learn"
[circulated on the Internet]

Coaches and Teachers

What Goes Around, Comes Around

The story most frequently told by the Greeks about the beginning of dancing upon the earth—a story which became a part of Greek mythology—went as follows: In the early days of the world, before the race of man peopled the land, the Titan Rhea, wife of Cronus, taught the art of the dance to the Curetes, sons of Earth, who dwelt in the island of Crete, and to the Corybantes, who lived in Phrygia, in Asia Minor. This act stood Rhea in good stead later. Cronus, so the legend goes, habitually devoured his children at birth. Rhea fled to Crete and there her youngest son, the god Zeus, was born. Rhea hid Zeus in a cave and gave Cronus, instead of the child, a stone wrapped in swaddling clothes. Cronus swallowed the stone, and Rhea placed the baby in the care of the Curetes. They, to prevent Cronus from hearing the cries of Zeus, danced over him a wild, noisy, leaping dance, in which they shouted lustily and beat their swords against their shields. Legend says that they later became priests of Zeus and that they and their descendants continued their dances for centuries, as cult rituals.

—Lawler, p. 12

The Rules

Savion Glover, who is considered by the most illustrious rhythm tappers in the United States to be the most virtuosic tap dancer in history, has worked with almost every leading exponent of rhythm tap in show business from the past quarter century—and been tutored by them. In the following passage, he speaks about the responsibility he feels to help transmit, through his dancing, the spirit of tap as he absorbed it from a generation of elders:

Honi [Coles] and Buster Brown and Lon Chaney and Jimmy Slyde and Ralph Brown and Chuck Green—they taught me the rules. And you have to know the rules, because that's respecting the tradition. Take the hoofer's line, for instance. That's where everybody's doing a paddle and roll and one dancer at a time takes a solo turn. There are rules, but the rules are unspoken, almost secret. The main thing is, you got to finish the phrase of the man before you, finish it and then add something of your own. And if you don't, you'll be cut by the next man, embarrassed, you'll have your own step flipped back on you. You can spit on someone through the dance. You can murder someone through the dance. Dancers do that all the time. It's part of our ritual to be competitive. And you know when you've been cut. It's terrible, especially if a lot of people recognize it. If it's like that, you'll get everybody going: "Oooooooooo. . . ."

—Glover, p. 33

Taste Always Flees from Difficulties

As for the positions, everyone knows that there are five of them. . . . I shall simply say that these positions are good to know, and still better to forget, and that it is the art of the great dancer to neglect them gracefully. Besides, all those positions in which the body is firm and well displayed are excellent. . . . Taste always flees from difficulties. . . . Let dancers keep them for study but banish them from execution, they do not please the public at all and only afford an indifferent pleasure to those who realize the efforts required for them.

—Noverre, pp. 102, 104–105

The Old One-Two

The Swedish-born choreographer and teacher Charles Louis-Frédéric Didelot (1767–1837) served as *premier maître de ballet* between 1816 and 1829 in St. Petersburg, where his ballets were much admired and where he introduced such innovations as "fleshings" (antecedents of the unitard, to be worn under abbreviated costumes to give the appearance of naked skin) and "flying wires" (with which dancers could give the effect of floating over the stage). However, as the British dance historian Cyril W. Beaumont noted, Didelot "in the classroom ruled his subjects with a rod of iron." Beaumont quotes a Russian witness, A.Y. Golovachova-Panaeva, as saying that "the children returned home [from Didelot's dance classes] with bruises on their arms and legs; even his son was not exempt from such treatment."

Beaumont also quotes Golovachova-Panaeva on Didelot's behavior in the wings during performances:

It was very amusing . . . to see Didelot behind the scenes watching his pupils. Sometimes he swayed from side to side, smiled, and took mincing

steps and stamped his foot. But when the little pupils danced he shook his
fist at them, and, if they missed the figures, he made their lives a misery. He
pounced on them like a hawk, pulled their hair or ears, and if any ran away
he gave them a kick which sent them flying. Even the solo dancers suffered
from him. Being applauded, a dancer went behind the scenes, when Didelot
seized her by the shoulders, shook her with all his might and, having given
her a punch in the back, pushed her on to the stage as if she were recalled.

And yet, Beaumont adds, "outside the theater, Didelot was very kind to his
pupils and helped and kissed those whom he had punched but an hour before." He adds, dryly: "These are the conditions under which the ballet was
formed and, however cruel and unjustifiable they may seem, it is of interest
to note that the members of the *corps de ballet* were uniformly talented."

—Beaumont, p. 18

In the Midst of Her Suffering, She Thought of Her Art

On November 13, 1862, a rehearsal was being held by the Paris Opéra of the
restored opera *La Muette de Portici* ("The Mute Girl of Portici")—a work whose
leading role of Fenella is always assigned to a dancer. (Anna Pavlova, a famous
Fenella, performs excerpts in a twentieth-century film.) On this occasion, the
Fenella was the young, brilliant ballerina Emma Livry. As the dancer, in the
wings, began to climb a scenic element that represented a mountain, on which
she would make her entrance to the stage, the flame of a gas jet touched her
tarlatan skirt, and its eight layers caught fire. By the time the audience (which
included her mother) heard her screams and a heroic stagehand had run forward to smother the flames without regard for his own safety, most of Livry's
body was charred. Unfortunately for the dancer, she was still alive, lingering
for another eight months of unspeakable agony. And yet, as dance historian
Lillian Moore chronicles, "even in the midst of her suffering, she thought of
her art, for she permitted some of the pantomimists of the Opéra to watch her
agonized struggles, and even tried to describe her sensations to them."

Emma Livry died, at the age of twenty-one, on July 27, 1863. Of the
many ballet dancers immolated across the world in theatrical fires during
the Romantic Era [see "The Theaters," p. 154], none was more admired
than this pupil of Marie Taglioni, who had already begun to achieve critical
and audience acclaim for her dancing and was expected to prolong the style
and standards of classicism that her eminent teacher had established.

—Moore, pp. 157–159

To Dance by the Light of the Moon

The following account, from the nineteenth-century British magazine *Dancing*, may be offputting to some readers for its politically incorrect language

and highhanded we-them presumptions. However, its story, ultimately endearing, relates an affectionate tutorial in a North American forest, conducted by a man from one cultural background for dancers from another
who were eager to learn it, and who did so in what was clearly a context of
mutual respect and pure love for dancing. And the results of such teaching
can still be seen in the unmistakable contradanse figures and partnering motifs
that mark some of the dances performed at pow-wows to this day by Native
Americans from the Great Plains. The dedicated dance teacher, once an aristocrat at the court of Louis XVI, whom Chateaubriand encountered was
only one of many itinerant teachers of French court dancing, with various
backgrounds, who carried their art and technique around the world during
the eighteenth and nineteenth centuries. Indeed, it is very difficult to discover any dance tradition on earth that is "purely" this or that. Dancing,
travel, and mass emigrations have gone together from earliest recorded time;
and dancers will not be surprised at all to find that the spirit of Marie
Antoinette lives on as part of the culture of Native Americans, whose most
intimate spiritual impulses, not to speak of their very histories, are embodied in their dancing:

> Chateaubriand, the many-sided Frenchman, who was poet, historian,
> philosopher, statesman, peer and party leader at the same time, felt so
> disgusted with the revolution and the horrible scenes which he had been
> obliged to witness that, in 1791, he went to America, then a young cava-
> lier full of romantic idealism. After having delivered a letter of introduc-
> tion to the President of the Republic of Washington, he started on a
> Quixotic tour through the wilderness of virgin forests, only accompanied
> by a giant-like Dutch servant, thus hoping to escape from every vestige of
> civilization. He was delighted when, in the western part of Canada, he
> did not any more meet either cities, people, houses, or roads. "True lib-
> erty," he exclaimed, "at last I have found thee. I am like the bird that is
> flying before me and choosing a resting place wherever it likes. Here I am
> a king of Nature, the water carries me in triumph, its inhabitants follow
> me, the birds sing their songs for me, the animals welcome me, and the
> trees of the forest bend their summits when I pass them." Besides such
> ejaculations he played a thousand foolish tricks just to prove to himself
> that he really lived in an absolute state of primitive liberty. His Dutch
> Sancho Panza, however, began by first shaking his head and finished one
> day by vanishing altogether, when his master played again at being a
> savage—but then, he had never read Rousseau's works.
>
> For days together, Chateaubriand remained lying about on the shores
> of the river and the lakes. He rested under trees the age of which was
> counted by centuries, shared his meals with the Indians, smoked the pipe
> of peace with them, and discussed politics with their chiefs. Once, when
> he was riding, deep in thought and dreams, through the wild forest, he
> felt startled by the sound of a violin. Indeed, he was not mistaken, it was

the tone of a real civilized violin—and still more wonderful! Getting nearer, he distinguished the tune of a quadrille, which he remembered having heard at the court of Marie Antoinette when he was quite a young captain. It was a tune the Queen had brought with her from Germany and introduced in Paris.

One can imagine the pleasant surprise this tune, reminding him of his civilized home, caused to Chateaubriand in the midst of the wilderness. He followed the sound of the music, and at last saw a little man with artistically dressed and powdered hair, in a coat of apple-green hue, with large ruffles in front and round his wrists, who was busily engaged in initiating the young Redskins into the secrets of Parisian style and elegant manners. One could have imagined that this was a fanciful picnic arranged in the forest of St. Germain with a dancing master as m.c. of this *bal champêtre*.

"*En avant deux, messieurs,*" commanded the apple-green gentleman solemnly in playing his violin, "*dos-à-dos, mesdames, balancez.*"

And the young Redskins of both sexes obeyed his orders like the pupils do in a dancing lesson of the civilized world. Sometimes only, the savage ladies and gentlemen gave vent to their natural inclinations by leaving their own partner, and courting in a primitive way somebody else's, but the apple-green gentleman knew how to put an immediate end to any such confusion. He scratched a fifth on the violin, and called, "*A vos places, messieurs et mesdames?*" And the Redskin ladies and gentlemen returned to their places and enjoyed themselves like children in learning the French dance.

This tiny, apple-green dancing master of the Redskins was Monsieur Violet, and his lessons were paid in kind, consisting of bear-hams and beaverskins. Poor Monsieur Violet, however, whose aristocratic finery of the *ancien régime* had become worn and threadbare, was a Count de Blanchefort, who, before the wholesale slaughter began in Paris, had saved his bare life, and after many strange adventures, accepted the still stranger appointment among the red Indians of North America. It was a great stroke of luck that his old violin helped him to make those ladies and gentlemen dance—he was thus enabled to earn some kind of a livelihood and found friends among the savages when his fatherland had forsaken him. When, in consequence of Chateaubriand's entreaties, he returned to Europe with him, he was deeply grieved to part with his nomadic friends, and they seemed to feel it as much that they should lose their dancing master. He left them as a memento his old violin, giving it to the most talented of his Indian pupils, who, in future, was to play it for the benefit of the others. And long afterwards, when again settled in Paris, the count remembered with grateful affection the times he spent in the forest, the beautiful moonlit nights, and the savage "ladies and gentlemen" whom he had taught to dance the latest quadrilles of the old French Court.

—Dancing, p. 238

It's Like Being Maria Tallchief

During the early 1960s, Margot Fonteyn asked the Balanchine star and Osage descendant Maria Tallchief if she would be amenable to conducting a private class for the president and first lady's daughter, Caroline, and "one or two of her cousins." The idea appealed to Tallchief, and with Balanchine's loan of a studio, she organized a class for Caroline Kennedy; her own daughter, Elise; and several other young girls. As Tallchief recounts in her memoir, a book filled with surprising stories,

I . . . seemed to develop a special rapport with Caroline. She was only eight, but she was fascinated by my background. One afternoon, while we were changing into street clothes after class, she stood alongside me and said in a whisper that she had a question. Her eyes were bright and she seemed all excited.

"I want to know what it's like being an Indian."

"Well, Caroline. It's no different from being anything else. It's my heritage, and I'm proud of it. You're Irish and French and American. That's your heritage. You should be very proud of that."

She peered at me directly with her father's shining eyes. "I'd rather be an American Indian, Miss Tallchief."

—Tallchief, pp. 297–298

Isadora on Grace

Dancing was always an experience to her, not merely a performance, and never movement for its own sake.

In 1911, I was privileged to hear her enunciate this principle to her pupils in a way I shall never forget. She had been teaching them the dance of the Happy Spirits in her *Orpheus* program. After they had learned the gestures and the groupings, there came a day when that was not enough, and she spoke to them something like this:

"Don't be merely graceful. Nobody is interested in a lot of graceful young girls. Unless your dancing springs from an inner emotion and expresses an idea, it will be meaningless, and the audience will be bored. I'll show you the difference. First, I will dance the music in the way I want you to dance it, then in the way I want you to avoid."

Whereupon she performed one of her marvels of apparent simplicity; a little skipping, a few upward and outward gestures of the head and arms, and heavenly beauty was created; the serene joy of the Blessed Spirits filled the studio. Then, she executed the same movements, with no perceptible variation, but in such a merely graceful manner that I was astonished at the different result. I would not have believed that she could make a dance look like that. And she was not exaggerating her effect by any least simper of face or body. She was simply leaving out the animating spirit, and what was left, unbelievable as it may sound, was, as she said, entirely uninteresting. Except as an object lesson. (Mary Fanton Roberts)

—Isadora Duncan, *The Art*, p. 22–23

Dotting the "I"s with Margot Fonteyn

When I asked to dance *Le Spectre de la Rose* in a Hamburg gala with Mischa Baryshnikov, Margot took it upon herself to teach me the choreography by post. She sent me a long letter, complete with the little differences that Mischa employed, and adorable drawings of eyes. They were heavily lashed "U"s, or ^ s, either open or shut. In addition to these valuable notes, she lent me her costume. (Lynn Seymour)

—Macaulay, unpaginated

Beyond Technique

Dance critic George Jackson:

The first time I saw Katherine Dunham was in 1947/8, in the student lounge, the Reynolds Club, at the U. of Chicago, where I'd dozed off in an easy chair trying to finish assigned reading—Dostoyevsky's *The Brothers Karamazov*. Drumming, out of the ordinary on campus at that time, roused me. The sound was insistent yet soft. In the middle of the large room stood a woman, a beautiful woman. She was dressed simply in a skirt suit, the jacket open on (I'm pretty sure) a flowered blouse. The cut and combination of what she wore seemed chic, yet she was a student. As she declared for one and all to hear, she—Katherine Dunham—had just come back from thesis work in Africa and wanted her fellow students to see what she'd found there. And so, after removing her shoes, Dunham began to dance. Remarkable was what she could do with rhythm. She took it into her body, and no matter how sharp and cutting the drum beat, she made it melt and flow. If the rhythm was complex and prickly, she combed it into sensuous strands. Even then, Dunham was a healer. And, she had unavoidable eyes. Margot Fonteyn was a dancer like that; one ended up being caught by her gaze. Photographs of Nijinsky lead to his eyes. It is a distinct gift.

—Jackson, unpaginated

Dancing School Dangers

Charles Dickens, who loved the theater, had a sharp eye for dance and wrote about it with verve and accuracy. His early (1836) journalistic collection, *Sketches by Boz*, chronicled a variety of lower-middle-class Londoners; in it he included an account of a student of social dancing, Mr. Augustus Cooper, a bachelor "just of age, with a little money," who lived with his stultifying mother. One day, on a leisurely walk, Mr. Cooper happened to notice an advertisement for the dancing academy of a Signor Billsmethi—"It was *very* select, the number of pupils being strictly limited to seventy-five"—and he procured Signor Billsmethi's home address, walked to the instructor's house, and signed up for lessons. In the following passage, we see Mr. Cooper at his first class, where he met other members of Signor Billsmethi's family as well as other aspiring dancers, and where one thing led to another—as Mr. Cooper's mother might have warned him would happen:

Well; Mr Augustus Cooper went away to one of the cheap shoemakers' shops in Holborn, where gentlemen's dress pumps are seven-and-six-pence, and men's strong walking just nothing at all, and bought a pair of the regular seven-and-sixpenny, long-quartered, town-mades, in which he astonished himself quite as much as his mother, and sallied forth to Signor Billsmethi's. There were four other private pupils in the parlor: two ladies and two gentlemen. Such nice people! Not a bit of pride about them. One of the ladies in particular, who was in training for a Colum-bine, was remarkably affable; and she and Miss Billsmethi took such an interest in Mr August Cooper, and joked, and smiled, and looked so be-witching, that he got quite at home, and learnt his steps in no time. After the practicing was over, Signor Billsmethi, and Miss Billsmethi, and Master Billsmethi, and a young lady, and the two ladies, and the two gentlemen, danced a quadrille—none of your slipping and sliding about, but regular warm work, flying into corners, and diving among chairs, and shooting out at the door,—something like dancing! Signor Billsmethi in particular, notwithstanding his having a little fiddle to play all the time, was out on the landing every figure, and Master Billsmethi, when everyone else was breathless, danced a hornpipe, with a cane in his hand, and a cheese-plate on his head, to the unqualified admiration of the whole company. Then, Signor Billsmethi insisted, as they were so happy, that they should all stay to supper, and proposed sending Master Billsmethi for the beer and spir-its, whereupon the two gentlemen swore, "strike 'em wulgar if they'd stand that"; and were just going to quarrel who should pay for it, when Mr Augustus Cooper said he would, if they'd have the kindness to allow him; and Master Billsmethi brought the beer in a can, and the rum in a quart pot. They had a regular night of it; and Miss Billsmethi squeezed Mr Augustus Cooper's hand under the table; and Mr Augustus Cooper returned the squeeze, and returned home too, at something to six o'clock in the morning, when he was put to bed by main force by the apprentice, after repeatedly expressing an uncontrollable desire to pitch his revered parent out of the second-floor window, and to throttle the apprentice with his own neck-handkerchief.

—Dickens, *Sketches*, pp. 305–306

Charles Dickens as a Dancer

My father insisted that my sister Katie and I should teach the polka step to him and Mr. Luck," writes Mamie Dickens in the second of her papers on "My Father as I Recall Him," in the December 1892 *Ladies' Home Journal*:

"My father was as much in earnest about learning to take that wonderful step correctly as though there were nothing of greater importance in the world. Often he would practice gravely in a corner, without either partner or music, and I remember one cold winter's night his awakening with the fear that he had forgotten this step so strong upon him, that, jumping out of bed, by the scant illumination of the old-fashioned rushlight, he diligently rehearsed its "one, two, three, one, two, three," until he was once more secure in his knowledge. My father was certainly not what in the ordinary acceptation of the term would be called 'a good dancer.' I doubt that he had received any instruction in 'the noble art' other than that which my sister and I gave him. In later years, I remember trying to teach him the schottische, a dance which he particularly admired and desired to learn. But although he was so fond of dancing, except at family gatherings in his own or his most intimate friend's house, I never remember seeing him participate."

—Dancing, p. 237

Don't Fall! That's an Order!

The German Emperor has been snubbing all the colonels of the garrison at Potsdam by telling them not to let their officers attend the Court balls unless they can dance. Dancing may not, strictly speaking, be a military accomplishment, and certain monarchs—the Great Frederick among them—have been known to sneer at officers who gyrated too gracefully to the tunes of the fiddle. . . . The Emperor's admonition to his colonels was made in consequence of one or two heavy tumbles, which gawkish dragoons procured for themselves while dancing with illustrious princesses. Such accidents, however, may perhaps as often denote nervousness as bad dancing, and an officer who is shy with ladies is frequently the best of soldiers. Some years ago, a brilliant cavalry officer had a bad fall in dancing with the Crown Princess Stephanie at a Court ball in Vienna, and the late Crown Prince was very angry. Once at the Court of St. Petersburg, under Nicholas, an officer brought a Grand Duchess to the floor with him, at which Her Imperial Highness called him furiously a "clumsy camel." The officer thought himself lost when the grim Czar approached him, seized him by the cuff and marched him deliberately out of the ballroom. Not a word was spoken as Nicholas and his captive strode through two empty chambers, but, on their reaching a passage, the Czar pointed to a corner where stood a pan full of powdered chalk, and said sternly: "Rub the soles of your boots into that." This was not so good as the *à propos* wit of Napoleon III, which turned a ball-room accident into the means of paying a graceful compliment to a mortified officer. As this gentleman scrambled to his knees, the Emperor gave him a helping hand, and remarked, with a smile: "Captain, this is the second time I have seen you fall. The first time was on the field of Magenta."

—*Dancing*, p. 101

To Learn at Any Price

I was 15 years old and a member of the de Basil Ballet Russe when I first came to London in 1933. During the long season at the Alhambra Theatre, Léonide Massine, our artistic director, arranged for a small group of the dancers to take classes with the renowned teacher Nicolas Legat. I was one of the group, together with Alexandra Danilova and Massine himself, who was perhaps the most ardent student of us all.

Monsieur Legat was small of stature, slim, and completely bald. He shaved what hair he had. He accompanied his classes seated at a grand piano, playing little tunes and chords of his own rhythmic phrasing. Many of his combinations were based on the count of five or seven, instead of the more conventional four or eight. He demonstrated the steps with his fingers on the lid of the piano, and we would crowd around him to catch his brief instructions. Returning to our places, we would go over the steps mentally. Legat rarely got up to demonstrate. If he did, it usually meant an inability on our part to grasp a step. This could put him in a furious mood, which we naturally tried to avoid, so we worked our brains full tilt. The master spoke very little English, and his few remarks were often sharp, but laced with wit. We were not dismayed by his piercing wit, or his devastating mimicry; after all, we had come to learn at any price, not to be praised. (André Eglevsky)

—Gregory, p. 5

Class of Perfection

During his decades of teaching at the Leningrad Choreographic School (later known as the Vaganova Choreographic Institute) between the 1940s and the 1960s, Alexander Pushkin (1907–1970) trained just about all the leading male dancers of the Kirov Ballet. His most famous pupils were Rudolf Nureyev and Mikhail Baryshnikov. The following portrait is by Gennady Albert, a Pushkin student from the 1960s:

Pushkin was not one of those teachers who gets results from students through sheer willpower and persistence. He didn't resort to shouts or demands. No one can remember his ever even raising his voice. His tactfulness and gentleness created a teaching atmosphere that put no pressure on the students. "Getting inspired himself during class, he enticed us along with him," remarked Nikolai Kovmir, one of the last of Pushkin's students, later a soloist of the Maryinsky Theater.

He used not the whip, but inspiration, to make students tirelessly repeat a difficult combination. He sincerely commiserated with his students' failures in class. It would have been so much easier to pour out accumulated impatience than to keep repeating in a quiet voice, "Take it softly, stand taller and push off harder with your left heel. You'll have two turns." The student, upset by his own inability, would get angry and sometimes raise his voice. Then the teacher would shrug in bewilderment and silently go over to his chair. It would grow very quiet in the room. The boy's face would turn red. Pushkin could teach important lessons in the course of his class: how to deal with people, with one's elders, how to appreciate the work of a comrade, a colleague, or a teacher. "It would be hard to find a more sensitive and kind person with both children and adults," said Nadezhda Bazarova, his partner onstage and a colleague at the school.

—Albert, pp. 73–74

Toast

The choreographer Paul Taylor didn't decide to study dance until he was a student at Syracuse University, where, as he told his swimming coach, he'd had a "flash" that he ought to give up competitive swimming and take up dance classes—which was why he was transferring to The Juilliard School in New York City. At Juilliard, his teachers included the choreographer Antony Tudor, a genius whose capacity for withering expressions of truth in public places could be seen as a mean streak. In the following anecdote, that capacity is front and center, although Taylor has also often spoken of how Tudor's ballets, with their innovative vocabulary and emphasis on the social and psychological implications of posture and gesture, have influenced Taylor's own dances. In the passage, the name "Tacet" refers to Taylor's literary personification throughout his autobiography of a mysterious and dark element he saw in his character—in this situation, an embodiment of arrogance:

The third high point of that year might also be called rock bottom. It was a dinner party given by my teacher Antony Tudor, a man not only known for his great ballets but for his deflating remarks. At this time there were certain things that I felt absolutely sure of, not the least of which was myself. The puffed-up Tacet part of me was getting the upper hand, and I had made the mistake of telling Tudor that I'd had a flash in college and felt practically foreordained to dance. Hugh Laing and other stellars were at the party. I was eating half an alligator pear stuffed with shrimp and listening hard to the interesting things being said when Tudor rose from the table like a bird of prey, quieted everyone, and sarcastically pro-

posed a toast to someone to whom he said the whole dance pantheon—
Nijinsky, Pavlova, Graham, and the rest—was but a mere footnote in
history, as compared with their new lord and master, the lately emerged
cock of the rock, the great (here I had a feeling something bad was about
to happen) Paul Taylor. My ears related to the rest of me in the way
purple relates to pink. I'd never before run across such an effective
method by which the older falcon generation puts young rabbits in their
place, and for a brief time took classes with new humility and much less
fluffy-tailed assurance.

—Taylor, pp. 45–46

Friendly and Tough

Dance critic Deborah Jowitt:

I first met Bella Lewitzky when I was 19 and chunky and she was Bella
Lewitzky. It was the middle of a Los Angeles summer—not much con-
certizing going on—and Bella was teaching evening classes in a large,
slightly shabby studio on Hollywood Boulevard. The only modern dancers I knew were all breath and spring and swishing ponytails; I had never
seen one with as many muscles as Bella had, and was trying to help us to
acquire. We began with a barre—which I thought alarmingly heretical—
and progressed through grueling floor stretches and center work to moving through space. She was friendly and tough and saw no reason why we
should be afraid of Lester Horton's famous "T fall," or clasp our thighs
and moan after a 20-count back-hinge to the floor, or totter when we
tried to follow her example and stand on one leg for eight measures while
waving the other around.

Bella has since said that she didn't know beans about teaching in those
days. . . .

—Jowitt, "Bella," p. 5

Quotas, Morals, and the Ziegfeld Follies

There are many reasons to admire the achievements in dance of Ruth St.
Denis and Ted Shawn, both in their joint project, Denishawn, and in their
individual careers. Their anti-Semitism, racism, and hypocrisy are not among
them, however. The following passage from the memoir of Denishawn
protégée Doris Humphrey, one of the most clear-eyed and damning ever
written by a dancer in English about his or her mentors, describes the final
conference at Denishawn that precipitated Humphrey's and Charles
Weidman's break with the enterprise that had trained them and fostered their
talents. (Nor is this the sole indictment of St. Denis's rigid views concerning ethnic and religious difference. The documentary *Free to Dance*, by Madison Davis Lacy and Adam Zucker, which PBS first aired in 2001, contains

88 DANCE ANECDOTES

the story of the tortured correspondence between St. Denis and fifteen-year-old African American dancer Edna Guy, whose desperate hope of studying at Denishawn was continually postponed by St. Denis, owing to Guy's race.)

In St. Denis's own 1937 biography, this meeting is vaguely characterized as "the nerve-wracking experience of a formal meeting where all the slumbering resentments and unresolved discussions which covered a period of months were brought up as the vital issues of the occasion," and the departures of Humphrey and Weidman are characterized as the result of these young choreographers' ambitions (aided and abetted by their friend, the costume designer Pauline Lawrence) to fledge their own wings artistically. Humphrey's account, which was not published until well after her death in 1958, is much more detailed. Humphrey's autobiography is in two parts: the section she had written in the first person about her early years and left unfinished, and the section in the third person that her editor, dance historian Selma Jeanne Cohen, wrote to complete the narrative. The following passage comes from the portion that Humphrey had written herself and left unpublished.

She begins with a report on St. Denis's remarks concerning her and Shawn's plans to create a permanent home for Denishawn and their vision of a string of satellite schools, called "Greater Denishawn":

... Continuing about the classes: they had decided on some overall policies, she said. The first one she mentioned was with respect to the Jewish students. It seemed best, she explained, to limit these to ten percent of the whole. This was the first time I had heard either director express a racial prejudice, and I was shocked. Also, I thought of the very talented young Jewish girls already in the school, and wondered what would become of them.

Then Shawn began to talk. There was another policy they intended to put into operation at Greater Denishawn, and this was with respect to the general moral tone. It had come to his attention, he said, that various affairs had been going on from time to time, and that these were questionable, if not downright immoral, as they did not result in marriage. A committee of faculty members would be established to hear the evidence in such cases. Permission to continue would be granted, or marriage would be advised. If the advice were flouted, there would be an instant cessation of the affair, or the guilty parties would be dismissed at once. I thought this was the most extraordinary proposal, but said nothing.

Next there was the practical consideration of finding the money to finish the house and make payments on the enormous mortgage. They had, he said, been carrying this heavy burden themselves, and had even accepted a grueling season with the Follies for no other purpose than this. The house was not complete, and thousands of dollars more were needed to make the Greater Denishawn come true. He was going to call on Doris and Charles to do their share in earning money next year, by putting them into the Ziegfeld Follies. In the meantime, others would be found to do the teaching at the school. All eyes were turned on me for comment on this proposal, which so stunned me that I could not speak for a moment. I thought of the exciting new experiments in movement, and of my hopes for composing in a new style, all of which would vanish. Also, I had a sharp remembrance of the current Follies. We had all traipsed over to Newark one night see it.

"I do not think I could do that," I said. "I saw what you did in the Follies, and I was shocked. The dances had been altered, the tempi were much faster, and you, Miss Ruth, had your skirts pulled up four or five inches higher than they should have been."

This statement had a most surprising result—Miss Ruth burst into tears. Then she began to ramble almost incoherently about how she had always been respectable, while Isadora Duncan was running all over Europe having babies by different men, while she herself had always been a model of virtue. Also that the mysticism of the East had been her ideal and always would be, despite any deviations. Seeing her emotionally out of control, Shawn took up the defense and said to me:

"Do you mean to say that Jesus Christ was any the less great because he addressed the common people?"

"No," I answered, "but you're not Jesus Christ."

"But I am," he said. "I am the Jesus Christ of the dance."

This statement fell into a startled silence. There seemed to be no answer to it.

—Humphrey, pp. 62–63; St. Denis, p. 321.

Every Emotion under the Sun

Sometimes, especially where dancing is concerned, not all the important lessons are learned in the classroom. When the movie star James Cagney was a teenager, he was holding down a number of jobs, including one as a first-floor bellhop at The Friar's, a club for actors in Manhattan. As a supplement to his modest salary, he received free passes to various shows. The theater interested him to some extent. He had read the plays of Bernard Shaw and studied a little dramatics at the Lenox Hill Settlement House with the married couple Florence and Burton James, for whom he appeared—in "a skimpy goatskin" and with marcelled hair—as the title character in a play called *The Faun.* On one occasion when Cagney received theatrical passes, he took a girl named Nellie Oliver, with whom he was enamored. In his memory of the date, his feelings for her created a climate in which he was able to appreciate what he saw on stage with an intensity he might not otherwise have experienced. The following account of that evening, in Cagney's own words, comes from one of the many conversations he had with John McCabe, who ghosted the 1976 autobiography *Cagney by Cagney* and continued his friendship with his subject after the book appeared. Decades later, with Cagney's blessing, McCabe went back to his transcripts and, after Cagney's death, published "an autobiographical biography," which drew extensively on personal details Cagney had vetoed from the earlier volume:

An angelic blonde. The stuff of which dreams, or at least my dreams, were made at the time. Fairy princess type, blue-eyed and blonde, classic figure. I was working at The Friars then, and I'd get passes for the theater or the movies, both new experiences for me. I had seen little comedy movies in Ridgewood, but now I could watch the big stars—Doug Fairbanks, King Baggott, Bessie Barriscale, Marguerite Clark, Sessue Hayakawa. The thing I remember most about Nellie is that she loved to dance, and I didn't know how. But she taught me, and I began to love it, too. We went only to parish and neighborhood dances. I couldn't afford taking her to dance halls, where we could have learned those great dances Vernon and Irene Castle were making popular: the one-step, the Turkey Trot, the Maxixe. Anyway, at the time, I thought they were cake-eater stuff. "Cake-eater" was current slang for "limp-wrist," the opposite of "manly." How wrong I was! When I saw Freddie and Ginger in *The Story of Vernon and Irene Castle*, I realized just how wrong I was. When I did *The Faun*, Florence James showed me some basic dance postures, which is where I first got the idea of line and extension. Then, God bless The Friars, I got passes to see Pavlova, and I sat there watching that beauty of motion so transfixed I could hardly breathe. I wept, it was so goddamned beautiful. I know that old wheeze "The Irish even cry at card tricks," and that is right, but this woman summoned up every emotion under the sun—just by moving.

McCabe adds: "Jim was to remember Pavlova and the superb simplicity of her movements and gesture when he began his life as a dancer. Some of those movements occur in the gentle, simple use of his hands, particularly in his early films."

—McCabe, p. 34

"Will You Work Hard to Learn the Part?"

Although Bill T. Jones, who is widely lauded for his ability to improvise as well as for his choreography, didn't train intensively as a dancer until he got to college, his innate gifts as a performer were recognized much earlier by Mary Lee Shapee, his drama teacher at Wayland Central High School in upper New York State:

During my sophomore year, the Drama Club was going to present *The Music Man*, and I, starved for any activity that might allow me to pretend, was honored when I was invited to join the club. A real-life couple—talented and elegant, with star quality—had the leads, and Mrs. Shapee had me read for the part of Marcellus. And read again. She then asked me if I would work hard to learn the part, if I would be willing to sing and dance. A tremor rose up through the sturdy cement floor of the drama room, registered in my knees, and had its effect on my "I'll do my best."

Wayland had its problems, and one of them was that no one there would have known how to deal with a black fifteen-year-old playing the randy lover of a white ingénue. In one of our afternoon chats, Mary Lee explained this to me as if it were absolutely reasonable. As a solution, she offered that I dance a solo in place of the romantic duet called for by the script. I was without the confidence to reason her into revolt, and I wanted the part no matter what, so I agreed.

"Sha-poopee" was the big production number where Marcellus sings out like a caller at a square dance about the virtues of a woman who won't kiss after the first, second, and third dates. I hadn't seen the movie version of *The Music Man*, so I sang the song from the Marcellus I imagined—a humorous, self-effacing man, a sexy blacksmith. Having no partner, I was unsure as to what I would do with the dance. I was told that a dance major from a nearby college would come and choreograph my part. During the rehearsals in the meantime, I pulled out all the old tricks, from our living-room dance contests, moves I had seen James Brown do, things I made up.

The choreographer never showed up, and, before we knew it, it was opening night. I was under the lights, center stage, and it was "Sha-poopee" time. I dove into the dance, trying things I had never tried even in rehearsal, even in the living room. I did my version of Estella and Gus's "Throw-It-Out-the-Window," a bit of "Buck-'n-Wing," the Jets' gliding step from *West Side Story*. And more. The audience stood up as my solo came to a close. For a brief instant I didn't know what they were applauding about. I was out of breath and out of myself. I was everything and nothing. I caught myself with a slight dip of the head and shoulders as acknowledgment and glanced to the wings, where Mary Lee, hiding her laughter, urged me to get on with my next line.

—Jones, pp. 66–67

A Girl's Best Friends

The projection of sexiness in a musical comedy is more than a matter of personal charisma: you've got to be carefully taught how to sing, dance, walk, gesture. Take, for instance, Marilyn Monroe's performance in Howard Hawks's 1953 *Gentlemen Prefer Blondes*, where Monroe's precise, iconic effects in the musical numbers were the results of Jack Cole's shrewd staging, bolstered by coaching from the great Broadway redhead, Gwen Verdon, who was serving as Cole's assistant on the set. As Martin Gottfried, the biographer of Verdon's husband and principal choreographer, Bob Fosse, relates, "Gwen showed the sex symbol how to be sexy while singing, 'I'm Just a Little Girl from Little Rock.' As another dancer put it, 'Nobody was able to satirize sexiness and be sexy at the same time the way Gwen could.'"

—Gottfried, p. 92

Curtain

Dance critic Robert Greskovic:

The detail that struck and amused me came just after the [onstage, open-to-the-public warm-up] class [given by Suzanne Farrell as part of "Suzanne Farrell Stages Balanchine," October 1995]. At its conclusion, the sizeable Farrell-watching audience took a cue from the dancers' applauding their dedicated teacher to send its own waves of applause, likely hoping that the object of the attention might respond with a ballerina bow. Not a chance. Even after Farrell's unceremonious exit, the applauding continued, but all it achieved was sight of the ballerina's slender, disembodied arm stretching out from the wing space to snatch her famous, talismanic floral shawl from the top of the piano, where she'd inadvertently left it. Curtain.

—Greskovic, p. 51

Hands and Things That Can Fill Them

The Spontaneous Dance Gestures of Maria Callas

During the early 1970s, the ballerina Natalia Makarova performed in a production of Verdi's opera *I Vespri Siciliani* at the Reggio Theater in Turin, Italy. The choreography was by Serge Lifar, but the invitation to dance came from Maria Callas, making her debut as an opera director. Makarova knew Callas's recordings; however, she had never seen the diva on stage and didn't realize how potent her gifts were for pure physical expression:

> Callas was an actress from head to toe. In her gestures and her manner of holding herself, there was something especially striking. I recall saying to her once that in classical ballet, particularly in the West, very few can use their hands expressively and make them speak. With most dancers, the whole arm moves from the shoulder without the palm opening, which it should, at the end of the movement. This final release of the hands is the dot on the *i*—while using her arms, the ballerina seems to be testing the density of air between them and her body. This is crucial for beautiful port de bras, since the final hand movement is extraordinarily expressive. Used correctly, it can express a great range of emotional shadings, almost an entire character. Maya Plisetskaya often spoke of this in her interviews. For instance, in *Giselle* almost no one can render Bathilde's gesture at that moment when Giselle, with simple-hearted delight, pats the hem of her gold-threaded dress. This gesture should be regal and at the same time a casual "turning with the hand" to Giselle, as if to ask, "What is the matter?" Usually it looks trivial, theatrical, because the hands and the wrists of Western dancers are not utilized properly. "I'm sure you could do this

gesture easily," I said to Callas, who instantly performed the very movement with such sovereign grace and simplicity that I was stunned. The
turn of the head, the neck, the expression in her eyes—everything came
of itself and was absolutely right.

—Makarova, p. 121

Imagine These Hands Awake!

... There they were, these dainty little dancing maids, like gazelles meta-
morphosed. Their long, slender arms as though in one piece drawn
through the shoulders, through the slender yet sturdy torso (with the full
slenderness of Buddha pictures), as though in a single finely wrought
piece as far as the wrists, out of which the hands walked out like players,
mobile and independent of action. And what hands! Buddha hands that
know how to sleep; that lie down easily when their time comes, finger
next to finger, to rest for centuries on their laps, lying palm upward or
standing straight up from the joint, bidding ceaselessly for quiet. Imagine
these hands awake! These fingers spread apart, open, radiate or turned
inwards like the petals of a Jericho rose; these fingers enraptured and
happy or anxious, pointing out from the very end of the long arms; these
fingers dancing. And the whole body in action—this ultimate in balance
dances suspended in the air, in the atmosphere of the body itself, in the
golden glow of the Orient. . . . (Rainer Maria Rilke, on Cambodian court
dance, ca. 1907)

—Sachs, pp. 40–41

Triggers in Celestial Fingers

Between 1936 and 1947, the ballet-trained dancer Xenia Zarina toured Asia
in the company of a pianist, with a project to study and perform the court
dances of Thailand, Cambodia, Bali, and Java as well as the classic dances of
India and Japan, working with the leading teachers of each tradition. Her
unparalleled *Classic Dances of the Orient* shows how well she accomplished
this project.

She also, of course, attended performances. Below is a description of one
dance she witnessed on a program of court dances in Java, at the Kraton of
the Susuhunan of Sukarta. In the description that follows, it is helpful to
know that the Bedoyo and Serimpi court dances, which go back to the eighth
century, are slow and lulling works exclusively for women, who, in both
cases, are arranged into exquisite geometrical patterns that require the dancers to maintain exact synchronization without ever looking anxious or even
intent. Nine women dance the sumptuous Bedoyo, a term that can be used
for both the dance and the dancer. The Serimpi—which, like the Bedoyo,
has been performed by visiting Javanese in New York in recent years in a
theatrical setting—is traditionally for four princesses who dance it in pairs,

exclusively for the sovereign, "one pair duplicating the other in a very attenuated story of love and jealousy for a historical king." Also, there are
several kinds of walking techniques in Javanese court dance. Mentioned here
is the "kapang-kapang," "a ceremonial entrance walk [which is] extremely
slow and trancelike, as though the executant were floating just above the
floor." (Zarina adds: "Must be learned from a teacher.") The other walk
mentioned is the "vatikangser": "a sideways progression done by a very
smooth shuffling of the feet that illustrates perfectly 'sand blowing in the
wind,'" the term's translated meaning.

The dance now began, figure after figure slowly, smoothly executed: hands
throwing the utdets [scarfs or sashes] now left, now right, now back, now
drawing them forward, the small feet flicking the little trains now to the
right, now to the left. The Bedoyos revolved to a new geometrical forma-
tion. Figure after figure—utdets floating in the air and falling again, heads
turning, bodies swaying softly like grasses in a gentle wind, while the
gamelan's clear, carillon melodies rippled against the sustained tones of
the great bronze gongs and, from time to time, a plaintive chant of the
women's chorus joined in. On and on they danced, like the movement of
stars across the night sky. Now and then, one of the two elderly women
attendants would hurry, crouching among the dancers, to straighten a
tangled train or to pick up an ornament that had dropped. These attendants symbolize ancestral protectors and are always present during the
dance performances.

Now each Bedoyo unobtrusively drew from her corsage a large, un-
gainly pistol, and wearily raised it to aim—but the arm and heavy pistol
dropped, and heads turned away as though the effort were too great. Again
the movement was repeated, again the arms dropped and the feet carried
the slender bodies with drooping heads across the floor in vatikangser
(sand blowing in the wind). A third time the movement was repeated,
and in the midst of the celestial tranquility a terrific explosion startled all
the guests. The Susuhunan beamed with pleasure. All nine pistols had
fired, and the Bedoyos, still floating in interstellar spaces, leaned languorously to the right, disposed of the pistols on the floor, and danced on as
the original Widadaris had danced—revolving to new positions, forming
new, perfectly spaced geometrical figures, utdets floating and falling, feet
balancing slender bodies in gentle undulations until, coming back to the
original pattern, they sank slowly to kneel again before the Susuhunan
and give the final Sembah [ceremonial salute]. For the last time they rose,
and with the kapang-kapang walk, disappeared as they had come—silently
floating into obscurity.

In earlier centuries, dancers of the Serimpi used not revolvers—which date
from the time of the East India Company—but bows and arrows.
—Zarina, pp. 106–107

Main Squeeze

At first, we practiced in the regular mirrored rehearsal hall. Then we found it more convenient to use a contraption that, when folded, looked like a wooden box, but, when unfolded, became three steps, up one side and down the other. At any spare moment, anywhere, we could practice.

"We'll have a hand-squeeze system," he proposed. "When I give you three quick squeezes, means we're coming to a hard part. One long squeeze, really good, darlin'! No squeeze at all? Well, let's do it again."

Before long, his system of signals became superfluous. "Now we just let those hands hang loose," he instructed. "Limp wrists, loose in the shoulders. There, that's it! Copacetic! Now let's get your feet attached to your ears." (Shirley Temple, on working with Bill Robinson)

—Frank, p. 92

Dagger Dance

Martha Graham's evening-length *Clytemnestra* (1958, with designs by Isamu Noguchi) was one of her greatest critical and popular successes. At the world première, in New York, Graham herself danced the title role, and Paul Taylor danced the role of Clytemnestra's lover, Aegisthus. In his autobiography, Taylor recalled the onstage events in the scene for himself and Graham in which she prepares to kill her husband, Agamemnon, for his sacrifice of their daughter, Iphigenia, during the Trojan War:

Great greedy gulps from an empty Noguchi wine cup. Rapturous reelings, slow darts. While in the midst of a cartwheel, I study the details of an upside-down proscenium. Hedonistic burning sensation of soles whisking across boards. Softness of a leap's superslow spongy landing. Softness of blue-carpeted ramp against rump. Softness of featherweight Martha in my arms.

For her safety, I shift into low gear, support her gently, treat her as spun glass. According to the whorls of my fingertips, her silky-smooth veil feels roughly corrugated.

Wantonly, we plot the murder of Agamemnon and the usurpation of his throne.

Aegisthus motions: "There is the dagger. Take it."

Queen motions: "Oh, no, I could not possibly."

Aegisthus motions: "Sure you can. Just let me help you to place your hand on it. It's over here in a pocket of the throne somewhere. Somewhere here . . . . Rats! The stupid prop man's forgotten to preset it. No, here it is after all. Grab on, O Queen."

Queen motions: "Mercy, it does feel nice. I do like daggers."

Aegisthus motions: "Wait a minute. Your dress has gotten caught up on something. May I be of assistance? There. Now you can go do your dagger dance."

Leaving me sitting on the throne with a purple veil in my lap, she begins a long, demanding solo. Since I'm downstage in bright light, it might be easy to draw the audience's attention away from her, but this wouldn't be cricket.

—Taylor, pp. 86–87

Salutes

For the past thirty years, statuesque Bettie de Jong has served as the indispensable rehearsal mistress for the Paul Taylor Dance Company. During the 1960s and 1970s, when both she and Paul Taylor were dancing with the company, she originated roles in *Scudorama, Big Bertha* (the title role), *Esplanade,* and many other dances; she was also Taylor's favorite partner. De Jong was born in Sumatra, Indonesia; when she was fourteen, her family moved to the Netherlands where she continued her studies in dance and mime. In New York, she studied at the Martha Graham School and performed for Graham and other choreographers before joining Taylor in 1962. One of her early Taylor assignments was in *From Sea to Shining Sea,* Taylor's 1965 work based on American history and legend:

We did *From Sea to Shining Sea,* with all sorts of American images in the third part, and when it came to Betsy Ross sewing the flag and saluting, I saluted with my palm out, and Paul said, "De Jong, we don't salute like that." I said, "Oh certainly, yes," and he said, "You're crazy." So, the next season, Eileen Cropley came from Britain and saluted the same way I had, and I said "See!" That's how we saluted in Europe: palms out, to show you have no weapon. Paul always made fun of me. Of course, I didn't even know who Betsy Ross was; I called her Betsy Roth. That's how new I was to this country!

—de Jong, unpaginated

Balletomania and
Other Thrills

Pavlova in Stockholm

In the crowd which escorted me when I left the theater, there were people of all stations: men and women belonging to the middle-class bourgeoisie, clerks and workmen, dressmakers' hands, shop assistants. They were all following my car, silently, and then remained standing in front of my hotel, until I was told that they wished me to show myself on the balcony. As soon as they saw me, they greeted me with a stormy outburst of cheers which, coming after the deep, protracted silence, sounded almost alarming. I bowed my head to them from time to time, and, all of a sudden, they started singing national tunes in my honor. I stood vainly seeking a way of expressing my gratefulness to them. Then an idea struck me. I turned into my room and came back with the wreaths and baskets of flowers which had been handed to me on the stage. But even after I had thrown roses and lilies and violets and lilacs to the crowd, they seemed loath to retire. I was deeply moved and quite embarrassed. I could not help asking my maid, "But what have I done to move them to so great an enthusiasm?"

"Madam," she replied, "You have made them happy by enabling them to forget for an hour the sadnesses of life."

—Franks, pp. 120–121

Woof!

Mlle Lola [Montez] first appeared in the costume of a Spanish lady—a basquine of black silk falling from her hips and weighted at the hem to stretch the folds, a black lace mantilla, a large comb in the chignon of her hair, a red carnation behind her ear, a fan that opened and closed like a butterfly's wing—and with a stance such as Goya might have sketched in a couple of strokes in one of his glowing water-colors. Then she returned, having changed into a fantastic dancing costume, all ablaze with sparkling sequins and flounces, to perform a *cachucha*, in comparison with which the most furious *pas* of Dolores Serral would have seemed like minuets and gavottes.

Never before had the somewhat plebian boards of the Porte-Saint-Martin received such an avalanche of bouquets and crowns. There was a hailstorm of camellias, Parma violets, and other fashionable flowers, of which at least a third were directed to the dancer's pretty feet and the other two thirds to her eyes, which are the most beautiful in the world and are used to ravishing effect. . . . Her teeth are as white and brilliant as those of a young Newfoundland dog, and shine like a burst of ivory when she smiles. . . .

Severe judges will say that she lacks good training, and that she does things in breach of the rules, but does that matter? (Ivor Guest, trans.)

—Gautier (1845), p. 160

Private Patron

Many years ago, when I was with the Ballet Russe de Monte Carlo, I had an admirer. He would only see me dance in New York. Sometimes he would take me out for carriage rides in Central Park, with the horses. He never laid a hand on me. Yet, when I did my first [performance as the lead in] *Swan Lake*, somewhere in the Midwest, he sent me a huge horseshoe—it took two men to carry it onstage—covered with two dozen white roses and two dozen white orchids. And, at Christmas, I received a wallet containing $250 or $300, which was a lot of money at that time.

—Ruthanna Boris, in conversation

Mistress of Rejections

Pauline Duvernay (1813–1894) performed at the Paris Opéra for only five years (1832–1837). However, during those years, when the Romantic ballet in Paris was at the height of its popular success, she was much appreciated by the ballet company and the public. As the dance historian Lillian Moore has written, Duvernay "was considered to be not only a great dancer but a magnificent actress and a sincere interpretive artist as well." As Moore describes her, she was brilliant, witty, willing to excel in any role, regardless of how small it might be, and also a brutal tease of the gentlemen who sought her personal offstage favors in the Foyer de la Danse, where "she had a reputation for coldness and cruelty," which, as the stories about her suggest, was earned:

> When another hopeful suitor asked what he might do to prove the strength of his affection, Pauline demanded one of his front teeth. Next day, he presented her with a dainty box containing the tooth. Pauline received the gift scornfully. "Sir," she complained, "I asked for one of your lower teeth, and you have brought me an upper!"
>
> —Moore, pp. 121–122

When You Get to the End of Night, Try *Swan Lake*

> "Those who talk about the future are scoundrels. It is the present that matters. To evoke one's posterity is to make a speech to maggots."
>
> —Céline, *Journey to the End of Night*

World War I national hero in his native France, World War II Nazi collaborator, the violently anti-Semitic physician and vehemently brilliant novelist born Louis-Ferdinand Destouches and known to readers worldwide as Louis-Ferdinand Céline (1894-1961) was a man of many parts. One of them was balletomania. In the early 1930s, a few years after the publication of his first novel, the celebrated *Voyage au bout de la nuit* ("Journey to the End of Night," 1932), Céline wrote his first ballet scenario, "The Birth of a Fairy," dedicated to an American dancer, Elisabeth Craig, with whom he was living at the time. In 1936, he took some of his ballet scenarios to the U.S.S.R. in the hope that a Russian company would perform them; however, there seems to be no record that any of them were ever staged anywhere. At the time of his death, his wife, another dancer, said that he had been hoping to write a book about the ballet. In 1959, Gallimard collected five of the ballet scenarios under the title *Ballets sans musique, sans personne, sans rien* ("Ballets without Music, without Dancers, without Anything"), which it published in an edition of 5,500 copies. Perhaps some of the theatrical challenges in Céline's ideas can be suggested by this scene, from the scenario "Scandal in the Deep" (ellipses are part of the original text):

> There he is, Captain Krog, with his spike in his hand . . . with his men . . . on the ice floe . . . massacring a thousand baby seals surprised in their little games . . . the blood of innocent seals runs everywhere on the ice . . . on the men . . . splattering Captain Krog . . . Captain Krog and his men dance with delight! . . . *The Dance of the Massacre!*
>
> —Céline, p. 38

Gooseflesh Is Only the Beginning

The Lindy Hop made its first official appearance in Harlem at a Negro Dance Marathon staged at Manhattan Casino sometime in 1928. Executed with brilliant virtuosity by a pair of competitors in this exhibition, it was considered at the time a little too difficult to stand much chance of achieving popular success. The dance grew rapidly in favor, however, until a year later it was possible to observe an entire ball-room filled with couples devoting themselves to its celebration.

The Lindy Hop consists in a certain dislocation of the rhythm of the fox-trot, followed by leaps and quivers, hops and jumps, eccentric flinging about of arms and legs, and contortions of the torso only fittingly to be described by the word epileptic. After the fundamental steps of the dance have been published, the performers may consider themselves at liberty to improvise, embroidering the traditional measures with startling variations, as a coloratura singer of the early nineteenth century would endow the score of a Bellini opera with roulades, runs, and shakes.

To observe the Lindy Hop being performed at first induces gooseflesh, and second, intense excitement, akin to religious mania, for the dance is not of sexual derivation, nor does it incline its hierophants towards pleasures of the flesh. Rather, it is the celebration of a rite in which glorification of self plays the principal part, a kind of terpsichorean megalomania. It is danced, to be sure, by couples, but the individuals who compose these couples barely touch each other during its performance, and each may dance alone, if he feels the urge. It is Dionysian, if you like, a dance to do honor to wine-drinking, but it is not erotic. Of all the dances yet originated by the American Negro, this most nearly approaches the sensation of religious ecstasy. It could be danced, quite reasonably and without alteration of tempo, to many passages in the *Sacre de* [*sic*] *Printemps* of Stravinsky, and the Lindy Hop would be as appropriate for the music, which depicts in tone the representation of certain pagan rites, as the music would be appropriate for the Lindy Hop.

—Van Vechten, pp. 184–185

Inspiration

Lone Star

Tommy Tune, the Broadway choreographer, remembers the time that Martha Graham visited his college, in his native Texas:

She was so dramatic, we were all in awe—we'd never seen a woman that looked like that! She said in her lecture, "All great dance stems from the lonely place." This little girl in the back of the room in a real Texas voice said, "Miss Graham, you said that all great dancing stems from the lonely place. Where is the lonely place?" Martha Graham raised herself up and said, "Between your thighs. Next question." We were never the same again.

—Grody, p. 152

No Short Cuts

Inspiration is not something that comes suddenly, like a stomachache. There is no such thing as inspiration. You have to work from childhood, and go through certain things, and sweat, and understand, and learn the métier. (George Balanchine)

—Gruen, pp. 281–282

Duende

Federico García Lorca:

The duende, then, is a power, not a work. It is a struggle, not a thought. I have heard an old maestro of the guitar say, "The duende is not in the throat; the duende climbs up inside you, from the soles of the feet." Meaning this: it is not a question of ability but of true, living style, of blood, of the most ancient culture, of spontaneous creation. . . .

Years ago, an 80-year-old woman won first prize at a dance contest in Jerez de la Frontera. She was competing against beautiful women and young girls with waists as supple as water, but all she did was raise her arms, throw back her head, and stamp her foot on the floor. In that gathering of muses and angels—beautiful forms and beautiful smiles—who could have won but her moribund duende, sweeping the ground with its wings of rusty knives.

—García Lorca, pp. 49, 54

The Constant Specter of Fear

Games—the powerful and raw, yet also deeply musical, urban street ballet based on children's game-chants, which Donald McKayle describes below— is still in active repertory in several dance companies. Choreographed in 1951, its alchemical mix of realistic and theatrical movement anticipates that of Jerome Robbins for *West Side Story* by six years:

It was a childhood memory that triggered my first dance. . . . It was dusk, and the block was dimly lit by a street lamp around which we hovered choosing a game. The street, playground of tenement children, was soon ringing with calls and cries, the happy shouts of the young. The street lamp threw a shadow large and looming—the constant specter of fear— "Chikee the Cop!" The cry was broken; the game became a sordid dance of terror. (Donald McKayle)

—Cohen, p. 57

Dances of Death

That the dead dance is a very ancient belief. A plaster relief from a grave in Cumae, near Naples, of late antiquity, shows them dancing—perhaps on the fields of the blessed, perhaps as ghosts. The latter is more probable, since they are represented as skeletons. In this case there is no question of the dead dancing as spirits in the heavenly paradise or in the fields of the blessed, but of a dance of the dead who have been buried in graves. People thought they saw lights shining on the burial mounds, and both heard and saw dancing and games, and heard the dead sing:

We warriors lie buried here below,
The soil above is heavy!
Happy he who is allowed to live
And enjoy his young life!

. . . The Dance of Death has found its way into purely profane dances. Among Hungarians and Slavs there is a social dance which is called the

Dance of Death. A dancer lies down "dead" and the others dance round him singing songs of sorrow. One or another leaves the ring and advances to the "dead" and changes his position in some way. Finally, somebody kisses the "dead." Then comes the resurrection, and then begins a wilder dance, with comic hopping steps, to the accompaniment of joyous songs. This Dance of Death persisted from the 15th to the 17th century in wedding dances in various parts of Germany. The procedure is essentially much the same.

—Backman, pp. 146, 152

Lift from Love

Eudora Welty:

In the primary department of Sunday school, we little girls rose up in taffeta dresses and hot white gloves, with a nickel for collection embedded inside our palms, and while elastic bands from our Madge Evans hats sawed us under the chin, we sang songs led and exhorted by Miss Hattie. This little lady was a wonder of animation, also dressed up, and she stood next to the piano making wild chopping motions with both arms together, a chair leg off one of our Sunday school chairs in her hand to beat time with, and no matter how loudly we sang, we could always hear her even louder: "Bring them in! Bring them in! Bring them in from the fields of sin! Bring the little ones to Jesus!" Those favorite Methodist hymns all sounded happy and pleased with the world, even though the words ran quite the other way. "Throw out the lifeline! Throw out the lifeline! Someone is sinking today!" went to a cheering tune. "I was sinking deep in sin, Far from the peaceful shore, Very deeply stained within, Sinking to rise no more" made you want to dance, and the chorus—"Love lifted me!"—would send you leaping. Those hymns set your feet moving like the march played on the piano for us to enter Davis School—"Dorothy, an Old English Dance" was the name of that, and of course so many of the Protestant hymns reached down to us from the same place; they *were* old English rounds and dance tunes, and Charles Wesley and the rest had—no wonder—taken them over.

—Welty, p. 874

A Book for a Book

In the foreword to the first edition of Lynne Fauley Emery's history, *Black Dance in the United States*, the choreographer and anthropologist Katherine Dunham called it "the first truly comprehensive book" on the subject. "In these times it may be surprising to many that Mrs. Emery is not black. She has written, however, with both care and dignity, and without exploiting the material she has uncovered for effect in the manner rather commonly prac-

ticed by white chroniclers of black fact." In her own preface, the author
explains why and how she got the idea to embark on the history:

> Seemingly insignificant experiences sometimes change the course of one's
> life; and it was just such an experience which led to the writing of this
> book. It is hard to believe that the reading of a single book could produce
> such change, yet *The Autobiography of Malcolm X* was no ordinary book. I
> had noticed the startling lack of dance literature with which my black
> students could identify. Nebulous thoughts which had been floating in
> my mind suddenly fell into place and became concrete ideas. *Malcolm X*
> provided the inspiration which eventually grew into *Black Dance in the
> United States*, and I will always be indebted to him for the understanding
> and insight I have gained.
>
> —Emery, pp. vii–ix

Papa's Waltz

> When I think about it, my father, Lord rest his soul, was the one who
> sparked my love for dancing. When I was a little girl, we lived in a neigh-
> borhood where there were social functions, parties, with sawdust on the
> floor. Everyone attended—even the kids. A band would play, and Papa would
> always waltz with me. He was a big man. We would waltz and waltz. And I
> was so proud. He would turn me around, say to the right, and then we
> would waltz a little more. He would lean over and whisper to me, "re-
> verse," which meant that he was going to spin me around the other way.
> And one day when Papa and I danced, he didn't have to say "reverse"—I
> just followed him. I was so happy you'd think I'd won the championship of
> the world! That was when I first realized what it was to dance. (Ruby Keeler)
>
> —Frank, p. 36

Beautiful Austerities

> Just before we sailed for home I went over to the Paris Exposition to visit
> Loie Fuller's tiny theater, which she was sharing with the remarkable little
> Japanese actress, Sadi Yaco.
>
> In America I had seen many imitations of Loie Fuller. She probably
> suffered more imitators than any woman alive, so I was somewhat pre-
> pared for her astonishing and beautiful performance. She was not, in the
> strict sense of the word, a dancer. She had a heavy body and never a very
> polished technique, but she was an inventive genius and brought a wealth
> of richness to both the dance and the stage. A little of this I recognized
> that night, but my real excitement and wonder was stirred to an unbeliev-
> able pitch by the extraordinary acting of Mme. Sadi Yaco.
>
> For the first time I beheld and understood the beautiful austerities of
> Japanese art. Here, in her dancing (she was, of course, both dancer and

actress), was the antithesis of the flamboyant, overblown exuberance of our American acrobatics. Here was a costuming in which the colors were vivid, yet so related to the mood that they seemed to emanate from a different palette. Her performance haunted me for years and filled my soul with such a longing for the subtle and elusive in art that it became my chief ambition as an artist. From her I first learned the difference between the words "astonishing" and "evoking."

—St. Denis, p. 40

The First Glow of Dawn in the Taj Mahal

During her landmark tour of India, where her company danced in Bombay, Calcutta, and Delhi, Anna Pavlova pleaded with the art patrons she met to show her examples of the country's native dance traditions, especially the temple and court traditions of Kathakali, Kathak, and Bharata Natyam. She was told that these had fallen into ruin long ago and were no longer taught or performed; and, as her biographer Keith Money explains, the performances by native dancers to which she was taken were sorry examples of noble traditions in deep decline. However, visiting the country's great monuments, Pavlova became overwhelmed with the depictions of India's dance heritage in its ancient art and resolved to help revive India's classical dances. In the passage following, the Bangalore-born dancer Ram Gopal (ca.1912–2003) quotes from a 1949 interview he conducted with the diplomat Diwan Chamanlall, who had met Pavlova in India in the 1920s. Gopal tells how the inspired ballerina in turn inspired three of the most important Indian dancers of the twentieth century:

She was amazed and inspired to see the Taj Mahal by moonlight and told me often that it was the most beautiful thing she had ever seen on this earth. In fact, she spent a whole night, till the early hours of the morning, watching the Taj Mahal by the light of a full moon until the first glow of dawn. She told me that somehow she seemed to have drunk so deeply of the spirit of India and the spirit of beauty, which she intuitively felt and understood, that she decided there and then to try and build an Indian ballet to express the essence and feeling that India's age-old monuments had inspired within her.

It is well known to lovers of ballet that her subsequent visits to Ajanta and its thousands of years' old Buddhist frescoes and sculptures had so inspired her that she created out of this in the twenties and danced a full-length ballet, *Ajanta Frescoes*, in London. With her unerring instinct and intuition, she had chosen Comalata Bannerjee, a gifted composer and one of the first young Bengali ladies of high-born family, to write the music, using the lyrical and enchanting Ragas and Raginis and Talas (time measures) of Hindu music for this Ajanta ballet, and also the Radha Krishna religious love theme. It was Comalata Bannerjee who introduced Uday Shankar to Pavlova as a suitable Sri Krishna to Pavlova's Radha. . . .

Uday Shankar, that great dancer and pioneer of Hindu creative dancing; the late Menaka, who revived interest in the Kathak dances of North India and her picturesque ballets; and Rukmini Devi, who made it respectable for Brahmin girls today to dance "Dasi Attam," a dance of the temple courtesans: these three great artists who have done so much pioneering and spadework for the younger generation of New Indian Dancers, were all alike inspired, bewitched, enraptured, and inflamed to "do something" for the almost dead art of India. It was the magic quality in the art of Pavlova, both by her incomparable dancing on the stage and her electrifying talk and the nervous energy that she radiated offstage to these three dancers from India, that inspired each of them with a determination to seek out, explore, create, and revive what Pavlova disconsolately found and was told was dead or dying.

—Franks, pp. 102–103

Emotional Impact

Natalia Makarova:

The concept of "spirituality" in the Russian ballet was born with the appearance of Anna Pavlova, the incarnation of the eternal feminine, of "the dancing of the soul," on stage. If you look through reviews of ballets in old Russian newspapers, you will be amused by the picture that emerges. In the beginning, the critics—and they were the best of the audience— approached the ballet from a strictly formal point of view: "Miss Andrianova executed grandes cabrioles en avant well." Or: "Instead of fouettés, Egorova danced la crème fouetté." In Russia, Andrei Levinson and Akim Volynsky were the first, inspired by Pavlova, to equate genius—not formal beauty—with spiritual dance. For me, a ballerina who does not have emotional impact is not a ballerina; she is merely a dancer, an artisan, even if her technique is fantastic. Ballerinas of formal virtuosity who spin like a top seem to me much more boring than a spiritualized but technically less-brilliant ballerina. Technical flaws can be corrected, but there is nothing to be done with a body capable only of what, in olden times, was called des morceaux de virtuosité. Luckily, no one yet gives formal classes in inspiration! . . . We were not given classes in inspiration at the Vaganova School, but we were taught how to express ourselves through the formal grammar of the classical dance, through that same arabesque.

—Makarova, pp. 34–35

Subconscious Solution

Just a few years ago, I was dancing the Queen Mother in Matthew Bourne's Swan Lake. I had had the idea of focusing on the nastier aspects of this woman. But Matthew really wanted me to make her rather an endearing person—adored by all, despite her rather inappropriate sexual appetite. He wanted me to show that her inability to understand her son was the result of upbringing, rather than having a truly horrid nature. I found this incredibly difficult to achieve and was never sure I had found the right balance, until an old friend and colleague came to see the performance. Afterwards, she delightedly remarked, "I know whom you based that on!" I was dying to know whom she had to say, for I truly didn't know myself. "Margot!" she announced, and I realized that it was true. I had searched hard and long and had come up with a subconscious solution, born of years of observation. And I had, at last, tried to dance like Margot Fonteyn. (Lynn Seymour)

—Macaulay, unpaginated

Locked

One New Year's Eve, I saw Rudolf Nureyev and Sonia Arova perform *Le Corsaire* in my hometown, Chicago. So, inspired to become a dancer, I quit college just before finishing my business degree and joined ballet classes. At first I was placed among children—eight-year-old girls. Then, quickly, I was moving ahead: I knew so little about ballet that I was taking beginning, intermediate, and advanced-level classes all in one day, without paying attention to the levels. The teacher asked me, "Don't you think you're too old?" I was 23.

When The Royal Ballet came to Chicago, I was a super in the third act. Nureyev and Fonteyn danced the principal roles. For my first role in a ballet, I was directed to stand at the back of the stage and hold a spear, then to exit as soon as the curtain came down. I stood in such a pulled-up first position the entire time that my body locked, and I was unable to move when the ballet finally ended. Everyone in the wings was yelling at me to, "Get off the bloody stage!" The curtain came back up for bows, and I was still, slowly, exiting.

Eighteen years later, as resident choreographer at the Boston Ballet, I was performing character roles and working alongside Nureyev, my inspiration. (Ron Cunningham)

—Hite, interview

No Words

In January 1980, the profoundly gifted and unreachably troubled American ballerina Gelsey Kirkland walked into the office of Lucia Chase, the founding artistic director of American Ballet Theatre, and resigned from the company. According to Kirkland's memoirs, the one person at ABT who understood her was the choreographer Antony Tudor:

While on the outs with ABT, I received a letter from Mr. Tudor. He sent along some belated criticism of my performance in *Swan Lake*, reminding me not to flap my arms, not to fall into personal melodrama. His deeper purpose was to defend the world of the theater. He counseled me not to lose my reverence for the stage. His sentiments made me burst into tears. I wrote him a brief message, unable to adequately express my gratitude for his thought and concern, saying that I had no words. He sent back a card emblazoned with the image of a lone red heart. There were no words whatsoever.

—Kirkland, p. 259

Seductions Attempted, Surmised, and Realized

Fantastic Legends

Geoffrey Gorer:

My friend Pavel Tchelitchew had introduced himself to Féral Benga after the latter's dance recital at the Théâtre des Champs Elysées in the autumn of 1933. Benga had already made a reputation for himself as a dancer at the Folies Bergère, a reputation that was enhanced by the "mystery" surrounding his private life—which, being translated into English from the Parisian, meant that if he had love affairs they were not known about and he was practically never seen in fashionable houses or night clubs. On this negative foundation were built the most fantastic legends; he was reputed to be extremely rich and impossible to meet, either on account of his mythical vices—at one moment or another almost every possible combination had been attributed to him—or of the jealousy of whichever keeper rumor gave him at the moment. Actually he was very shy, much distressed by the fact that, because he was a Negro and a dancer, everybody considered that they had a right, if not a duty, to make sexual advances to him, and so poor that after the failure of his dance recital he had barely enough to live on. For although his dances in the recital had had enormous success, and the critics had been uniformly and superlatively eulogistic, his associates had been laughed off the stage and had refused to continue with the recitals projected for the future; Benga had no money to continue alone.

—Gorer, p. 15

Corrupt Spirits and Depraved Minds

The German-born scholar Otto Kinkeldey (1878–1966), who is frequently called the father of American musicology, made a study of Italian treatises on the art of dancing from the second half of the fifteenth century and concluded that they proved the art "was assiduously cultivated in the circles that gathered around the Tuscan and Lombard princes, who did so much for the arts in this most fruitful period of the Renaissance." He goes on: "From the days of Boccaccio, the manuscripts of the early Renaissance . . . showed that the art of dancing played no small part in the lives of educated men and women of the 14th and 15th centuries. As practiced in the upper strata of society, it was a refined and complicated art, differing greatly from the simple and spontaneous folk or peasant dance, which must have existed contemporaneously."

One of the fifteenth-century authors whose work Kinkeldey studied was Guglielmo Ebreo of Pesaro, a Jewish dancing master about whose life nothing whatsoever is known but whose single treatise on dancing has been preserved in a number of manuscript copies, indicating that "his position was not obscure." Furthermore, Kinkeldey adds, "from the care displayed in the actual copying of his text and from the bindings in which some of the copies are preserved, it is quite clear that he wrote for people of taste and culture. If our author's meaning was always as clear as the handwriting of some of his scribes, our knowledge of the subject would have reached a more advanced stage than it has."

One of the crystal-clear passages from Guglielmo's treatise:

The art of dancing is, for generous hearts that love it, and for gentle spirits that have a heaven-sent inclination for it, rather than an accidental disposition, a most amicable matter, entirely different from and mortally inimical to the vicious and artless common people who frequently, with corrupt spirits and depraved minds, turn it from a liberal art and virtuous science into a vile, adulterous affair, and who, more often in their dishonest concupiscence under the guise of modesty, make the dance a procuress, through whom they are able to arrive stealthily at the satisfaction of their desires.

"Guglielmo, we see, had a very lofty conception of his art," Kinkeldey adds.
—Kinkeldey, pp. 2, 21

Splendor and Wickedness

The last of Balanchine's ten productions for Diaghilev [was] given in 1929, shortly before the death of the latter. *Le Fils prodigue* ["Prodigal Son"], composed by Prokofiev, and costumed by Rouault, was marvelously interpreted by the young Lifar, with Dolin and Woizikowsky as the companions of the Prodigal and Doubrovska as the courtesan. In this ballet, Balanchine made contrasting use of the elements of pantomime and acrobatics in new and startling fashion. The dance of seduction was particularly effective. Agnes de Mille has vividly described it: "Doubrovska as an ancient biblical courtesan full of splendor and wickedness hangs over the Prodigal's body, her arms locked over his bent elbows, her wrists dangling, her long slender legs bent so that her toes trail in the air, her knees moving slowly in rhythm with his steps. He crosses the stage languorously under this sensuous burden. She sits before him and with frenzied strength jumps to her toes. He wraps her about his waist like a belt . . . and with feet spread apart watches her slide down his body to the ground where she lies in a coil, hand clutching ankle, spine tense as a sprung trap. He sits beside her, swings toward her, away from her, tries to lift himself from the floor, sinks back, and twists himself into her arms in an inextricable tangle. This constitutes one of the most important seductions to be found on any stage. . . .

"It is with vigorous wiles that the courtesan lures the Prodigal into her power, as we have seen, and vigorously she makes known her triumph. Her attendants immediately smother him in her crimson train. She mounts to the shoulders of one of them and stands looking down a good ten feet at her subdued lover. In this device, a tumbling trick, Doubrovska opens up an entirely new field for theatric expression. Literally she towers over her prey. No actress by voice or presence could dominate the situation more completely. . . . (Agnes de Mille, 1930)

—Moore, pp. 243–244

The Rapture of Fonteyn and Nureyev

When I admit that—based on what Rudolf-told-Fred-told-Kenneth-told-Deborah-told me—yes, I *do* believe that Margot and Rudy were lovers, you must understand that I, like the rest, am telling you more about my personal prejudices and predilections than ever I could about what really went on between those two people who, as if sharing some complicit laugh, took their secret, undivulged, to their separate graves. And the frustration which they have bequeathed to us endures for a very good reason—in order to lead us to the real question, and to its true answer: namely the fact that rapture has a realm beyond the bedroom, and that whatever took place behind closed doors, out of our sight, was as *nothing* compared to what happened on the stage, in front of our eyes.

—Daneman, p. 408

Half Mad and Ready to Swoon

The waltz and Romanticism made their entrance together into nineteenth-century Europe, and for well over a half century, both of them were fraught with the peculiar tension that arises when attraction to the unknown is countered by the terror of it—a tension that Danish dance critic Erik Aschengreen has discussed (in Patricia McAndrew's translation) as "the beautiful danger." There have been many vivid literary attempts at crystallizing the powerful feelings of the dance, both for those who practice it and those who observe it, beginning with Goethe's in his tragic, 1801 novel, *The Sorrowings of Young Werther*. ("Never have I moved so lightly. I was no longer a human being. To hold the most adorable creature in one's arms and fly around with her like the wind, so that everything around us fades away. . . .") The following cameo, by Ernst Moritz Arndt, of a waltz at an actual party in a Bavarian village articulates the anxieties and anticipations that the dance stimulated in many onlookers:

> The dancers held up the dresses of their partners very high, so that they should not trail and be stepped on, wrapped them tightly in this shroud, bringing both bodies under one covering, as close together as possible, and thus the turning went on in the most indecent positions; the hand holding the dress lay hard against the breasts pressing lasciviously at every movement; the girls, meanwhile, looked half mad and ready to swoon. As they waltzed around on the darker side of the room, the clasps and kisses became still bolder. It is the custom of the country, and not as bad as it looks, they say: but I can now quite understand why they have forbidden the waltz in certain parts of Swabia and Switzerland.
>
> —Sachs, p. 430

Duels de Deux

Giacomo Casanova (1725–1798) had one of those titanic lives (and libidos) that defy attempts to summarize them. Venetian-born and the holder of a doctorate from the University of Padua, he served at various times as a soldier, a professional violinist, a librarian, the secretary to the Cardinal of Padua, a clergyman, the founder of a workshop for the making of printed silk, a historian, a translator, a novelist, an essayist, a gambler whose invention of the lottery netted him millions, and—oh, yes!—the most famous womanizer in Western letters. At one point, he "retired" to dash off a dozen volumes of memoirs chronicling his exploits as a libertine. The jury is still out on how much of them is actually true (beginning with Casanova's accounting that he had bedded 122 women); however, modern appreciation of the writing is practically unanimous. A critic no less formidable than Edmund Wilson proclaimed them the most interesting memoirs ever written; and readers who dip into them will discover that it isn't only the content that makes for their fascination. Casanova knew how to juggle the threads of several stories at once; in every endeavor he embraced, it seems, he was a master of multitasking. The son of an actor and an actress who both hoped he would become a priest—a hope that had to be revised when at the age of sixteen he

was expelled from the seminary for conduct unbecoming a man of the cloth—
Casanova enjoyed attending theater and opera, wrote precisely and authori-
tatively about actors and dancers, and occasionally contributed personally to
the stage events. (When he went to see Mozart's opera *Don Giovanni*, he
discovered that the libretto by his pal Lorenzo Da Ponte incorporated some
of his own exploits, which he had related to Da Ponte in conversation.)

The following episode from his memoirs concerns a seventeen-year-old
"comic dancer," a ballerina named Marina, who specializes in soubrette roles
and with whom Casanova is enjoying a dalliance; a ballet master named
Antonio Stefano Balletti (1724–1789), who, unbeknownst to Casanova, is
about to become Marina's dancing partner and who clearly, from Casanova's
version of events, comports himself with a revealing grace worthy of his
surname; and a professional gambler and pimp named Count Celi, whose
insult of Marina in Casanova's presence leads Marina to respond in kind,
which prompts the Count to "throw a knife in her face." She sidesteps it.
The count begins to pursue her. Casanova unsheathes his sword and places
the point at the Count's throat. The Count demands a meeting the next day,
to take the conversation out of doors. Casanova sets the time at 4 P.M. and
arrives early, looking forward to a duel:

Going into a coffeehouse to wait until four o'clock, I fall into talk with a
Frenchman whose appearance I liked. Enjoying his conversation, I warned
him that, upon the arrival of someone who was to be alone, my honor
demanded that he was to be alone, too, for which reason I must ask him
to disappear when he appeared. A quarter of an hour later, I see him arrive with a companion. I tell the Frenchman that I should be glad if he
would stay.

He comes in, and I see that the fellow with him was wearing a sword at
his side a good 40 inches long and looked a perfect cutthroat. I rise, saying
coldly to the bas . . . :

"You told me you would come alone."

"There's no harm in having my friend along, since I have only come to
talk with you."

"If I had known that, I would not have gone to the trouble. But let us
make no disturbance and go and talk where no one can see us. Follow me."

I go out with the Frenchman, who, knowing the place, takes me where
there is no one, and we stop to wait for the two men, who were coming
slowly along, talking together. When I see they are ten paces away, I draw
my sword, telling Celi to be quick and draw his, and the Frenchman unsheathes his sword, too.

"Two against one?" says Celi.

"Send your friend away, and this gentleman will leave, too. Besides,
your friend has a sword, so we are two against two."

The man with the long sword said he would not fight with a dancer;
my second replies that a dancer is as good as a bas . . . , and, so saying, he

advances on him, gives him a blow with the flat of his sword. I pay the same compliment to Celi, who falls back with his friend, saying that he only wanted to have a word with me and that he would fight after that.

"Speak."

"You know me, and I do not know you. Tell me who you are."

It was then that I began to hit him in good earnest, as my brave dancer did the other; but only for a moment, for they ran away as fast as their legs could carry them. So the whole pretty affair was over and done with. My brave second was expecting company, so I went back to Milan alone after thanking him and asking him to sup with me after the opera at the "Pozzo," where I was lodging. For that purpose I told him the name I had given for the register.

I found Marina just going out; when she heard how the whole thing had gone off, she promised me she would tell it to everyone she saw; but what delighted her was that she was certain that, if it was true that my second was a dancer, it could be no one but Balletti, who was to dance with her at Mantua.

After putting my papers and my jewels back in my trunk, I went to the coffeehouse then took a place in the parterre of the theater, where I saw Balletti pointing me out as he told our comical story to all his acquaintances. At the end of the opera, he met me, and we went to the "Pozzo" together. Marina, who was in her room, came into mine as soon as she heard me speak, and I enjoyed Balletti's surprise when he saw his future dancing partner, on whose account he had to prepare to dance *demi-caractère* parts. Marina simply could not risk appearing as a serious dancer. When we sat down at table, these fair votaries of Terpsichore, who had never met before, declared an amorous war, which kept me amused throughout supper, for, confronted with a dancer, Marina, who knew what she was about in matters of love, adopted an entirely different behavior from that which her catechism instructed her to use with "gulls." In any case, Marina was in excellent spirits because of the extraordinary applause which greeted her appearance in the second ballet, by which time the story of Count Celi was known to the whole parterre. (Willard R. Trask, trans.)

—Casanova, Volume Two, pp. 279–281

Critical Lines

The Puritan Maypole

... Thus each alternate season did homage to the Maypole, and paid it a tribute of its own richest splendor. Its votaries danced round it, once, at least, in every month; sometimes they called it their religion, or their altar; but always, it was the banner staff of Merry Mount.

Unfortunately, there were men in the new world of a sterner faith than these Maypole worshippers. Not far from Merry Mount was a settlement of Puritans, most dismal wretches, who said their prayers before daylight, and then wrought in the forest or the cornfield till evening made it prayer time again. Their weapons were always at hand to shoot down the straggling savage. When they met in conclave, it was never to keep up the old English mirth, but to hear sermons three hours long, or to proclaim bounties on the heads of wolves and the scalps of Indians. Their festivals were fast days, and their chief pastime the singing of psalms. Woe to the youth or maiden who did but dream of a dance! The selectman nodded to the constable; and there sat the light-heeled reprobate in the stocks; or if he danced, it was round the whipping-post, which might be termed the Puritan Maypole. . . .

It was the Puritan of Puritans; it was Endicott himself!

"Stand off, priest of Baal!" said he, with a grim frown, and laying no reverent hand upon the surplice. "I know thee, Blackstone! Thou art the man who couldst not abide the rule even of thine own corrupted church, and hast come hither to preach iniquity, and to give example of it in thy life. But now shall it be seen that the Lord hath sanctified this wilderness for his peculiar people. Woe unto them that would defile it! And first, for this flower-decked abomination, the altar of thy worship!"

And with his keen sword Endicott assaulted the hallowed Maypole. (Nathaniel Hawthorne)

—Klein, pp. 22, 24

Nuts

That was awful, no dementia to it at all. (Jack Cole, Hollywood choreographer, speaking to a young Tommy Tune about Tune's choreography for the show *Wildcat*)

—Grody, p. 154

Beauty?! Get Real!

The music of Mr. Tchaikovsky does not suit the dances at all. It's not even possible to dance to it. In places it is a symphony, and in others unsuccessfully imitates ballet rhythms. There are two or three music phrases, but the composer repeats them endlessly.

In general, *Sleeping Beauty* will interest those who don't look for choreography in the ballet, but only amusement for the eye in the décors and costumes. (Unsigned review, in the January 4, 1890, edition of the *Peterburgskaya gazeta*, of the world première by the Imperial Ballet of the Marius Petipa–Peter Ilyitch Tchaikovsky production, *The Sleeping Beauty*, January 3, 1890, at the Maryinsky Theater in St. Petersburg)

—Scholl, p. 176

The Choreographer Weighs In:
7/20 November 1904. Sunday.

In the morning, the opera *Dubrovsky*—my dances. In the evening, the 105th performance of *The Sleeping Beauty*—my ballet—Mme. Trefilova. They left out the Blue Bird. It's the first time. It's sad to see so large a troupe [saddled] with such bad management.

Went to the theater. Receipts: 2,935.70. The whole ballet went very badly. It's a disgrace. . . . (Lynn Garafola, trans.)

—Petipa, *The Diaries*, p. 57

Unfair

The following passage, by Peter Ilych Tchaikovsky, by common consensus the greatest composer for the ballet in history, responded to a cutting remark by the composer Sergei Taneyev that Tchaikovsky's Fourth Symphony had elements of "ballet music":

I completely fail to understand what you call ballet music and why you won't accept it. Do you mean by ballet music any cheerful and dancelike tune? But in that case you can't accept most of Beethoven's symphonies, in which it can be found at every turn. Are you trying to tell me that the trio of my scherzo is written in the style of Minkus, Gerber, and Pugni?

This seems to me unfair. I totally fail to understand how the expression *ballet music* can be something *disapproving!*

—Warrack, p. 5

Knees Don't Please

From the Maryinsky prima ballerina assoluta Mathilde Kschessinska:

In the jealousy scene [of *Esmeralda*, where Kschessinska danced the title role], in which I see Phoebus with his fiancée and have to dance a pas de deux before my rival, I express my despair, in the final coda, like a wounded bird. It so happened that the dancer who was playing Phoebus' fiancée murmured quite loud: "Her knees aren't even turned out." It was not even annoying! It was simply . . . stupid!

Such a remark gives an only too clear picture of the way in which certain dancers think of ballet technique. I was not one of those who dance themselves silly and think of nothing but details of execution, of turning out their knees, who are hypnotized by technique at the expense of acting. Where there is no mime, technique must obviously be followed; but in scenes of powerful drama, where everything rests on the emotion, one can safely forget one's knees! The dancer who made this remark had not the slightest conception of what a dramatic interpretation should be. (Arnold Haskell, trans.)

—Kschessinska, p. 75

Nothing Is Left but the Debris

In 1928, a year before his death, Serge Diaghilev was interviewed in Paris by a Russian-language newspaper about classical dancing and the company of Ida Rubinstein, whose novelties—outrageous to Diaghilev on aesthetic grounds—were also in competition with those of his own Ballets Russes for audiences. Diaghilev, in fact, had introduced her to the Parisians in 1909, in the title role of Michel Fokine's *Cléopâtre*. However, when Rubinstein, a wealthy Russian heiress with intense entrepreneurial ambitions yet only a modicum of ballet training, founded her own company and hired some of Diaghilev's chief artists at wages he couldn't match, Diaghilev was incensed. The fact that her pet panther attacked him (see "Fauna") probably didn't help. Nor did her company's repertory, which, when measured against Diaghilev's own exacting standards, seemed to him senseless. Indeed, few working dance critics would ever venture to critique an artist with the unsparing severity—and also the authority—that Diaghilev displayed in this interview.

After explaining that "if theatrical creativity is to evolve . . . it is not enough to remain faithful to our teachers. We were not taught algebra and ancient Greek in order to spend our lives solving problems or speaking the language of Sophocles," he goes on to give an example from architecture: "The gifted innovators who have created American skyscrapers would find it easy to restore arms to the Venus de Milo, because they have a profound knowledge of classical art. But what, precisely, offends our eye in New York is the Greek portico of the Carnegie Library and the Doric columns of the railway stations. Skyscrapers represent our classical art." (Diaghilev visited New York in 1916.)

The interviewer then asks him for his opinion "of Ida Rubinstein's attempts at classical dance," to which Diaghilev replies:

> Rubinstein's performance confirms what I have been saying. It reveals the desire to cling to the traditions of classical ballet, but no coherence, no harmony, is ever apparent in her work. . . . Rubinstein herself has not realized that classical dance is the most difficult, the most delicate, and the most ungrateful of all the arts. It does not forgive errors.
>
> Her arched silhouette, her bent knees, the utter confusion in all her striving after a futile "classicism" largely account for the fact that a dancer in her company, of second rank but still knowing her job, looked to us like a star according to the old precepts of a routine invented half a century ago. When classical dance represents only a "monument of antiquity," one must not only *not* preserve it, one must condemn it, for it becomes a poison that can contaminate the organism of modern choreography.
>
> That is how the "classicism" of Rubinstein's choreography looked to us, and I think I have the right to say so because, 20 years ago, it was I who introduced an exotic, mysterious, hieratic Ida Rubinstein to choreography.
>
> How has she had the temerity to alter so mercilessly the image we had of her? To us that image seemed unforgettable, but she has erased it forever. Nothing is left but the debris, which does not even have the usual beauty of ruins silhouetted against the sky. (Text of Diaghilev's December 1928 interview with a reporter from *La Renaissance*)
>
> —Kochno, pp. 286–287

Premonition

The ballerina Alexandra Danilova died peacefully in her sleep in New York on July 13, 1997, at the age of 92. Her funeral, at Frank Campbell's on the upper East Side, was open to her adoring public, and the chapel was filled to overflowing. Among the speakers who, from their various vantage points as friends, family, and colleagues recalled her life and career, was Louis Uffland, her manager and confidant of several decades. He related that shortly before her death, the ballerina had a premonition, which came to her in the form of a dream, that she would die. She told Mr. Uffland that she foresaw herself in heaven, meeting all her ballet friends from her youth. Among them was Serge Diaghilev, who had treated her at the Ballets Russes with affection and forbearance bordering on indulgence. In the dream, he recognized her and cried out happily, "Chourutska!"—his old pet name for her. Then, after a pause, he added, "Late again."

—Mindy Aloff, July 1997

Russian Salad

Any readers who are feeling blue about their artistic careers might take heart from the next anecdote, which suggests that even giants go through tough times and scalding criticism. In June 1933, Lincoln Kirstein—then working as a ghostwriter for Vaslav Nijinsky's wife, Romola, on her radically edited version of her husband's diary, which she was preparing for publication— took her to see the London debut of Les Ballets 1933, the company that the twenty-nine-year-old George Balanchine had just founded with Boris Kochno. The repertory, which Balanchine had choreographed over a period of a few months, featured the "baby ballerina" Tamara Toumanova in several ballets, including Balanchine's first staging of *Mozartiana*, as well as Tilly Losch in his *Errante* and, with Lotte Lenya, in his first staging of the Kurt Weill-Bertolt Brecht cantata, *The Seven Deadly Sins*. (The note to Serge Lifar that Kirstein mentions would have been significant, incidentally, as Lifar was Balanchine's nemesis at the time.):

July 8 . . . . Took Romola to the opening of *Les Ballets 1933* at the Savoy. Nervous as to what she might think of it all. She said Toumanova was too big and slow and should still be at school; some of Balanchine's *adagio* ideas not bad; the whole evening like a school demonstration, a sort of *salade russe*. During the entr'acte, she left a note next door at the hotel desk for Serge Lifar. She showed me the spot, behind a column, where 20 years ago she used to watch Vaslav pass, going down to dinner with Diaghilev. Afterwards, backstage, Balanchine came out looking haggard and tired. Romola said he had actually to make the very theater dance, since he had no dancers; "old Pa Diaghilev would be pirouetting in his grave." Rather depressed; a letdown.

—Kirstein, *By*, p. 147

Incidentally, Kirstein didn't seem to be dissuaded from his enthusiasm for Balanchine's ballets in Les Ballets 1933, as the next entry shows that he kept going back to the theater.

Oh, She Adored It!

The painter and scenic designer Pavel Tchelitchev is best known in the dance world as Balanchine's friend and collaborator during the choreographer's early years in America. They shared a somewhat mystical temperament as well as an appetite for theatrical surprises—qualities embodied by Tchelitchev's lighting, costumes, and theatrical effects incorporating silks for Balanchine's 1933 *Errante* ("The Wanderer," to Schubert), which featured a dress of green silk with a ten-foot-long train, a costume conceived by Tchelitchev (inspired, apparently, by costumes designed by Loïe Fuller for a spectacle about the sea) and realized by the Paris-based fashion designer Edward Henry Molyneux. To appreciate the delicious diary entry by Kirstein concerning Tchelitchev's hunger to learn the opinion of Janet Flanner, Paris correspondent at the time for *The New Yorker*, it's helpful to know a little bit of background on the names that Kirstein's diary entries mention. Edward James, the husband of the dancer Tilly Losch, was the primary backer of the Balanchine-Kochno company Les Ballets 1933, where *Errante* had been given its première, with Losch wearing the silk dress. Tamara Toumanova, a teenage ballerina whom Balanchine had discovered (along with the teenagers Irina Baranova and Tatiana Riabouchinska) at the class of Olga Preobrajenska in Paris, performed with Les Ballets 1933 as well, and Balanchine loved her as both an artist and a person. [Kirstein's diary, June 17: "Balanchine is in love with Tamara Toumanova, whose mother says he is old enough to be her father (at twenty-nine?)"] However, Toumanova was also contracted to appear with the Ballets Russes de Monte-Carlo of the wily and unscrupulous Col. de Basil, who ultimately stole her away from Balanchine through a contract dispute. "Virgil" refers to Virgil Thomson, the American composer and music critic. Edith Sitwell, of course, was the British poet and a member of a wealthy family, many of them figures in the arts. "Bérard" was Christian ("Bébé") Bérard, the peerless theatrical designer of Balanchine's *Cotillon* and *Mozartiana*.

Kirstein traveled in very privileged circles in Europe, among both artists and socialites, as his amused diary entries concerning Tchelitchev make clear. It is also a measure of the regard in which Janet Flanner was held that the artist would be so keen to know her assessment of his creation:

June 10 . . . . *Errante*, stupendous climax with the falling chiffon cloud; Virgil says this is the private life of Pavel Tchelitchev: love, revolution, tempestuous love affairs, etc. Tchelitchev looking like an angry, intelligent horse; with Edith Sitwell swathed in white chiffon, with a white-and-gold mobcap and huge gold plaque. . . .

June 21 . . . . To Pavel Tchelitchev's studio with Noël Murphy, whom he is painting. George Lynes (the photographer), Glenway Wescott (the novelist) already there. Discussion of the great Bérard-Tchelitchev feud; scandal and gossip around the ballet world. The French dancers deliberately stepped on Tilly Losch's ten-foot sea-green train in *Errante*, and she screamed onstage (in German). Tchelitchev's long lecture on the nature of stagehands, without whom nothing can be accomplished in any theater; how the French ones were either idiots or (obviously) bribed to sabotage him because he was Russian, or because they were helpless idiots; but German and English ones were the best, giving effortless aid, like clockwork. Tons of beautiful sketches in heaps, rejects from *Errante*; he pressed one on me; like an idiot I was too slow accepting it, so he gave it to George Lynes. "Oh, so it's not good enough for you?"

June 24 . . . . To Tchelitchev's studio, 5 rue Jacques Mawas. Says he is tired of working for snobs and amateurs. I tried to describe the marvelous new stage at Radio City Music Hall, what wonderful things might be done there. He said toe dancing was finished, ridiculous; that Balanchine was on the verge of abandoning classic academic dance (under his influence?), but had a strong instinct for spectacle. He is sick to death of *scandales*, European intrigues, French (Parisian?) society, fashionable dressmakers; New York was obviously the place to be during the present *crise mondiale*. Edward James phoned: The Monte Carlo company is suing him over the defection of Toumanova; he is countersuing for libel, harassment, or something. Tchelitchev says James's passion is for litigation rather than patronage; he thinks real property is a real asset but only the poor understand the stock markets. Tchelitchev particularly wanted to know what Janet Flanner thought of his *Errante*. I said she adored it. I did not say she had been unable to see it, and that I had described it to her in great detail for her "Paris Letter," which covered the two rival ballet companies. Julien Levy took me to Brancusi's studio. Magnificent. . .

—Kirstein, *By*, pp. 134, 140, 142; Zafran, pp. 23–34 *passim*

Artists! To the Barricades!

The trouble with the modern dance now is that it is trying to be respectable; the founders of the modern dance were rebels; their followers are bourgeois. The younger generation is too anxious to please, too eager to be accepted. For art, this is death. To young dancers, I want to say: "Do what you feel you are, not what you think you ought to be. Go ahead and be a bastard. Then you can be an artist." (Anna Sokolow)

—Cohen, p. 29

You Think I'm Kidding?

Mary Fanton Roberts, author of this remembrance, was an editor in New York who was one of Isadora Duncan's most reliable and helpful friends.

Isadora's uncompromising attitude on the subject of art often made her enemies, for she was ruthless in her absolute artistic integrity. I remember an incident at the *Masque of Caliban*, given in the Lewisohn stadium, New York City, in 1916. The author, Percy MacKaye, had persuaded Isadora to inaugurate it, and while waiting to begin, she found herself near a group of "Greek" dancers, trained by one of her imitators. One of these girls, excited by the occasion and the proximity of the great dancer, said to Isadora archly, "If it weren't for you, we wouldn't be doing this. Don't you feel proud?" Isadora looked at the poor child and said, "I regard what you do with perfect horror."

Of course, the girl could not be expected to understand the grounds for this rebuff, and must have gone away much hurt. Later, in relating the occurrence to us, Isadora explained what she meant, putting her unerring finger on a fundamental and too frequent fault in dancing. "Their movements are all *down*," she said, "grovelling on the earth. They express nothing but the wisdom of the serpent, who crawls on his belly."

—Isadora Duncan, *The Art,* pp. 18–19

Cheap Show

Michel de Montaigne:

I note that the good poets of Antiquity avoided any striving to display not only such fantastic hyperboles as the Spaniards and the Petrarchists do but even those sweeter and more restrained acute phrases which adorn all works of poetry in the following centuries. Yet not one sound judge regrets that the Ancients lacked them nor fails to admire the incomparable even smoothness and the sustained sweetness and flourishing beauty of the epigrams of Catullus above the sharp goads with which Martial enlivens the tails of his. . . . Those earlier poets achieve their effects without getting excited and goading themselves on; they find laughter everywhere: they do not have to go and tickle themselves! The later ones need extraneous help: the less spirit they have, the more body they need. . . .

It is the same with our dancing: those men of low estate who teach it are unable to copy the deportment and propriety of our nobility and so try to gain favor by their daring footwork and other strange acrobatics. And it is far easier for ladies to cut a figure in dances which require a variety of intricate bodily movements than in certain other stately dances in which they merely have to walk with a natural step and display their native bearing and their usual graces. . . . (M.A. Screech, trans.)

—Montaigne, p. 462

Intuition and a Stud Button

In her memoir, *Castles in the Air,* the darling of American ballroom dancing, Irene Castle, praises a review by Gilbert Seldes of her and her husband, Vernon. "She danced from her shoulders down," the review went in part. "The straight scapular supports of her head were at the same time the balances on which her exquisitely poised body rested. There were no steps, no tricks, no stunts. There was only dancing, and it was all that one ever dreamed of flight, with wings poised, and swooping gently down to rest."

Castle explains:

I have a great fondness for that description, because it describes the way it was, or at least the way I felt when I danced. Vernon *did* invent the steps, often on the spur of the moment, and by keeping my eyes firmly fixed on the stud button of his dress shirt I could anticipate every move he was going to make and we made it together, floating around the floor like two persons sharing the same mind. It was intuitive dancing, to be sure, because I never practiced if I could help it, and if it had been difficult, I'm sure I never would have had the patience to carry on with it.

—Castle, p. 87

What Makes a Ballet Critic

The Rose and the Star, a book (alas, long out of print) from which several passages in this anthology have been drawn, is one of the most idiosyncratic and wonderful dance volumes in English. It consists of a conversation between the critic and British ballet fan P.W. Manchester (represented in this entry) and the writer and Russian-ballet enthusiast Iris Morley at a moment—the late 1940s—when both countries were enjoying ballet of very high quality, beginning with their respective national prima ballerinas assoluta: Margot Fonteyn in Britain and Galina Ulanova in the U.S.S.R. Manchester and Morley compare and contrast the two cultures and their ballet with an authority and a literary passion that makes the reader ache to join in. They still believe in the magic.

Obviously anyone who can write an article and persuade an editor to print it can call himself a critic, while some of the best judges of Ballet I know have never put pen to paper and have no urge to do so. No one who has had less than a dozen years of ballet-going, which means several years of pre-war Ballet, or else has been able to see a good deal of Ballet in other countries, has any very solid basis today on which to found public expressions of opinion. One needs to have seen a very great deal of many ballet companies and one *must* have got the "glamour" aspect thoroughly out of one's system—which alone takes a few years. One must also know exactly how far personal prejudices, favorable and unfavorable, play a part in one's views and take steps to neutralize them before they are perpetuated in print. A music critic who really likes Ballet is usually extremely sound in his judgments—Ernest Newman and the late Edwin Evans were two of the best ballet critics we ever had—but if they are not interested they are apt to concentrate on the music and sometimes make astonishing remarks about technique, which leave the rest of us pop-eyed.

—Manchester, pp. 182–183

The Critic as Anthropologist

Deborah Jowitt's highly personal essay *Time and the Dancing Image* is yet another book—this one thematically organized according to imagery (veils,
Salomes)—that believes in the magic of the theater.

A dance critic, attending performances night after night, devises strate-
gies for keeping eye and mind fresh. Some years ago, no doubt influenced by a longstanding addiction to *National Geographic*, I began to find
it useful, on occasion, to blot out all expectations based on knowledge of
styles or techniques. Instead I imagined myself an anthropologist skulk-
ing in ambush, observing the activities of members of a hitherto undis-
covered tribe—trying to discern their customs and social hierarchy before
I stepped out of the bushes and made myself known to them.

—Jowitt, *Time*, p. 7

"Criticism as Ethnography": Keynote Address by Sally Banes, Dance Critics Association Conference, 1989

About a month ago, I told a philosopher friend the topic of my talk for
today. "I can immediately think of two important differences between
dance critics and ethnographers," he said. Now this friend, the son of an
African statesman and an upper-class British woman, grew up in Ghana,
was educated at Oxford, and teaches at Cornell. Not only does he literally embody cross-cultural experience; he is also one of the leading contemporary philosophers of mind. "This is great," I thought. "I'm about to
get a brilliantly insightful theoretical groundwork for a complicated topic.
The talk is as good as written." "So . . . ?" I asked, taking out a mental
notebook, and gearing up for some subtle philosophical discourse. "It's
this," he replied: "Ethnographers get a lot more grants to go to *much* more
interesting places."

—Banes, p. 16

The Mission of a Dance Review

Edwin Denby:

A dance journalist's business is to sketch a lively portrait of the event
he is dealing with. His most interesting task is to describe the nature of
the dancing—what imaginative spell it aims for, what method it proceeds by, and what it achieves. In relation to the performance, he describes the gifts or the development of artists, the technical basis of
aesthetic effects, even the organizational problems that affect artistic

production. The more distinctly he expresses himself, the more he exposes himself to refutation and the better he does his job. But beyond this the dance public wants him to be influential in raising the level of dance production in their community; to be enlightening on general questions of theater dancing, its heritage, and its current innovations; and to awaken an interest for dancing in intelligent readers who are not dance fans already.

—Denby, Dance Writings, p. 534

Saint Edwin

Edwin Denby, a leading candidate for the title of greatest dance critic in history, was dubbed "Saint Edwin" by his colleagues for his luminous yet lightly displayed intelligence, his patience in the face of ignorance, and his unfailing courtesy when confronted with views that contradicted his own. However, as his friend the poet Frank O'Hara noted in the introduction to Denby's second collection of criticism, *Dancers, Buildings and People in the Streets*, "He will not just put up with anything." As an example, O'Hara recounted the following anecdote:

> Recently, at the première of Balanchine's *Don Quixote*, he was asked what he thought of the new work. Denby said, "Marvelous! I was very moved."
> "I was moved right out of the theater," his interrogator replied.
> "That's where you belong then," Denby said in the gentlest of tones.

—Denby, Dancers, p. 8

Turning Points

Bigger

Suzanne Farrell, the ballerina whom George Balanchine called "my Stradi-varius," has recounted the precise moment when she understood what he wanted and when he saw that she was capable of both surrendering more to him as a dancer and projecting his choreography more fully than any artist with whom he had ever worked. It occurred in the studio, during a class, around 1962:

> Although I was convinced he was a genius, it also occurred to me that he might be just a little eccentric . . . until he challenged me to pirouette his way in class one day and changed my life.
>
> It was shortly after moving into the State Theater, and we were in eleven o'clock morning class in the huge, windowless main hall on the fifth floor. Like every other ballet dancer on earth, I had been taught to turn from a fourth position with one leg directly in front of the other, both knees bent in plié ready to push off into as many pirouettes as possible. I was what is called a "natural turner," having no fear of spinning around on one leg as fast as I could, and the results more often than not were smooth multiple pirouettes. Turning was not one of my problem areas, but Mr. B made it a problem, or so I thought. He asked me to start my pirouette, and I settled into a nice, comfortable fourth position.
>
> Thinking I was ahead of the game, I straightened my back leg, know-ing that he liked it that way, although it still felt foreign and unorthodox. I thought I was giving him what he wanted, but he didn't think so at all.
>
> "Why don't you try a big fourth?" he said. I shuffled my legs a little wider and looked at him for approval. "Bigger." Again I shuffled a few more inches. "Bigger." Now I was feeling really uncomfortable with my legs so far apart that the notion of pushing off for a turn was becoming a fantasy.

"More," was the next suggestion, and though I silently tried to accommodate him, he knew what the rest of the dancers were thinking—no self-
respecting ballerina would ever take such a wide stance before a turn.

"More." By now my legs were so far apart that I risked losing my grip
and slipping to the floor in a split. If this was a Balanchine experiment,
I wished he had used another guinea pig. Now that I felt thoroughly
ridiculous—which was not helped by nervous twitters from the other
girls, all hoping they weren't next on the turning block—he smiled in
triumph and said with enormous satisfaction, "*Now* turn." Never in my
life had I turned from such a deep lunge, and my instincts told me to
shuffle back to where I had begun, but I looked at Mr. B and thought
better of it. He seemed so happy and excited, and I did after all want to
please him. Half defiantly (I was sure that I would fall on my face) and
half curiously I turned . . . and turned . . . and turned. . . .

The turn that had begun with such painstaking resistance and hard
labor resulted in such a wonderful sensation that I decided then and there
that this man knew exactly what he was doing—even when he asked for
what seemed physically impossible. "Impossible" went out of my vocabulary; things were merely "different." If he wanted wider, he would get
wider; if he wanted smaller, he would get smaller; and if he wanted me to
stand on my head I would ask only whether I should be facing front or
back. That pirouette was really the beginning of our spiritual understanding; indeed, it was not about pirouettes at all, it was about believing in
someone even when you might doubt.

—Farrell, pp. 94–95

The Hell I Will

In the early 1970s, after she had given up performing, Martha Graham suffered from tremendous depression and drank herself into a coma. It was at
this time that a young fan, Ron Protas, a photographer, visited her constantly,
cared for her unstintingly, and won her confidence.

Then, one morning, I felt something welling up within me. I knew that
I would bloom again. That feeling, an errand into the maze, over and
over in my mind, sustained me to go on. It was my only way to escape the
constant fear of what might come.

Finally, the turning point came. By then, I was sitting up, out of the
coma. I had for the only time in my life let my hair go white.

Agnes de Mille came to visit. She was a good friend through it all, and
courageous soul that she is now, still stands with me, but, at times, Agnes
can say the absolute wrong thing for the finest and most heartfelt reasons.
This visit was no exception. "Oh Martha," she said with a smile, "I am so
glad that you decided to let your hair go natural." When she left, I turned
to the window and said to myself, "The hell I will." The next morning I

had a colorist in, and somehow I would fight my way back. And I did, but it was more of a fight than I had anticipated.

—Graham, p. 145

A Man's Work

As a child in Mexico, I had been fascinated—as any child would be—by Spanish jotas, Mexican jarabes, and Indian bailes. Later, across the border, I had seen tap dancers and ballet dancers. All this seemed interesting enough to watch, but to me it was something for girls to do. It never occurred to me as something a man would be caught dead doing. Then pure accident brought me to a performance by Harald Kreutzberg. What I saw simply and irrevocably changed my life. I saw the dance as a vision of ineffable power. A man could, with dignity and a towering majesty, dance. Not mince, prance, cavort, do "fancy dancing" or "show-off" steps. No: dance as Michelangelo's visions dance and as the music of Bach dances. (José Límon)

—Cohen, p. 23

Falling, and Falling, and Again Falling

The first time I saw pictures of Isadora Duncan, I simply fell in love with her with all the ardent tenderness that a young man of 17 brings to such a love. Later on, I saw pictures of Shanta Rao and fell in love again, and later still, when I saw her on stage—with her irresistible, sensuous feminine radiance—I fell even more in love with a passion that a grown man can bring to something he knows is a treasure. Whatever discoveries I have since made in perception or attention or the pure fact of movement I owe to these loves. (Erick Hawkins)

—Cohen, p. 39

Stunned into Study

Merce Cunningham knew as a child that he had to learn how to dance. His epiphany came as he watched a performance in his native Centralia, Washington, by a dancer named Mrs. Maude Barrett, who would become his first teacher:

She came on stage dressed in a yellow gown with white pantaloons and little black patent leather shoes, swinging Indian clubs. I'd never seen anyone do that, and she was also talking to the audience because they were all her friends; that was quite a sight. Then she put the clubs down at the side of the stage. She really didn't stop talking. And she put something over her skirt. I couldn't figure out what it was at first, but I later realized it was a big rubber band. Then she got up on her hands and walked around the stage and didn't stop talking. It was such a sight to see this woman, who was no longer young, with this kind of energy. It stunned me. I thought, I have to study dancing.

—Lesschaeve, p. 34

Something Sacred

Alastair Macaulay, the author of this remembrance, is the drama critic for *The Financial Times* and one of Britain's leading dance critics:

The first time I saw Margot Fonteyn perform, she was dancing Juliet at the age of 56. I had already seen Kenneth MacMillan's *Romeo and Juliet* twice before with a younger ballerina as Juliet, and now, though I knew little about ballet, I could tell that sometimes (notably in the balcony scene) Fonteyn was dancing a simpler version of the choreography and that sometimes (especially in the ballroom scene) she was in pain. When I left the theater, I was aware that I had seen an extraordinary artist, but I had no clue that my life had been changed. Only the next day—and then every day for six weeks, several times each day—did visions of Fonteyn's Juliet start to burst into my head unbidden. Neither before nor since have I been so haunted by a performance: I might be attending a seminar (I was then an undergraduate), or cycling down the road, or in mid-conversation, and suddenly all I would see would be Fonteyn, Fonteyn, Fonteyn for a few moments.

If there is one moment that I—like many others—would single out from these once-blinding memories, it is when Romeo-Nureyev knelt to kiss the hem of Juliet-Fonteyn's robe. They were both in profile to the audience, and Nureyev took time—as if her very hem was precious. Fonteyn, in turn, looked down at him in complete stillness and wonder, as if something sacred was occurring. Suddenly, she hurled her arms up into the air and looked up through them and past them into heaven. Again, she held this moment in complete stillness. Then she brought her arms down—down over her face; down over her body; down in an astonishing wave; down on the crest of the music. All around the theater, dozens of people were gasping out loud in emotion; I later heard such gasps again, but only ever at Fonteyn performances. It seems to me now that Fonteyn was a less marvelous Juliet than Lynn Seymour, and that the role of Juliet did not show me the greatest virtues Fonteyn had as a dancer. But it was that performance that—as Frederick Ashton said of Anna Pavlova— "injected me with her poison" and made me a devotee not just of Fonteyn but of all ballet.

—Macaulay, pp. 36–37

Sudden Realization

In her memoir, *The Amateur: An Independent Life of Letters*, the writer and editor Wendy Lesser devotes a chapter ("Portrait of a Ballerina") to a meditation on a photographic portrait from the 1930s by George Platt Lynes. The subject is Tamara Toumanova, seated in an odd yet lovely way, while wearing a long black tutu, trimmed with metallic streaks, from an early Balanchine ballet. "George Lynes' pictures will contain, as far as I am concerned, all that will be remembered of my own repertory in a hundred years," reads an appreciation signed by Balanchine from 1956. Lesser became fascinated with the photograph, which, as she observed, seems to encapsulate Balanchine's concern with off-balance movement, exactitude, irony, seductive feminine beauty, and the contrast between "coherent, artificially manipulated composition" and an energy that is "wild, free, unconfined." Lesser arranged to interview Toumanova, then living in Los Angeles, for the now-defunct magazine *Dance Ink*. At the end of the interview, Lesser showed Toumanova a copy of Lynes's image:

> After studying the photo for a moment, she identifies it as being from *Cotillon*, the first ballet Balanchine made for her, in 1932. What is odd, she comments, is that in the photo she is wearing not her own costume (that of a young girl at her first ball), but the costume of another role, "the woman in black." Balanchine, apparently, was not present during the photography session; it was Lynes who got her to pose in this theatrical, purely invented position. Toumanova nonetheless agrees with Balanchine's assessment of Lynes's choreographic evocation. "It's so outstanding," she says, looking at the picture. "I don't say this because it is me, but because it is a beautiful picture. The hand, resting . . . the quality of the look. They don't take photographs like that anymore."
>
> Later she elaborates on this theme. "It is an epoch that is going away. I look at it and it is like another world." She looks at me hard, as if to instill in me the importance of what she is about to say. "In life, you never realize how everything changes. It changes suddenly."
>
> I look down at the photograph in my hand, at the dreamy look, the softly resting hand, the delicately balanced pose, and I realize that the woman in the photograph is silently telling me just the opposite. *I will be this way forever*, she is saying.
>
> —Lesser, pp. 193–194

From Stage to Page

Eggsactly

During the eighteenth century, "blind" dances with eggs were popular theatrical acts in both the United States and Europe, one of many bits of unexpected knowledge to be found in *The American Musical Stage before 1800* by scholar of theater history Julian Mates. The passage below, from Thomas Carlyle's translation of Johann Wolfgang von Goethe's popular novel *Wilhelm Meisters Lehrjahre* ("Wilhelm Meister's Apprenticeship"), describes a version of this wonderful stunt. In the scene, the young street dancer Mignon is performing the egg dance for an audience of one—the protagonist of the novel:

> She carried a little carpet below her arm, which she then spread out upon the floor. Wilhelm said she might proceed. She thereupon brought four candles, and placed one upon each corner of the carpet. A little basket of eggs, which she next carried in, made her purpose clearer. Carefully measuring her steps, she then walked to and fro on the carpet, spreading out the eggs in certain figures and positions; which done, she called in a man that was waiting in the house and could play on the violin. He retired with his instrument into a corner: she tied a band about her eyes, gave a signal; and, like a piece of wheel-work set a-going, she began moving the same instant as the music, accompanying her beats and the notes of the tune with the strokes of a pair of castanets.
>
> Lightly, nimbly, quickly, and with hair's-breadth accuracy, she carried on the dance. She skipped so sharply and surely along between the eggs, and trod so closely down beside them, that you would have thought every instant she must trample one of them in pieces, or kick the rest away in her rapid turns. By no means! She touched no one of them, though winding herself through their mazes with all kinds of steps, wide and narrow, nay, even with leaps, and at last half-kneeling.

Constant as the movement of a clock, she ran her course; and the strange music, at each repetition of the tune, gave a new impulse to the dance, recommencing and again rushing off as at first. Wilhelm was quite led away by this singular spectacle; he forgot his cares; he followed every movement of the dear little creature, and felt surprised to see how finely her character unfolded itself as she proceeded in the dance.

Rigid, sharp, cold, vehement, and in soft postures, stately rather than attractive,—such was the light in which it showed her. At this moment he experienced at once all the emotions he had ever felt for Mignon. He longed to incorporate this forsaken being with his own heart, to take her in his arms, and with a father's love to awaken in her the joy of existence.

The dance being ended, she rolled the eggs together softly with her foot into a little heap, left none behind, harmed none; then placed herself beside it, taking the bandage from her eyes, and concluded her performance with a little bow.

—Goethe, pp. 108–109

A Half-Ethereal Splendor

The Russian poet Alexander Pushkin (1799–1837), whose craftsmanship approaches Dante's, was a connoisseur of dancing, theatrical and social; and in his heroic poem *Eugene Onegin* he chronicles both ballet and ballroom practices with considerable knowledge and specificity. One of the most celebrated dance passages in *Onegin* concerns a performance by Avdotia Illyinichna Istomina (1799–1848), a dancer of considerable beauty who is considered Russia's first Romantic ballerina and who earned success in ballets by Charles Didelot that were based on Pushkin's works. It's even possible to glimpse the steps she dances in John Bayley's translation of stanza XX: *rond de jambe* (perhaps *rond de jambe en l'air*), some kind of *grand jeté*, pirouettes to both sides, and a small beaten step, such as an *entrechat* or an *assemblé battu*. Didelot's biographer, Mary Grace Swift, has written that "the soulful flight—the union of performing virtuosity with deep sensitivity to the dramatic impact of the movement—was then, and still is, a fundamental aesthetic goal of the Russian performer, and Didelot was a prime force in instilling that special spirit, that happy combination of soulful expression with faultless technique in Russian ballet." For Pushkin's jaded, arrogant young Onegin to find even the marvels of Didelot boring is one of the poem's keenest jokes. Below, the ballerina's entrance:

> The house is packed out; scintillating,
> the boxes; boiling, pit and stalls;
> the gallery claps—it's bored with waiting—
> and up the rustling curtain crawls.
> Then, with a half-ethereal splendor,
> bound where the magic bow will send her,

Istomina, thronged all around
by Naiads, one foot on the ground,
twirls the other slowly as she pleases,
then suddenly she's off, and there
she's up and flying through the air
like fluff before Aeolian breezes;
she'll spin this way and that, and beat
against each other swift, small feet. (John Bayley, trans.)

—Pushkin, p. 43; Swift, p. 169

Dickens on . . . Could It Be Juba?

In 1842, during his American tour, Charles Dickens was taken to a dance hall
in the vibrant (and dangerous) Five Points section of lower Manhattan—the
gang-ridden turf that served Martin Scorsese as a subject in his movie *The
Gangs of New York*. Among the things that nineteenth-century Five Points
was also known for, though, was the explosion of tap dancing—a hybrid
kind of virtuosic stepping that evolved through competitions between African American buck-and-wing dancers and Irish clog dancers. During his
first visit to America, in 1842, Dickens toured Five Points and, in a dance
hall called Almack's he observed an African American virtuoso who was said
to be the legendary Juba. In the first volume of his *American Notes*, the great
novelist immortalized the performance. A portion of the passage is also cited
in the remarkable history *Dan Emmett and the Rise of Early Negro Minstrelsy*, by
Hans Nathan:

Our leader has his hand upon the latch at "Almack's," and calls to us from
the bottom of the steps. For the assembly-room of the Five-Point
fashionables is approached by a descent. Shall we go in? It is but a moment.

Heydey! The lady of Almack's thrives! A buxom fat mulatto woman,
with sparkling eyes, whose head is daintily ornamented with a handker-
chief of many colors. Nor is the landlord much behind her in his finery,
being attired in a smart blue jacket, like a ship's steward, with a thick gold
ring upon his little finger, and round his neck a gleaming golden watch-
guard. How glad he is to see us! What will we please to call for? A dance?
It shall be done directly, sir: "a regular break-down."

The corpulent black fiddler, and his friend who plays the tambourine,
stamp upon the boarding of the small, raised orchestra in which they sit,
and play a lively measure. Five or six couples come upon the floor, mar-
shaled by a lively young negro, who is the wit of the assembly, and the
greatest dancer known. He never leaves off making queer faces, and is the
delight of all the rest, who grin from ear to ear incessantly. Among the
dancers are two young mulatto girls, with large, black, drooping eyes, and
head-gear after the fashion of the hostess, who are as shy or feign to be, as
though they never danced before, and so look down before the visitors,
that their partners can see nothing but the long fringed lashes.

But the dance commences. Every gentlemen sets [advances towards] as long as he likes to the opposite lady, and the opposite lady to him, and all are so long about it that the sport begins to languish, when suddenly the lively hero dashes in to the rescue. Instantly the fiddler grins, and goes at it tooth and nail; there is new energy in the tambourine; new laughter in the dancers; new smiles in the landlady; new confidence in the landlord; new brightness in the very candles. Single shuffle [sideways dance step], double shuffle, cut [diagonal step] and cross-cut [second diagonal step across the first one]: snapping his fingers, rolling his eyes, turning in his knees, presenting the backs of his legs in front, spinning about on his toes and heels like nothing but the man's fingers on the tambourine; dancing with two left legs, two right legs, two wooden legs, two wire legs, two spring legs—all sorts of legs and no legs—what is this to him? And in what walk of life, or dance of life, does man ever get such stimulating applause as thunders about him, when, having danced his partner off her feet, and himself too, he finishes by leaping gloriously on the bar-counter, and calling for something to drink, with the chuckle of a million of counterfeit Jim Crows [i.e., white minstrels in blackface], in one inimitable sound!

—Dickens, *American*, pp. 101–102

A Secret

In this passage, from Edwin Denby's "Superficial Thoughts on Foreign Classicism" (1953), one sees how a dance performance can have a moment-to-moment "story," even though there may be no overall scenario or literary narrative:

I was astonished and delighted watching a Parisian dancer save an awkward passage in performance. She seemed to be saying to the audience, "I'll tell you a secret: this is a passage of no consequence at all, and it doesn't suit my style either, such a stupid choreographer—oops, that elastic—again!—where was I? Oh yes, I'll just sketch in a few steps, I'm delicious at sketching in, you know—and then, just in a moment more, there's a bit—oh really so clever, you'll adore seeing how divine I am in it—ah, here goes now!" "How adorably alive," the audience whispered to its neighbor.

—Denby, *Dance Writings*, p. 547

Modest and Absolute

For three years during the late 1980s, the brilliant modern-dance choreographer Mark Morris was the choreographer in residence at the Théâtre de la Monnaie in Brussels. Although the residency began well—with Morris using the resources of the large opera house to choreograph what is considered to be his Handel masterpiece, the evening-length *L'Allegro, il Penseroso ed il Moderato* (with a singing text predominantly provided by John Milton)—the audiences in Brussels were not pleased with other new works. Indeed, in the European manner, they (or claques of them) frequently and brutally booed the dancers, and the Brussels critics followed suit.

And yet, despite—or, perhaps also because of—the many woes and disappointments that Morris endured in Belgium, he made a spectacular repertory there. As his biographer, Joan Acocella, puts it: "That city taught him sorrow in a new way. He responded by smiling and saying that everything was fine—and indeed, much of the time, by feeling fine. And then he went into the studio and, one after the other, created six completely different works about the darkness of life."

Acocella goes on to make a literary animation of one of those dances. The passage is taken from the galleys of her biography, which differ slightly from the published volume:

The most unusual of them was *Behemoth*, long (38 minutes), cold, abstract, and silent: the only full-scale piece Morris has ever made without music. The dance is in eleven sections, separated by slicing blackouts. In each section the dancers engage in strange, ritualistic maneuvers whose only emotion seems to be a quest for precision. Twisting their torsos, turning on the floor like the hands of a clock, the dancers get each angle just right—38 degrees, not 37—as if they had worked out a system by which, against all odds, they might be able to survive, but any deviation from which would spell disaster. The disaster is already there, however. Again and again, one dancer will be set off at an angle to the group, in frightening isolation. Often, the dancers are headless; they lie on the floor upstage-downstage, so we can't see their heads. Elsewhere they are faceless. They look at each other without recognition. (They acknowledge us even less. They end the piece with their backs to us.) Now and then the terror implicit in all this is given some meager expression: the dancers fall to their knees, their hands shiver, they look upward. But for the most part the piece makes no emotional appeal whatsoever. It is modest and absolute.

—Acocella, *Mark Morris*, p. 184

A Half Century of *Ivesiana*

Although not frequently invoked in discussions of Balanchine's repertory, *Ivesiana*, the choreographer's dark vision of New York City, has exerted a renewed power on New York dancegoers since 9/11, as if a seed somewhere deep within the work had been waiting to burst open in response to the catastrophic events of that day in 2001. (Key to the theatrical effect, too, is its palpably nocturnal lighting design, by Jean Rosenthal.) Critic Tobi Tobias, who has followed the ballet from its inception, reflects on a 2004 New York City Ballet performance:

I wish I understood better why Balanchine's *Ivesiana* made such a piercing impression on me when I first saw it with its original cast and why every subsequent encounter with it—I got to see it twice last week—has confirmed its power. Is it Balanchine's acute response to the music? His piercing imagery? His ability to set up scenes that clamor for lurid melodrama and responding waves of kitsch sentiment and then play them out with tranquil objectivity?

Created in 1954, the ballet is set to four small, unrelated pieces for orchestra by Charles Ives—eerie, idiosyncratic music that is both spare and complex. Often it seems to be a kind of ambient sound going on inside your head as you try to live in a contemporary urban America that harbors faint, fragmented echoes of its past. The ballet's four sections are named for their music.

Central Park in the Dark: The light has almost failed in a space without boundaries. A large cluster of female figures—hair unbound, shrouded in unitards as dark and dull as mud—moves out from a faraway corner to fill the area, with the humdrum gait and pace of pedestrians in a train station. The bodies then bend over head first, kneel, and sway back and forth, crouching at intervals in fetal position. A pale bare-legged girl in a plain white sundress, "victim" written all over her, enters and picks her way through their midst as they begin to resemble tombstones or, raggedly waving their raised arms, trees in a forest rife with dangers. The girl, arms outstretched before her, fingers like antennae trying to palpate anything they might encounter, seems to be blind.

A man enters, clad like the anonymous figures. The girl goes to him immediately and, at his touch, swoons in relief or fear. Logic would have it that this lone male is the girl's potential attacker, yet sometimes he seems as lost and terrified as she. They wander through the not-quite-human matrix as if through a tangled wood, jumping over the low obstacles formed by the bodies pairing up to link arms. Slowly, inconspicuously, the figures arrange themselves into a mound. Then, as the music rises to a crescendo of muted cacophony, the man flings the girl's body onto this half-animal, half-vegetable hillock and flees. The body lies there, inert, for some terrible moments in which nothing happens. Finally the girl rises, only to return to her sightless wandering. The ensemble recedes, reassembling in its opening position way back in the space, as if the same story were about to unfold again, and the fragile girl, isolated in the middle of nowhere, walks tentatively out of our view.

The Unanswered Question: Another dark space. Light falls on only two people. The first is a woman in a white leotard, limbs and feet bare, long hair streaming over her shoulders, face expressionless. The other is a near-naked man whose existence lies in reaching out for her eternally. The woman is an icon. She's borne by four men swathed in black who are nonentities apart from their function. They hold her high above their shoulders, in standing or seated position, so that she resembles the statue of a saint paraded before a worshipping crowd. They swoop her downward towards her yearning pursuer, sometimes sweeping her over his recumbent body. They pass her along among themselves in a horizontal circle, as if she were a belt binding them. They wheel her backwards and bring her up head first, as if she were emerging from deep waters. Not once do they allow her feet to touch the floor.

The theme is central to Balanchine. The yearning man is the artist-lover. The woman is his muse, by definition—indeed, of necessity—unattainable. The idea is commonplace; the marvel is the way in which Balanchine has found a series of images operating in time to convey it.

In the Inn: A man and woman meet casually at a club, enjoy a sophisticated danced flirtation—they're worldly wise, attractive and mutually attracted—then go their separate ways with insouciance. No strings, no regrets, just that gorgeous interlude in which they charm and challenge each other and we get to watch, relishing their savoir-faire. There is no indication whatsoever of how this section relates to the darkness that prevails in the rest of the ballet. You're left to figure that out for yourself—if you need to.

In the Night: The landscape of the first section has now become the sole action. Once again, in the gloom, the anonymous figures trudge cross-stage on their knees—until the inexorably failing light makes them invisible. Matthew Arnold's "We are here as on a darkling plain" verses would seem to apply but for the fact that what Balanchine gives us here is not a cri de coeur like "Dover Beach," with a proposed escape route ("Love, let us be true to one another"), but a simple, uninflected statement of fact that proves to be ineradicable.

No one mentions *Ivesiana* when lists of Balanchine's masterpieces are being drawn up, but it is one nevertheless. And, half a century from the date of its making, it remains as new as tomorrow.

—Tobias, "Ballet"

Fauna

Catastrophes

Ida Rubinstein (1885–1960), the charismatic and beautiful performer, impresario, and heiress to storied riches, was born in Russia to a family of Ashkenazi Jews. Although she studied music and dance as a child, and would go on to become a student of Michel Fokine's, by most accounts she was less of a dancer than a kind of specialist in living sculpture. Her attenuated figure and her dramatic presence led Serge Diaghilev to cast her in some exotic roles with overtones, as her biographer Michael de Cossart writes, of "decadence and sadism." Eventually she founded her own company and, thanks to her inherited wealth, hired away some of Diaghilev's collaborators at fees that he could not hope to match—for which he never forgave her or them.

Rubinstein was theatrical outside the theater in many ways, and one of them was her habit of keeping large wild animals as pets. She was well known for walking a leopard on the streets of Paris, and she also owned a black panther who liked to eat hats and gloves and to try to crawl up curtains, "chewing them until they fell down." (Her pets would accompany her on shopping trips, and when couturiers heard she was coming, they tended to close up early.) Once, when the painter and scenic designer Léon Bakst was visiting, the panther got "stuck inside an immense waste-paper basket and became agitated." Rubinstein pulled it out, but, as Bakst remembered, "when she let the animal go, I was horrified to see that Madame Rubinstein had her chest and arms literally starred with claw marks. She hadn't said a word, and she declared that it was nothing."

On a later visit from Diaghilev, the panther, awaking from a nap, took exception to Diaghilev's "large frock-coat." De Cossart relates that, when the cat "bounded in Diaghilev's direction . . . he [Diaghilev] promptly leapt up onto a table with a cry of terror," which scared the wits out of the panther, who "took refuge in a corner where it crouched, howling and snorting, its whiskers bristling." Rubinstein, laughing heartily, picked up the cat by the scruff of the neck and pitched it into the adjacent room. "Diaghilev was saved." Saved to take strong measures, it seems. A few days following, the panther was taken away from Rubinstein as "experts had declared that it was a danger to human life."

—de Cossart, pp. 45–46

Groan and Bear It

The ballroom dancer Irene Castle was one of the very few vaudevillians to take notice of the animal acts with which she and her husband, Vernon, shared the stage. What she noticed was not pretty. "Viewed from the audience, these acts were charming," she wrote in her memoir, *Castles in the Air.* "Little dogs jumped through hoops or paraded around in human clothing and monkeys rode on their backs in a steeplechase. The backstage conditions for these animals were not so charming. We saw dogs beaten unmercifully after the curtain fell and given the water cure in the alley, with the trainer holding a powerful hose to the dog's nose and filling his lungs with water. We saw animals shocked with electricity, stuck with needles, and starved except for the few tidbits of reward which made them do the things they were afraid to do. There was little affection between the trainer and his animals. Affection might make a dog unpredictable on the stage. So the animals were cowed, afraid to make the slightest mistake."

At first, until they refused to perform at all on programs with animal acts, the Castles would try to save the animals they saw being mistreated by buying them from their owners and giving them away, in the hope that whatever their fate with new owners, they couldn't be worse off than they were in the theater. One animal they managed to save was a roller-skating bear, which they encountered in Chicago's Palace Theatre:

> During the first few days of that Chicago engagement, we were disturbed by a plaintive wail coming from beneath the stage, and at first we thought there was a sick child in the basement. As we finished our act and went to the head of the stairs, determined to investigate, we were startled by the appearance of an Italian trainer, leading a huge brown bear up the steps.
>
> The Italian pushed the bear into a chair in the wings and then shoved a Coke filled with honey through the end of the cone-shaped muzzle. When the hungry bear tipped his head back to guzzle the honey, the Italian clamped roller skates on his feet. Once the honey was gone, a small poodle was shoved into the bear's arms and he was pushed onto the stage.
>
> He was the most talented bear I have ever seen. Bottles were placed on the stage in such a manner that he had to do a figure eight to get around them. This he could do on one leg. He skated very well indeed. After the performance he was led away to his cage in the basement. Aside from the brief moment when he got his bottle of honey, the bear's

life was not a happy one. The iron-barred cage was so small he could not even turn around in it. The room where he was kept was frequented by musicians who went there to smoke between acts. A persistent blue layer of smoke hung suspended in the room, and when the musicians left the lights were clicked out and the bear was left to spend his time in complete darkness.

Eventually, the Castles purchased the bear from his trainer, and after a series of attempts to find a home for it, did: in a Chicago zoo, where it was put in a pen with an old black bear. Although Irene Castle was fearful that the black bear would maul the one the couple had rescued, in fact, as she relates the story, the two bears immediately took to one another, "rolling like kittens, slapping playfully at each other and apparently having a field day."

"In the years to come," she concluded, "I could not help but picture the brown bear watching the children roller skating past the bear pen as they do in zoos, then turning to the old black bear with a belittling expression and saying, 'You think that's good? Boy, you should have seen me wow 'em in Dubuque.'"

—Castle, pp. 105–106

Steed

In [Anna Pavlova's production of] *Don Quixote* . . . Rosinante was played by a real horse. Although petted, pampered and fattened by every member of the company, who constantly fed it tidbits, this creature was so ingeniously made up that onstage he did actually bear some resemblance to the emaciated creature of Cervantes' imagination. So convincing was his appearance that certain members of the audience complained to the R.S.P.C.A., who sent an inspector to investigate.

—Franks, pp. 38–39

Beasts, Birds, and Butterflies

The Japanese stage seems never to have contemplated the use of live animals in the way we sometimes see patient old horses on the boards in the West. The Kabuki stage horse is a work of art, a splendid structure of wood and velvet borne by two specialist assistants. These assistants have exercised a monopoly for generations, and there is very little about the behavior of horses that they do not know and reproduce. Their beasts toss their heads, paw the ground, back away from obstacles, and fret at the bit like any thoroughbred. Trotting is a proud specialty, and the authors have even seen a gentle canter. The actor who rides such horses must give a tip known as "hay money" to the artists if he does not wish to risk an undignified fall—the pleasing tradition persists at least, even if present-day stage discipline militates against any such calculated mishaps.

Lesser beasts—boars, foxes, dogs, monkeys—are played by small boys in skins, while dragons, serpents, sea monsters, and other such monstrosities are direct borrowings from the popular animal dances of Chinese origin and may require the coordinated efforts of several assistants.

Birds make frequent appearances, either as omens or as bearers of messages. They are more or less realistic and are manipulated by the *kurombo* [assistant stage manager] who waves them on long rods called *sashigane*. This technique is also used for butterflies (which are much in demand for enraging lions) and for bouncing balls in games. Rats and other small animals can be made to run about the stage in this way.

—Halford, p. 405

Dead Meat

The choreographer Kenneth MacMillan worked out his internationally popular version of *Romeo and Juliet* (1965) on Lynn Seymour and Christopher Gable, two young dancers at The Royal Ballet. At the end of the evening-length work, Romeo dances in the crypt with a Juliet whom he can't revive and believes has died. Gable relates to dance writer Barbara Newman the choreographer's inspiration for that pas de deux and the dancers' development of it:

And then Ken had a wonderful idea: "When you've tried and tried and tried and it won't work," he said, "then I want it to be just like a big piece of dead meat on the stage." A gorilla at London Zoo had a baby—did you read about this?—and didn't know how to look after it, and it died. But they couldn't take it away from her. She dangled it around and played with it sometimes, and it didn't do anything, and she kept walking around with it. It bashed onto chairs and things, but she just kept pacing and wouldn't let it go. Well, that was the image I had in my mind. I used to drag Lynn around the stage, and she'd just let her legs fall apart, all open and exposed and other ballerinas make pretty shapes on the floor. And I used to rock, the way you rock when you go into that bad, grief place.

—Newman, p. 281

Swalloween?

Owl dances are frequently spoken of in Greek literature—humorous dances, in which the strutting of the bird, the twitching and twisting of its neck, and its intent, peering gaze were imitated. We are told that bird-catchers used the dance to hypnotize owls which they wished to capture! Also, there is clear evidence for a cock dance in Greece. On the island of Rhodes there was performed annually a famous swallow procession or dance, in which children apparently disguised as birds and carrying a replica of a swallow, went from house to house, singing, demanding gifts of food, and threatening to steal the food if it should not be given freely.

Furthermore, the ancient playwrights Aristophanes, Crates, and Magnes "each wrote a comedy called *Birds*; also, Aristophanes wrote one entitled *Storks*, and Cantharus one entitled *Nightingales*. In all of these plays the members of the chorus were garbed as fantastic, colorful birds, and, as in all early comedy, the chorus danced."

—Lawler, pp. 61–62

Scandals

Fury, Beauty, and Depth

When Serge Diaghilev's Ballets Russes gave the world première of *Le Sacre du printemps* in Paris, on May 29, 1913—with music by Igor Stravinsky and choreography by Vaslav Nijinsky—the uproar in the audience was so violent that the evening has remained the standard in ballet history for avant-garde provocation and hostile audience reaction. The young Jean Cocteau summed up the mêlée as, "*Quel bombe! Quel chef d'oeuvre!*" Although the Ballets Russes was already somewhat notorious in certain circles for Nijinsky's 1912 ballet, *L'après-midi d'un Faune*, and was to provoke other *scandales* through its productions in later years, such as that precipitated by the 1917 *Parade*, with its walking Cubist sculptures by Picasso, the one associated with *Le Sacre* overshadows all.

Historian Cyril W. Beaumont reported on the fateful first evening of Nijinsky's ballet, as well as on subsequent performances, where audiences responded quite differently:

> *Le Sacre du printemps* was an attempt to show the birth of human emotion in a primitive age. It is the story of herd reaction under the tribal rites of prayer and sacrifice in worship of the earth and the sun. . . . The movements generally were symbolic rather than emotional, and, on account of their complexity, sometimes carried to a fantastic degree, required the greatest precision of execution. It may be mentioned that this ballet required one hundred and twenty rehearsals and was given at Paris and London only six times in all.
>
> At first acquaintance, this ballet was so completely novel in its outlook, so starkly primitive in its conception, so brutal in its movements, that many found it utterly repellent. No other Diaghilev production roused such a storm of protest and furious indignation. So great was the tumult on the

first night that Diaghilev stood up in his box and called out, *"Je vous enprie, laissez achiever le spectacle!"* ["I beg you, let the work proceed."] Behind the scenes, the dancers, harassed and overwrought, were on the verge of tears. When the second act began, the tumult in the theater was so great that the music could not be heard, and Nijinsky had to stand in the wings and beat out the rhythm with his fists. But after the first shock had passed, and the ballet had been witnessed a second and a third time, it was seen to possess much primitive beauty and to evoke a deep inner emotion.

—Beaumont, pp. 654–655

Lolapallooza

In August of 1845, mourning the death in a duel of her lover, Henri Dujarier (co-owner of *La Presse* and, until his death, her major source of support), Lola Montez (ca.1820–61)—a native of Limerick born with the name Eliza Gilbert who was pretending to be a Spanish aristocrat, a dancer of charm more than sufficient to overcome the realities of her modest and late training, and a courtesan of fantastic virtuosity—decided to leave Paris for diversion and, perhaps, to discover another patron. She made her way to a music festival at Bonn, during which she mildly scandalized the populace by wheedling her way into a dinner largely attended by men, seating herself as the only woman among a group of them, staying on for brandy after the few other women had departed, and then—during a fracas that erupted when Franz Liszt, in the course of a toast to the nationalities represented at the festival, forgot to mention the French—jumped up and shouted her two centimes' worth. From Bonn, however, she moved on to heavy-duty scandalizing, as her biographer, Bruce Seymour, recounts:

> With the festival over, Bonn was quickly slipping into summer somnolence, so Lola journeyed up the Rhine to elegant Baden-Baden, a scene of far greater excitement. Baden-Baden was one of the most fashionable resorts in Europe at that time, and its elite clientele, including royal vacationers from every ruling family on the continent, was drawn as much by its famous gaming tables as by the curative powers of its waters. Lola said that although gambling was never a passion with her, she enjoyed trying her luck at the tables. The casinos were probably also a good place to meet men with money to spare.
>
> But whatever luck Lola may have been having at the gaming tables, her eccentric behavior attracted the disapprobation of Baden-Baden's official guardians of public morality. Cries of outrage rose after the dancer one evening gave a public demonstration of her agility by throwing a leg over the shoulder of a gentleman standing next to her. But when, in the great hall of the spa, she dazzled an admirer sitting beside her by raising her skirt up to her thigh, the resulting outcry led the police to order the shameless beauty to leave town. Baden-Baden joined Ebersdorf, Berlin, and

Warsaw on the list of cities that had expelled Lola Montez. Lola returned
to Paris and the life she enjoyed.

—Seymour, p. 88

Make That *Eight Sinatra Songs*?

Twyla Tharp and Mark Morris are two of the very greatest choreographers
currently practicing. However, their visions, backgrounds, and experiences
are radically unlike; and given the ego that is fundamental to the production
of outstanding art, it is no surprise to learn that they aren't the best of friends.
Morris, in particular, can be quite outspoken in public; however, the incident to which his biographer, Joan Acocella, refers below was so withering
and also so unexpected that it has become one of the definitions of scandal at
a dance concert in America in recent times. Knowledgeably and elegantly,
Acocella places the event in the context of Morris's character and inclination
to call attention to his subject matter through provocative means. (His suite
Lovey features a cast, dressed in what look like nightclothes, who seem to be
tormenting and/or abusing baby dolls.)

To round out the picture, though, one might add that the dance by Tharp
to which Morris took exception seems to be a version of the Apache [pro-
nounced ah-POSH], a physically grueling duet for a man and woman, de-
pendent on split-second timing in the partnering and with images of savage
brutality on the part of the man, that was popular in French dance halls just
prior to World War I. Other choreographers have borrowed elements from
it as well, including Vaslav Nijinsky, in his own, scandalous, 1913 staging of
The Rite of Spring. Tharp, who knew that Frank Sinatra's music succeeds
with audiences on a number of levels, not all of them benevolent, rounded
out her suite of dances in homage to him with one of the most exciting
stunts she has ever devised: the woman throws herself horizontally at the
man, like a tomahawk, from across the stage while he, apparently about to
leave, begins to put on his jacket; and he must complete that action while
she's still flying before he insouciantly catches her, as if he were plucking a
feather from his lapel:

> Morris is in many ways an old-fashioned moralist—one of the few ways
> in which he resembles the other choreographers of his generation. He
> believes that art has discussable content, and he will happily explain the
> content of his dances, even if you haven't asked. Queried about some
> detail, he will say, "That's because that piece is about death" or "That's
> because they're in love." And if the dance is about something terrible, he
> believes it can be justified by redeeming social value. "I think the most
> important thing in a work of theater is that it be presented with a good
> spirit, humanely," he said once in a television interview. "Art can cer-
> tainly be very ugly"—he was introducing *Dogtown* here—"if the point is
> the opposite of that." If the point is not the opposite of that, the work is

objectionable. Once, in 1984, at a performance of Twyla Tharp's *Nine Sinatra Songs*—a piece that in its final section shows a woman being yanked around by a man—he stood up in the audience, yelled "No more rape!" and walked out of the theater. "I can defend every single measure of my choreography . . ." he said to Alan Kriegsman of *The Washington Post.* "I can hold it up in a court of art."

—Acocella, *Mark Morris*, p. 107

Touring

A Hands-On *Schéhérazade*

The Diaghilev ballerina Lydia Sokolova told the dance historian Richard Buckle of a one-night stand by the Ballets Russes in Spain when the town insisted on seeing the famous *Schéhérazade*, even though the company hadn't brought the production on that tour. So, troupers that they were, the dancers found themselves performing Michel Fokine's Middle Eastern harem fantasy in the set for his *Carnaval* and in a conglomeration of costumes from his *Les Sylphides* (Romantic tutus), *Daphnis and Chlöe* (chitons), and *Cléopâtre* (sheer, pleated skirts).

Speaking of *Schéhérazade*'s climactic scene, when the potentate catches his unfaithful wife and concubines cavorting with slaves and orders his guards to slay them all, Sokolova recalled: "Nobody knew who anybody was, or who to make for. . . . There were no swords, so they had to strangle us. My *dear*, we put *everything* into it. We never had such an ovation, before or since."
—Denby, *Dancers*, p. 208; Buckle, *In Search*, p. 41

And Now for Something Completely Different

Dance critic Marcia B. Siegel:

> The computer broke down at Hunter College a couple of Saturday afternoons ago, and it took a flustered box office half an hour to get the audience in to see the religious and ceremonial dances given by the Tibetan folk opera, Lhamo. Twenty minutes after curtain time, a young man in a Western suit and tie, who later appeared in some of the dances, came out and announced that the program would be delayed ten minutes, and that they were cutting four numbers originally scheduled. He assured the audience that we weren't missing anything—the dances were

pretty much like some others we would be seeing, and they were kind
of boring, anyway.

The Tibetans have that kind of charm. . . . (1975)

—Siegel, p. 269

"I Want to Dance for Everyone in the World"

In the history of ballet, no one is recorded to have toured more intensively
than Anna Pavlova (1881–1931). In her memoir, "Pages from My Life," translated into English by Sebastian Viorol for *Dance Magazine*, she speaks of having been inspired to tour by reading about the life of the Romantic-era
ballerina Taglioni, "for the celebrated Italian used to appear everywhere. She
danced at Paris, at London, and in Russia, where she is still remembered."

Pavlova went way beyond that. The writer A. H. Franks records that during the five years of World War I, the ballerina and a company of some twenty-
two dancers toured North and South America, and that during the last eleven
years of her life, she and her company visited every country in Europe as
well as made repeated visits to the United States, Canada, Argentina, Brazil,
Chile, Costa Rica, Cuba, Ecuador, Panama, Puerto Rico, Uruguay, Venezuela, Mexico, China, Japan, the Philippines, Malay States, Burma, India, Egypt,
South Africa, Australia, New Zealand, and Java. Nothing seemed to stop
her. She took her company to Guayaquil, Ecuador, during an epidemic there
of yellow fever (which, owing to elaborate hygienic precautions, none of the
dancers contracted); at an outdoor performance in Mexico, she danced her
entire signature solo *Le Cygne* during a downpour as the rest of her company
ran for shelter.

During Pavlova's entire career, it is estimated, she toured about 500,000
miles. During one tour in 1925 of the United States, she and her company
played in seventy-seven towns over twenty-six weeks, giving over 238 performances—and Pavlova danced in every one of them. During another tour
in 1927, of Great Britain, she performed in forty-seven cities over ten weeks.
Franks writes that for most of the millions of people who saw her, she represented "an introduction to ballet, for she was the only dancer they had ever
seen." He adds: "Undeniably, Pavlova more than anyone else interested the
world in ballet and inspired young people themselves to dance. . . In every
country she visited she was received and entertained by the leaders, whether
kings, presidents, viceroys, or mayors. In Madrid, the King of Spain sent a
nightly bouquet to her dressing-room. In Canada, she received a golden key
and the freedom of the City of Quebec; in Venezuela, a magnificent jewel
case from the President. In Huddersfield, the town council considered the
occasion of her visit with careful deliberation and had a performance stopped
so that the mayor, clad in all the authority of his chain of office, could make
her an address of welcome—and present her with a bottle of vodka."

What everyone associated with these tours seems to have remembered
most vividly was Pavlova's relentless pursuit of perfection:

From Bundaberg to Kidderminster, Tennessee to Llandudno, the Royal Opera House, Covent Garden, to a bullring in Mexico, from dingy assembly halls to Europe's grandest theaters, her life consisted of work. Her "girls" still speak with bated breath of her vitality; lost in wonder they vie with each other in recounting tales of Madame practicing in darkened theaters when everyone else was exhausted. According to present-day standards, these girls worked fabulously hard, but never half as hard or for such long periods as Pavlova.

—Franks, pp. 25–28 passim

Fleeing Hitler

The ballerina Yvonne Mounsey, interviewed here by Emily Hite, was at the beginning of her career as a ballet dancer with the Ballet Russe de Monte Carlo, when World War II began:

Paris, 1939. August 31 or September 1. Massine and Picasso were discussing the ballet, and Picasso was throwing aside sketches. Of course, then, he wasn't "Picasso." We were in a rehearsal room in Paris. On the street below, the military was declaring martial law. Germans walked into Czechoslovakia. It was the day or the day before my birthday, September 2, on which day war was declared. That day, the company also disbanded. I took a train to the coast, and a boat across the English Channel, and then another back to South Africa.

The boat was dangerous; the water was full of German submarines. We had to zigzag our way to South Africa in order to avoid them; it took forever. How did I survive on that boat? I danced. People would ask me to do acrobatics. I had learned as a kid—back bent, legs up here. [She shows an acrobatic maneuver; I am amazed. –E.H.] I was a natural. I was very limber.

Igor Schwetzoff, my teacher in London, had to get out of England, too. He was affiliated with the other Ballet Russe—Col. de Basil's. When we got off the boat in Capetown, Igor got a telegram from Australia, and he went to go work with Col. de Basil. My teacher sent for me soon after, and I was on the next boat to Australia. I was there a whole year during the war—not working; I don't know how we had any money. The dancers were housed somewhere—a beach house—six of us in some woman's house. They had a vegetable garden and chickens. We lived on spinach and poached eggs. And they lent us bicycles.

After a year, de Basil's company got an American contract, and we all came over on a huge boat. The corps de ballet girls slept down in the hold—where they put the cargo—on cots. I never felt there were hardships; we always had enough to eat, slept enough. I was about 19 or 20 years old. We got off in Hawaii and went to some restaurant or bar. Whoever was in charge of us told us, "You can only have Zombies [a mixed

drink] and you can only have one, because they make you drunk." They
tasted so good—like milkshakes—we drank more than one. We all were
so drunk and got so sick!

—Hite, interview

Respect

During the late 1940s, four leading dancers from the Ballet Russe de Monte
Carlo—Alexandra Danilova, Frederic Franklin, Sonya Tyven Lindgren, and
her husband, Robert—made a six-week tour of South Africa. Danilova was
the leader of the group, and she took her responsibilities quite seriously.
One can see, just in the accounts of her deportment and discipline on this
trip, which many people might have regarded as a working holiday, how her
presence in the larger company would have inspired the dancers to give their
very best during the grueling, whistle-stop tours through America for which
the Ballet Russe was noted—tours that sometimes could last for the better
part of a year. In a book of reminiscences about the various Ballets Russes
companies, published following a large reunion of their dancers, organized
by Douglas Blair Turnbaugh in New Orleans in 1999, one finds a quintessential "Choura" moment related by Robert Lindgren from the South African excursion:

> In the theater, she was all business and gave class every night. She would
> give us barre and combinations, which, she said, she had learned as a
> student in Russia—but we would laugh and everything turned into a joke.
> It was winter in South Africa—very damp and chilly. Choura caught cold
> and had a miserable cough. When we tried to ask her how she felt, she
> would reply sharply, "don't ask me how I feel or I will break down and
> cry, and if I break down, I will not dance—the performance will be can-
> celled, and we will not be paid. Please, I'm fine." She could not stand
> complainers. . . .
>
> Capetown is a beautiful city, and we enjoyed it. One evening in the
> theater, Choura learned that [the conductor] Willie McDermont and I
> had taken a trip to the top of Table Mountain, where one could view the
> Pacific, Atlantic, and Indian Oceans. After the performance, Choura took
> me aside and thoroughly scolded me. "Bobitchka, you are professional
> artist, and the performance is the most important thing. You must not
> come to the theater tired. You must always respect the audience." I felt
> thoroughly admonished.
>
> —De Mari, pp. 51–52

Rainmakers

Deep in the Bengali forest, in India, live a village of people called the Chhau.
In 1973, Beate Sirota Gordon, the New York scholar and impresario of

Asian dance traditions, traveled to the village of Purulia to see their dances. "Indian dance has four classical styles—Kathak and Manipuri in the north, Bharata Natyam and Kathakali in the south," she wrote in her memoir. "But Chhau is a separate form, a ritual folk dance performed to bring rain to the fields."

By 1975, Gordon had arranged for eleven of the Chhau dancers to travel to New York to perform at Carnegie Hall. They were accompanied by Dr. Battacharya, a professor of anthropology, who served as their chaperon. When they arrived, Gordon wanted to show the dancers something of New York City, suggesting the Empire State Building, a Broadway musical.

"That isn't necessary," the professor advised. "Leave them at the hotel, where they can watch television, eat and sleep. That's all they need."

I thought this was unkind; he seemed to be speaking from the standpoint of his Brahmin caste. So I had them taken to the Empire State anyway. Looking suspiciously at the elevator, they refused to enter. "We are not getting into this box," declared one, and the others instantly agreed. When their guide suggested going somewhere else, they asked to be taken back to the hotel. They wanted to watch television, eat and sleep.

At Carnegie Hall, they were a sensation. Rain actually fell on Manhattan when they did the rain dance.

—Gordon, p. 167

Cinderella in China

In May of 1980, Boston Ballet was the first American company to perform in the People's Republic of China. We took our production of *Cinderella*, which I had choreographed. The Chinese had carefully selected the companies and the ballet by looking at the repertories of several companies around the United States before happening upon my *Cinderella* in Boston.

It was an historic occasion, and, as the choreographer, I was very nervous. I was also playing the role of a Step-Sister. My wife, Carinne Binda (we were married in 1982) was performing the Winter Fairy. During the Step-Sister dance, which is designed to be funny and usually gets a lot of laughs, the audience was *silent*. After a variation of difficult dancing, no one clapped. I was standing in the wings thinking, "They must not like it! What a mistake to come!"

"Winter" is the fourth variation of the Seasons, and Carinne finished with an amazing pirouette. Once again, dead silence. Some Westerners who were traveling with the company—including Clive Barnes and some board members—applauded spontaneously. Then the entire audience began applauding, and it was show-stopping. From that point forward, the audience was laughing and applauding for everything, and the performance was a huge success. We found out afterward that the Chinese thought it was impolite to make noise during a performance because it would break the concentration of the dancers. Thankfully, we went from thinking they hated it to knowing they loved it. The performance was televised across China and reached over 30 million viewers—the largest TV audience both in China and ever recorded for a televised ballet anywhere at that time.

In my version of *Cinderella*, I have 12 ten-year-old children as Clock Dwarves who tell Cinderella when it's time to go home. We didn't know if we would be able to use children in China; the answer had several times been, "It's possible." So I prepared two versions—one with the children, one without. When the company arrived in China, 20 or so political officials interrogated us about what would be done with the children and how they would be represented. This was just a few years after the Cultural Revolution ended, and these children were the first crop to begin dance training.

We were able to have Clock Dwarves. The students, dressed in plaid shirts, gymnastic pants, and shoes, marched into the studio like grim soldiers. They thought they weren't supposed to have fun. Carinne and I worked with them for a while and got them to enjoy themselves. Their teachers then took care of the rest of the rehearsals, and drilled them to perfection, like a corps de ballet—but they were still having fun. The audience was thrilled and delighted to see their own children onstage. (Ron Cunningham)

—Hite, interview

The Theaters

The Bolshoi

Iris Morley, in *The Rose and the Star*:

I know of nothing more exciting than to cross the huge Theater Square on a really cold winter evening. There are the towering classic columns of the façade rising dark from acres of snow, and the air where the electric light falls is so cold that it sparkles like diamond dust. Once inside, however, winter is eliminated. Everything seems to be made of crystal, gilt, vermilion damask, or white marble. Neither the icy winds of spring nor the sultry torpor of summer penetrates its columns. Everything has a special air of festivity and make-believe and even the cream cakes sold at the buffet have an exotic shape, like the third act [i.e., "Land of Sweets" scene] of *Nutcracker*. If the feminine portion of the audience possessed rubies and diamonds, they would undoubtedly wear them, for the Russians love magnificence. As it is, they have to make do with silk dresses and blouses and skirts. However, when all of us—three thousand odd—are gathered in beneath the great crystal chandelier, we feel that premonitory glow which precedes the satisfaction of a deep instinct. Nowhere in the world—not even in Leningrad—shall we see a more splendid scene than that which will be revealed to us when the curtain rises.

—Manchester, p. 19

Immolations of Nineteenth-Century Ballet Girls

Prior to the substitution of electricity for gas in theaters as a means of illuminating the stage, one of the most dangerous professions in the theatrical world was that of danseuse in a theater: the flammable layers of tarlatan or tulle used for their tutus only needed to catch a spark from the gas jets to go up in flames. The gaslight made astounding theatrical effects possible, which is why theaters continued to use it, despite the dangers. Those effects, however, were purchased at the price of living death: many of the dancers, burned extensively, suffered the misfortune of lingering in life for weeks or months in agony. Among them was Emma Livry, the prodigious young star of the Paris Opéra Ballet and protégée of Marie Taglioni, who had so hoped that Livry would carry on her standard of classical purity. (A number of studio photographs of Livry in ballet costume, notably by Nadar, show her to have had perfect proportions for ballet and beautifully shaped legs and feet.) The skirts of the promising young English dancer, Clara Webster, caught fire during a performance, and she began to burn in full view of the stunned audience, no one having had the presence of mind to ring down the curtain. Between the 1840s and the end of the century, flocks of dancers also perished in this hideous way in Marseilles, Hamburg, New York, Liverpool, Trieste, Rio de Janeiro, Naples, and many other places.

In 1873, the chief officer of the London Fire Brigade, one Captain Shaw, published an article in *Practical Magazine*, which, as dance historian Ivor Guest wrote in a book chronicling the short, incandescent life and long, bleak death of Clara Webster, drew "a terrifying picture of the risks of fire backstage in theaters." Guest goes on to quote from the report:

The quick shifting of light scenery in the immediate vicinity of powerful gaslights," [Shaw] wrote, "the intense heat caused by the lights in the upper parts over the flies and slides, the rapid manipulation of gas, oil, lime, and other lights for scenic effect, and the occasional use of explosives in the midst of a vast quantity of highly dessicated wood, a labyrinth of cordage, and a quantity of hanging drapery moving about with every draught and blast of wind; these and others hardly sufficiently important for special notice . . . constitute legitimate risks which may be sometimes capable of reduction, though they cannot be altogether abolished." The suggestion he made (and he was by no means the first to make it), that all costumes, fabric, and woodwork should be saturated in a non-inflammable solution, may have been adopted by one or two managers, but they were at most very few, despite the fact that several such solutions had been patented and were inexpensive to prepare.

As early as 1859, Guest remarks, "Messrs Cochran and Dewar of Glasgow were then retailing a preparation which would give "perfect protection from fire to our ballet-girls for a sum than which few would offer less to a beggar—certainly not more than twopence each." However, this attempt to shift responsibility for preventing immolations from the theater managers to the endangered performers, themselves, was not a success. The "preparation" discolored the tutus and disfigured their contours, and the dancers refused to use it.

One would think that the theater managers would have tried to fireproof their theaters, if only for the sake of their paying audiences. Indeed, in 1882, in the wake of a resolution passed by the Fire Brigade Committee of the Metropolitan Board Works of London, Captain Shaw "presented a lengthy report on the 41 London theaters which he had inspected." Guest adds that "his main concern . . . was with the 55,000 spectators who congregated nightly in these theaters; the dangers that dancers had to face was only one facet of a very much greater problem." Forty years after the "problem" was observed, some attempts were being made to fix it, at least in London. Why did it take so long? Guest puts the burnings of the earlier decades in context:

> The enlightened 20th century was still a long way off in the 1840's. Then—in the heyday of the Romantic Ballet, when fashionable society flocked to the Haymarket to applaud the great singers and dancers who came to London in the summer season—thousands of impoverished, ignorant creatures were herded in the filthiest squalor, sometimes two or three families to a single rat-infested room, in the foul Rookery of St Giles, not a mile away from the Opera House.
>
> But there were other evils, too, that cried out to be abolished: the appalling exploitation of human beings, slavery in all but name, in the sweat-shops; the apprenticing of young boys to chimney-sweeps; child-labor in the mines; the conditions of the seamstresses, forced during the season to work often 18 or 20 hours a day, making dresses for ladies of fashion; the horrors of the lunatic asylums; the lack of proper sanitation; the dangerous conditions in the factories. To give a complete picture, the list would fill many pages. Against this mountain of wrongs, it is hardly surprising that lesser evils, such as the lack of fire precautions in the theaters, were often overlooked.
>
> —Guest, pp. 1–2, 4–5

Finishing Touches

When Colette, the novelist and dancer, made a tour of French music halls with her manager, they arrived, after a long and tiring train trip, at a town Colette called "X" ("whose name is of no consequence"), where they had to rush to a rehearsal for the performance later:

> This evening we are to inaugurate a brand new music-hall, called the "Atlantic," or the "Gigantic," or the "Olympic"—in any case, the name of a liner. Three thousand seats, an American Bar, attractions in the outer galleries during the intervals, and a gipsy band in the main hall! In the meantime it makes no difference to us, except that we are certain to cough in the dressing-rooms, since new central heating never works, making the place either too hot or not warm enough. . . .
>
> Brague turns left—I turn left; he stops short—I stop short.

"Good Lord!" he exclaims. "It isn't possible!"

Wide awake, I, too, judge at a glance that it really is not possible.

Huge dust-carts, laden with sacks of plaster, obstruct the street. Scaffolding screens a light-colored building that looks blurred and barely condensed into shape, on which masons are hastily molding laurel wreaths, naked females, and Louis XVI garlands above a dark porch. Beyond this can be heard a tumult of inarticulate shouts, a battery of hammers, the screeching of saws, as though the whole assembly of the Niebelungen were busy at their forges. . . .

The rehearsal takes place. It passes all comprehension, but the rehearsal takes place. We go on through the dark porch under a sticky shower of liquid plaster; we jump over rolls of carpet in the process of being laid, its royal purple already bearing marks of muddy soles. We climb a temporary ladder leading, behind the stage floor, to the artistes' dressing-rooms, and finally we emerge, scared and deafened, in front of the orchestra.

About 30 performers are disporting themselves here. Bursts of music reach us during lulls in the hammering. In the conductor's rostrum, a lean, hairy, bearded human being beats time with arms, hands and head, his eyes turned upward to the friezes with the ecstatic serenity of a deaf mute. (Raymond Postgate and Anne-Marie Callimachi, trans.)

—Colette, pp. 126–128

Sweetening the Unfamiliar with Eye Candy

On May 18, 1909, the night before the Ballets Russes was scheduled to make its debut in Paris at the Théâtre du Chatelet (completely renovated for the company's appearance at the insistence of the Ballets Russes' founder and director, Serge Diaghilev), a gala dress rehearsal of the opening-night program was held in the theater for the benefit of socialites, artists, writers, and reporters; among those in attendance were Rodin and Ravel. The company's Parisian presenter, Gabriel Astruc, prepared a little surprise for the occasion, too:

It was always my principle to devote as much thought to my preview audiences as though they were themselves part of the production. In May 1909, the night the Russian Ballet was first revealed to the public, I offered the prettiest actresses in Paris front row seats in the balcony. Fifty-two were asked; 52 accepted. In the seating, I was careful to alternate blondes and brunettes; they all arrived on time, they were all very pleased; and the sight of this row of smiling beauties caused the rest of the house to burst into applause. That most serious of newspapers, *Le Temps*, devoted a front-page article to this innovation, referring to it as my *corbeille*— my "flower basket." Since then the first balconies of all new French theaters have been called not balconies, but *corbeilles*.

—Steegmuller, p. 68

Taormina

On a tour to Italy in 1982, Boston Ballet performed at the 10,000-seat Greek amphitheater in the town of Taormina, overlooking the Mediterranean Sea. A stage had been put down over the remains of the one built by the Greeks thousands of years ago.

We had been performing Nureyev's *Don Quixote* all over Italy. My wife, Carinne Binda, was the ballet mistress; I was playing the character Gamache, and Nureyev, himself, was Basilio. It was nearly midnight by the time we took curtain calls. Standing onstage to bow, we faced the vast audience that rose above us and stretched out before us, as all the people held lit candles in appreciation. We aren't sure how they got the candles; we think they may have brought them into the theater. It was a most moving experience to be in a performance with the legendary Nureyev, an icon in Italy, on this 3,000-year-old stage. What an amazing profession we were a part of. How privileged each of us felt to be an artist and a dancer. (Ron Cunningham)

—Hite, interview

New York, New York

The most enduring dance craze of the interwar years, the Charleston, may have been popular in South Carolina as early as 1903, but it became a national enthusiasm when it was first performed in a Broadway play, *Runnin' Wild*, in 1923. The plays which were performed at theaters across the nation were those which had enjoyed success in New York. The decision by booking agencies to form a road company was taken by men behind desks in New York. The books which became bestsellers were increasingly likely to have been published by other men, behind other desks, in New York City.

—Homberger, p. 117

Costumes, Footgear, and Hair Do's and Don'ts

Nailing It

Dancing courtesans provided popular entertainment at the after-dinner events of ancient Greece known as *symposia*. The dance historian Lillian B. Lawler notes that archaeologists have unearthed "a vase cleverly made in the shape of a courtesan's shoe" and that "Nails on the sole seem to indicate that it was a dancing shoe—perhaps even a forerunner of the modern tap-dancer's footgear! Even more interesting is the fact that the nails are arranged so as to form the word *akolouth(e)*, 'Follow (me)!'"

—Lawler, p. 133

What Dancers Should Wear

From *The Art of Dancing: A Poem in Three Cantos*, 1729 edition, by Soame Jenyns. In the first line, the word "suits" is being used as a verb:

> . . . each man's habit [customary way of dressing] with his business suits;
> Nor must we ride in pumps, or dance in boots
>
> But you, that oft in circling dances wheel,
> Thin be your yielding sole, and low your heel:
> Let no unwieldy pride your shoulders press,
> But airy, light, and easy be your dress;
> Let not the sword, in silken bondage tied,
> An useless weight, hang lugging at your side;
> No such rough weapons here will gain the prize,
> No wounds we fear, but from the fair-one's eyes.
> The wooly drab, and English broadcloth warm,

Guard well the horseman from the beating storm,
But load the dancer with too great a weight,
And call from every pore a dewy sweat;
Rather let him his active limbs display
In camblet thin and glossy paduasoy. [peau de soie]

—Jenyns, pp. 16–17

I Would Like to Go Dressed Up

The following excerpt from a letter of January 22, 1783, by Wolfgang Amadeus Mozart to his father refers to a masked ball (a "redoute") in Vienna, where the composer and his wife, Constanze, were living:

. . . Please, send the Sinfonies I requested as soon as possible;—I really need them!—And one more favor because my wife won't give me any peace about it—you know, of course, that we are in the middle of a carnival season and that there's a lot of dancing here just as there is in Salzburg and Munich.—and I would like to go dressed up, but please don't say a word to anyone, as a Harlequin—because around here there are so many— indeed nothing but—asses at the Redoute;—therefore, I would like to ask you to send me your Harlequin costume—but it would have to be very soon—we are not going to the ball until we have the masks, although everything is already in full swing.—We actually prefer house balls.— Last week I gave one in our apartment.—Of course, each of the gentlemen had to make a contribution of 2 guilden.—We started at 6 o'clock in the evening and ended at 7;—what, only one hour?—No, No!—we ended at 7 o'clock in the morning. . . ." (Robert Spaethling, trans.)

—Mozart, pp. 139–140

Skimpy Outfits, But the Walking Is Worse

For a grand lady arriving with her cavalier to preside over a ceremonial ball to remove her silk robe, and reappear in a transparent tunic reaching to just above her knee, with rose-colored legs and feet, in order to dance one of those famous *pas de deux* with a stranger dressed as a rope dancer, seems to me to be overstepping the limits of the ridiculous. . . . I once found myself laughing at a print representing the interior of the *Circus*, but, three steps away, I saw one of a backstage scene at the Opéra, and I was seized with indignation by the caricature which had been made of the cradle of my apprenticeship!—Well! I have once again seen that cradle, and that print had in no way exaggerated the immodest dress of the female dancers. Sitting in the stalls, I was astounded at the sight of Diana's Nymphs making their entrance—with their *heels turned out* towards the audience!—Was this a coquettish affectation or simply the innocent behavior of the daughters of the Southern sea?" (Knud Arne Jürgensen, trans.)

—Bournonville, *Letters*, p. 67

Letting It All Hang Out

The choreographer Marius Petipa recounts in his memoirs how a director of the Imperial Theater in St. Petersburg—a M. Saburov—had the habit of conducting meetings with members of the ballet in his office while he wore a dressing gown:

> From the day he began his duties, he received all the artists, men and women, in this costume. He had even had a little "unpleasantness" with one of the lady artists, about this. His Excellency was carried away and did not notice that the skirt of his dressing gown had fallen open, but the artist noticed. She also observed that the Director had nothing on under the dressing gown, and gave him a resounding slap in the face. As you see, in those days also, as in our time, there were directors who were willing to swallow physical punishment.

Petipa adds that "this did not stop Saburov from continuing his directorial functions." (Helen Whittaker, trans.)

—Petipa, *Russian*, pp. 50–51

Authenticity

In the mid-1970s, Beate Sirota Gordon, then director of the performing arts department at Manhattan's Asia Society, brought over Sitara Devi, an outstanding dancer from India, to perform at Carnegie Hall.

> Sitara was a fiery personality who didn't take kindly to any kind of criticism. I once questioned the authenticity of her costumes, which were very showy, with hundreds of sequins on them. Why couldn't she wear her beautiful Benares saris? Because they wouldn't show up on the stage, she said. I complained that it made her look like a nightclub act. She was furious.
>
> "You want authentic?" she shouted. "You want really authentic? Then I'll go topless! *That's* authentic."
>
> . . . A week later, in the Midwest, a party was given in her honor. Her brother, a drummer given to drink, was usually kept on a short leash by her. But someone forgot to watch him, and before long he was weaving around muttering, "She thinks she's so great, without me she's nothing!"
>
> Without saying a word, Sitara took off a high-heeled shoe, hit him hard on the head with it and walked away. We lugged him out and had

him taken to his hotel. Quite unconcerned, Sitara went on entertaining
the party for another six hours.

—Gordon, pp. 168–169

The Loveliest Costume the World Has Ever Seen

When the Castles starred on Broadway in *Watch Your Step*, Irving Berlin's first
show, on opening night (December 8, 1914) Irene Castle wore a dress designed by the London dressmaker and *Titanic* survivor, Lady Duff-Gordon,
which the wearer described as "probably the loveliest costume the world has
ever seen":

Elsie de Wolfe [the actress and interior decorator] likened it to a Fragonard.
To me, it was sheer heaven. It was the first dress with a torn hem line and
was made of a blue-gray chiffon that looked like smoke and was 12 yards
around the bottom. The bodice was silver with long, full chiffon sleeves,
carrying a wide band of gray fox at the wrist. The cloak was made of a blue-
gray and silver brocade (using the wrong side), very full in the skirt, and a
tight bodice that laced down the left side with chartreuse and emerald-
green satin streamers. The huge skirt part of this handsome brocaded
cloak was garlanded in light gray fox, which had been tinted slightly mauve.
. . . Besides being beautiful, the dress was perfect for dancing. It molded
the legs and trailed out behind like smoke, giving a fluid grace to anything you did in it.

—Castle, pp. 134–135

Fitting In

In the old days of the Ballet Russe companies . . . they never sent costumes to the cleaners. In [Michel] Fokine's *Firebird* I was a monster—I
was about 17—and those costumes SMELLED to high heaven. They stank!
You just had to hold your nose, put them on, and go dance. . . . In [Fokine's]
Le Coq d'Or ["The Golden Cockerel"], I was the king's nurse. It's a Russian story with Russian costumes. I had to fasten cushions around me, to
look fat, and stuff cotton wool in my cheeks and wear a false nose. I wore
a big Russian hat. I was a rather good actress; I had to cry because my king
had died. What an honor it was to be given the part by Fokine, himself.

[At the New York City Ballet] we used to go to the dime store and
make things for our costumes in the early days. We didn't sit there and
have our costumes handed to us. Sometimes we were lucky and were
sent to Karinska's atelier (shop), and you got your *own costume.* Then you
didn't have to wear someone's stinky costume. Maria [Tallchief] was the
first one fitted for a *Prodigal* costume—she only did the Siren two or three
times—then they gave it to me, and they made it fit me. (Yvonne Mounsey)

—Hite, interview

Those Were the Days

At a recent fancy ball in Washington, an ingenious young woman went as the Meteorological Bureau. On her head she wore a silver helmet, crested with a weather-vane. Her waist drapery was confined with a close-fitting blue bodice, ornamented with white stars and bordered by rows of real silver dollars. The bodice was laced in front over a thermometer, in which the lady kept the mercury moving up and down in an excited manner. She wore from her shoulders a heavy bearskin cape from Montana, while her frilled skirts were of the lightest Chinese silk. (August 1892)

—*Dancing*, p. 173

"The Red Shoes are never tired. . . ."

At the conclusion of the 1948 film *The Red Shoes*, created by Michael Powell and Emeric Pressburger, the ballerina Victoria Page (played by the Royal Ballet ballerina Moira Shearer) is driven mad by the demand that she choose between dancing and her marriage (to a composer, played by Marius Goring) and, refusing to make the choice, jumps off a balcony into the path of an oncoming train. For full ironic effect, she's made up and dressed in full costume as the young girl of the ballet-within-the-ballet—based on Hans Christian Andersen's tale "The Red Shoes"—in whose world première she's about to appear. The problem is that the fatal jump takes place before Vicky's performance, while the orchestra is tuning up—that is, before the character that Page-Shearer will impersonate on the stage has had the chance to go into the shoemaker's shop, buy the Red Shoes, and wear them:

Excuse me, Mr. Powell"—it was the wardrobe mistress speaking—"the script says that Moira runs out onto the terrace and jumps into the railway cutting, wearing the Red Shoes. But how can she be wearing them? The ballet hasn't started yet. She hasn't even tried them on."

This was a poser, but it would never do to turn tail before a wardrobe mistress. "She's wearing the Red Shoes," I said firmly. "She is wearing the full costume for the ballet, plus the Red Shoes."

"But how *can* she be," wailed the wardrobe mistress.

"You just do your job and I'll do mine," I advised her kindly. "It's the Red Shoes that are dancing her away to her death, and so she's got to be wearing them."

By now, even Emeric was against me. "I'm not sure that you are right, Michael," he said mildly. "Vicky cannot be wearing the Red Shoes when she runs out to commit suicide."

"But it isn't Vicky who's running away from the theater, it is the Red Shoes that are running away with Vicky. We'll invent a reason for her wearing the Red Shoes when we get back into the studio. But tomorrow morning she wears the Red Shoes or I don't shoot the scene."

"Why not shoot it both ways?" suggested George Busby, the peacemaker.

But I already had an image in my mind of the shattered body of the ballerina lying on the railroad track, and her Red Shoes, red with blood, and I said: "No."

Next morning we were shooting the scene in the toy railway station of Monte Carlo, which still existed then, and which I had known since I was a child. Our cameramen struggled to maintain their position as the excited and sympathetic French crowd pressed in and around the two lovers. Marius knelt between the rails beside the dying girl, and with a passionate flinging out of his arms appealed to Heaven whether this was just. Moira, with her beautiful blue ribbons and her peach-colored dress smeared with blood, whispered: "Julian! Take off The Red Shoes."

I was desperately trying to see what was going on, when I felt an arm around my shoulders and looked round into the face of the stationmaster, who had joined the crowd. Tears were pouring down his face as he watched the dying girl, and he stammered: "*Oh! Mon dieu! C'est terrible! C'est terrible!*"

Nearly all the British critics, having failed to understand the rest of the picture, picked upon this final scene as typical of the bad taste of the Archers, and particularly of Michael Powell.

—Powell, pp. 650–651

Cleopatra's Feast

One night I took Monsieur B to a program of Japanese dances at the Kabuki Theater. Though his work was in a different field, he numbered many dancers among his friends, since they were all artists, so that there was always much to listen to his excellent views on Japanese dancing, but the riot of color and design in the foyer seemed to have intoxicated him again.

"The dancing is good, but this scene is still better," he said, dropping down on a sofa in the lobby and watching with all his eyes [sic] a stream of kimonos drifting by. . . .

"Once I read a translation of a Japanese novel and was struck by one of the scenes in it. On the night of a ball, a man goes to meet his sweetheart in a suffocatingly sweet greenhouse. Of course on that night his sweetheart was more beautiful than any of the white lilies blooming there. She was dressed in gala attire like a red rose in her glory at Cleopatra's feast. She was really there in the gloriously blossoming greenhouse, but the man was literally dazzled and did not know which were flowers and which his sweetheart. At last he came out weary of searching. Just now I vividly recalled that passage, and I thought, 'Only in Japan, could there be such a fanciful composition.'"

—Kawakatsu, pp. 21, 39–40

The Gorgeous Childhood of a Fairy-Tale Princess

When the novelist and dancer Colette embarked with her manager on a tour of French music halls, one of the performers she met was a young ballet dancer, barely out of childhood, named Bastienne, whom Colette described as leading "the indigently, happy-go-lucky but hardworking life of little motherless ballerinas who have no lover." Colette explains: "Between the morning lesson, starting at nine, the afternoon rehearsal, and the nightly performance, they have next to no time left for thought. Their wretched phalanstery does not know the meaning of despair, since solitude and insomnia never afflict its members." When Colette first sees Bastienne, the dancer is five months pregnant and requires help to lace herself into her dancing corset. After Bastienne gives birth and begins to bring her infant backstage during performances, Colette offers an indelible word-painting, in which the theatrical fantasies represented by the costumes and postures of the theater personnel and the reality of the child's needs indelibly coalesce into three brief, incandescent paragraphs:

Today, in the warmest corner of the big dressing room, there stands, supported on two chairs, the tray of an old traveling-trunk with a canopy of flowered wallpaper. It is the piteous crib of a tiny little Bastienne, hardy as a weed. She is brought to the theater by her mother at eight, and is removed at midnight under her cloak. This much-dandled, merry little mite, this babe with scarcely a stitch of clothing, who is dressed by small clumsy hands that knit for it, awkwardly, pilches and bonnets, enjoys, despite her environment, the gorgeous childhood of a fairy-tale princess. Ethiopian slaves in coffee-colored tights, Egyptian girls hung with blue jewelry, houris stripped to the waist, bend over her cot and let her play with their necklaces, their feather fans, their veils that change the color of the light. The tiny Bastienne falls asleep and wakes in scented young arms, while Peris, with faces the rose pink of fuchsias, croon her songs to the rhythm of a far distant orchestra.

A dusky Asian maid, keeping watch by the door, shouts down the corridor, "Run, Bastienne, run! Your daughter is thirsty!"

In comes Bastienne, breathless, smoothing her tense billowing skirts with the tips of her fingers, and runs straight to the tray of the old travelling trunk. Without waiting to sit down or unfasten her low-cut bodice, she uses both hands to free from its pressure a swollen breast, blue in color from its generous veins. Leaning over, one foot lifted in the dancer's classical pose, her flared skirts like a luminous wheel around her, she suckles her daughter. (Raymond Postgate and Anne-Marie Callimachi, trans.)

—Colette, pp. 184, 186

An Earwig with a Difference

Allegra Kent:

The Cage, created by Jerome Robbins in 1951 to music by Stravinsky, uses stylized choreography to investigate an insect society, somewhat like that of preying mantises or black widow spiders, in which the female finds the male's existence superfluous after mating and kills him without compunction.

For the lead role of the Novice, Robbins envisioned a black wet-looking wig. Nora Kaye's freshly showered hair was the original inspiration for this look. Perhaps Robbins, a keen observer of flora and fauna, noticed that Kaye's head uncannily resembled a pupa—in insect life the tender stage between the larva and the imago. In contrast, the hairstyle for the corps girls was to be a disheveled mop, arranged ad hoc.

A long time ago—perhaps in the late 1960s—while I was performing the Novice with New York City Ballet at the New York State Theater, I had a hair-do disaster of alarming magnitude. Mid-ballet while I was whirling, twirling, and executing the ferocious movements that would eventually kill the first boy bug in my life, I felt two bobby pins slip from their place, slither down my neck, and fall to the floor. An excess of hair gel and centrifugal force were at the root of the problem. As more and more of the foundation around the wigband became unhinged, and I continued with the head-snapping, foot-stomping choreography, I realized my wig was leaving me. It was half on and half off, hanging down near my ear. This in-between state was intolerable, so, in a panic, I ripped it off and tossed it into the wings—but not the one where Mr. Balanchine stood calmly observing my performance. Yes, Mr. B was watching this particular *Cage* from his favorite off-stage viewing position downstage right. I felt humiliated, anticipating his negative response to my unexpected hair change. Would he ever take me seriously again, or would he regard me as merely a prankster? Yet there was no time to think of my liberated locks. The only thing I could do was plunge into my part with more intensity.

After the final bows, I hoped to avoid Mr. B, but he started walking towards me. At that moment I despised myself, as I started to imagine what he might say: "That was awful dear. You ruined the ballet."

I steeled myself for an upbraiding of supreme vehemence. I had been dancing professionally for over 15 years and arranging my own hair since day one. I had no excuse.

But then I saw that Mr. B was smiling. "That was wonderful," he said in an enthusiastic tone. "You should lose the wig in every performance."

—Kent, "To Toss," p. 104

Bow-Tied

Vaudeville-burnished George Burns played straight man to the character of the gentle birdbrain developed by his beloved wife, Gracie Allen, and then, after her death in 1964, eventually carved out a solo career in the movies; he was also a polished writer of considerable charm. *The Most of George Burns*, a compendium of four books he published between the ages of eighty and ninety, is nearly 800 pages long and serves as an authoritative memoir on twentieth-century American show business. The following anecdote, brilliantly constructed down to the punctuation, so that the timing of an oral delivery is built in, comes from *Living It Up*, first published in 1976, when Burns (who lived to 100) was a mere lad of eighty:

One of the vaudeville acts I did which I forgot to mention in the book was called "Ruby Delmar and Friend." I was Friend. It wasn't great billing, but by that time I did so many acts I ran out of names. Ruby was a beautiful girl except that she was bowlegged. She always looked as though someone had stolen her cello. From her waist up, she was stunning. From her waist down, I was prettier.

In those days all the girls wore short skirts. But Ruby was self-conscious about her legs, so she always wore long skirts. Even on the stage her dress was right down to the floor. She was a great whirlwind dancer, but nobody knew it because everything she did was hidden by that skirt. When I was on the stage with her I'd look out at the audience, and they looked so confused—they knew something was going on under that skirt, but they didn't know what. So I had to explain to the audience that she was dancing. Once I had to explain it to the police.

Anyway, our agent said he couldn't get us any more work with Ruby wearing those long dresses. So I figured out the answer. I had Ruby wear a short skirt, changed the act to Latin music, and got Ruby a bongo drum. She was a sensation. She was the only girl who could do a whirlwind tango and still have room for the bongo. She was such a big hit that she teamed up with a bowlegged fellow and got rid of me. I really couldn't blame her; I had no place to hold my bongo.

There's a finish to this story. Ruby married her partner and I went to the wedding. It was a beautiful affair except for one thing—they had to walk down both aisles.

—Burns, pp. 246–247

Makeup

Unmasked

Gaetan Vestris [1729–1808], the "God of the Dance," was the first to follow [Jean Georges] Noverre's suggestions and substitute make-up for the mask. Prompted perhaps by his extraordinary vanity, he appeared displaying his own features in an abbreviated version of Noverre's own ballet *Medée et Jason* at the Paris Opéra in 1770, and revealed an unsuspected talent for acting. Next to follow suit was Maximilien Gardel [1741–1787], who had been unable to obtain permission to dance without a mask until he made it a condition of his appearance as substitute for the indisposed Vestris as Apollo in *Castor et Pollux*.

—Moore, pp. 39–40

Caked

Doris Humphrey—the dancer, choreographer, and theoretician of choreography—began her performing career, like her colleagues Charles Weidman and Martha Graham—in the Denishawn company, co-founded and directed by Ruth St. Denis and Ted Shawn. American dance companies, such as Denishawn or the Ballet Russe de Monte Carlo, supported themselves through frequent, backbreaking tours across the country, often for the better part of a year:

Denishawn programs were strenuous. The first part called for a pink and white make-up, including a body make-up of glycerin and powder, as we danced barefoot and bare-legged. Then came the more exotic ballets. These were elaborately costumed; usually we wore wigs. In a Spanish ballet we were laden with petticoats, ruffled dresses, shawls, stockings, and satin shoes. There was also a dark-skinned make-up, which had to go over the pink and white. Often at the end there wasn't time to remove it all, so we would board Pullman trains in dirty feet and two layers of body make-up.

—Humphrey, p. 40

And Try Not to Drop Any on Your Eyeball, Either . . .

In the well-known documentary film, *A Dancer's World*, Martha Graham is shown in her dressing room, preparing herself to dance the role of Jocasta in her version of the Oedipus tale, *Night Journey*. Among her ministrations is the action of lighting a candle and melting some substance in its flame, then applying the molten result to her eyelashes. What Graham was doing in that 1957 film (and is rarely, if ever, done anymore) was "beading" her eyelashes, a common practice from the nineteenth century that had its risks. In the following passage from his 1925 manual, *The Art of Stage Dancing*, Ned Wayburn—a dance teacher and choreographer in New York between the 1910s and the 1930s, whose illustrious list of students included Fred and Adele Astaire, Gilda Gray, Marilyn Miller, and Gertrude Lawrence—explains the correct method:

> Beading the lashes consists in placing a small bead of cosmetique on the extreme tip of each lash. This is best done on the upper lashes only, leaving the lower ones free. The Lockwood Cosmetic Stove is a small affair that holds a piece of candle and a baby-size frying pan, or skillet, and is one device for its purpose that has the approval of fire insurance companies and so will not be objected to by the theater fireman. There are some heating devices that you are not permitted to use in any theater, and persistence in their use after being once cautioned has caused arrest more than once. . . .
>
> You light the candle, place a small amount of Roger and Gallet black cosmetique in the little pan and heat it over the candle flame till melted. Take up some of this molten cosmetique on the flat end of your orangewood stick and apply it with a deft quick stroke to the upper lashes, painting each one separately and without clotting, so that a little bead hangs to the tip of each upper lash. Use care not to drop any of the black on your make-up. The effect of this beading is to beautify the appearance of the actress by bringing out her eyes in a wonderful manner under the strongest of spot lights.
>
> —Wayburn, p. 158–159

Melting

On one occasion during her tour of French music halls, the novelist and dancer Colette was scheduled to perform in a matinee on a day when the thermometer registered 96 degrees F., and that was before the audience packed itself into the unair-conditioned theater. She sits, made up, at her dressing table backstage:

> My cold cream is unrecognizable, reduced to cloudy oil that smells of petrol. A melted paste, the color of rancid butter, is all that remains of my white grease foundation. The liquefied contents of my rouge jar might well be used "to color," as cooks say, a dish of "*Pêches Cardinal.*"
>
> For better or worse, here I am at last anointed with those multicolored fats, and heavily powdered. I still have time, before our mimodrama, to survey a face on which glow, in the sunshine, the mixed hues of purple petunia, begonia, and the afternoon blue of a morning glory. But the energy to move, walk, dance and mime, where can I hope to find that? (Raymond Postgate and Anne-Marie Callimachi, trans.)
>
> —Colette, p. 145

Painted Lady

The ballerina Yvonne Mounsey danced for Balanchine at both the Ballet Russe de Monte Carlo (where she was given "a lovely role" in his 1941 *Balastrade*) and at the New York City Ballet in its early years, where she danced the lead role of the Siren in his *Prodigal Son.* In 1950, the company was scheduled to perform in London, at Covent Garden:

> Balanchine said, "When we go to Covent Garden, you have to do *Prodigal.*" In England they liked story ballets, so we had *Firebird* and then *Prodigal* on the same program.
>
> I was a princess in *Firebird* sometimes. One night, when I was doing the Siren, Vida Brown [the ballet mistress] begged me to do princess, too, in *Firebird,* which was going on first: "I don't have anybody!" Balanchine was there, and I told him I couldn't do both. I was nervous and needed to prepare for *Prodigal,* do my make-up and things. But Balanchine said, "You do princess. You look beautiful as woman, then as Siren. Maybe Mr. Metro-Goldwyn-Mayer in audience, he take you to Hollywood." He thought I was going to fall for *that*? . . .
>
> So I did princess first, with my *Prodigal* tights underneath my costume and half my *Prodigal* make-up on already. In those days, the company was only about 60 people. We didn't have a huge company, so everybody danced.
>
> The Siren wore white tights with those black strings, which were actually painted on. Eddie Bigelow used to come to my dressing room at night after a performance [of his own] and paint my legs. That was the only time available. I would stand on the table, and he would paint my legs! I wore black tights underneath the white ones, to keep the paint from reaching my skin, but the paint came through the tights onto my legs anyway. The paint came off in the wash, you see, so we had to repaint them every time.
>
> —Hite

Conductors

Dancers? There Are Dancers Onstage?

British citizen Vernon Castle, of the famous ballroom partnership, wanted to return to England to enlist to fight in World War I. Just prior to his returning to Britain, a last performance featuring the Castles dancing together, to John Philip Sousa's band, was arranged for the couple's many fans in New York, at the Hippodrome. Vernon's wife and dancing partner, Irene Castle, described the evening:

> There was one small complication. John Philip Sousa was a bandmaster, a very famous bandmaster, and I am sure he was convinced that most of the people had come to listen to his music. He peeped out of the corner of his eye to make sure we were on the stage, then turned his back to us and began to pump away, paying no further attention to us. He ignored our frantic signals to pick up the tempo, and his uniformed arms flailed away with the precise beat of a man conducting a military march, which was exactly what he was doing.
>
> I was boiling mad. I could have kicked him. But Vernon laughed and whispered in my ear that it didn't matter—and added, "I love you." It didn't; nothing did for the moment. We had each other and we were dancing!
>
> —Castle, p. 141

Beecham

Music critic Irving Deakin:

> The conductor of the orchestra at a ballet performance, if he be a good one, is an extremely important part of the whole. It is true that, on occasion,

the conductor is himself the star performer, which can be extremely annoying. One of ballet's most spectacular occasional conductors is Sir
Thomas Beecham, and without the genius of that supreme master of the
orchestra, he could be a source of constant irritation. In his association
with the Diaghilev Ballet, for which he accepted no fee, he inaugurated
the highly admirable custom of having one of the interludes between the
separate ballets going to make up the program a purely orchestral one,
giving young composers first hearings of their works or else very old and
rarely played compositions. Beecham will perform no music he feels to
be uncongenial; he conducts conspicuously and with some mannerisms
that seem superfluous; he sometimes exaggerates a tempo either on the
slow or the fast side; occasionally he over-points music that should be
kept quite simple; in short, he has his little perversities which indeed can
become fascinating, because, after all, one knows from the intoxicating
beauty of his musical phrasing and shaping that he is passionately in love
with ballet as an art, precisely as he is in love with music.

—Deakin, pp. 16–17

A Conductor's Révérence

At the Apollo Theater in London on January 25, 1931, the newborn
"Carmargo Society" was giving its second performance. Two days before,
Anna Pavlova had died in her sleep in The Hague. The first ballet on the
program had just been performed, and the audience was waiting for the
second. Suddenly, the conductor, Constant Lambert, turned around and
announced, "The orchestra will now play "The Death of the Swan" ["Le
Cygne," from *The Carnival of the Animals*, by Saint-Saëns] in memory of
Anna Pavlova." Philip J. S. Richardson was present:

> The curtain went up and disclosed an empty, darkened stage draped in
> grey hangings, with the spotlight playing on someone who was not there.
> The large audience rose to its feet and stood in silence while the tune
> which will forever be associated with Anna Pavlova was played. It was an
> unforgettable moment.
>
> —Franks, pp. 67–68

Universal Billing

The following story, told by Eleanor Powell's biographer, Alice B. Levin, is
based on several interviews, including an interview that Powell gave to Miles
Kreuger, president of the Institute of the American Musical:

> While Eleanor was on an MGM sound stage rehearsing the ballet num-
> ber for *Broadway Melody of 1940*, word arrived from Louis B. Mayer that
> Arturo Toscanini, the world-renowned conductor, shortly would be vis-

iting the set. Mayer requested Bobby Connolly, the film's dance director, to prepare a routine for the Maestro to view. Meanwhile, Connolly told the crew that "a famous man was to come onset to watch Ellie."

Toscanini was escorted onto the sound stage and sat in on the rehearsal. Afterwards, he seemed curiously disappointed. After explaining that what he really wanted to see was "the dance with the noise," Eleanor promptly switched her ballet shoes and skirt for her tap shoes and tap costume. Then, for almost two hours, she tap-danced for Toscanini. Dona Massin Carn watched the Maestro watching Eleanor dance, and never saw anyone so enthralled.

Toscanini left the sound stage with tears streaming down his cheeks. He later wrote Eleanor that his three greatest memories of his visit to the United States were the sunset, the Grand Canyon, and her dancing! That letter hung on Eleanor's wall for the rest of her life. "I will never get billing like that, ever again—and from the man I adored so much," Eleanor told Miles Kreuger.

—Levin, pp. 71, 73

About *Appalachian Spring*

The Brooklyn-born composer Aaron Copland won a Pulitzer Prize in 1944 for his score for Martha Graham's work. He also conducted it for the Graham company on a number of occasions:

> I have conducted all of my own compositions as well as works by other composers, but *Appalachian Spring* is the one I know best from a conducting point of view. I have often admonished orchestras, professional and otherwise, not to get too sweet or too sentimental with it, and I have reminded performers that *Appalachian Spring* should be played cooler than Tchaikovsky and lighter and happier than Stravinsky's *Sacre du Printemps*. My own favorite place in the whole piece is toward the end, where I have marked a *misterioso*. I would tell string players that we don't want to know where the up and down bows are. They must have a special sustained quality there—kind of organlike in sound, with each entry like an Amen.
>
> —Copland, p. 50

English Quick-Stepper

One of the finest conductors for ballet and dance in the twentieth century was Robert Irving (1913–1991), who served the New York City Ballet as its principal conductor between 1958 and 1989. Before then, he conducted for the Sadler's Wells (later The Royal Ballet), and, during the 1960's and 1970's, he frequently conducted for Martha Graham as well.

In an interview with the magazine *Music Journal* in 1960, he explained that "Ballet conducting . . . requires, in addition to everything needed for symphonic conducting, an ability to fuel the rhythm." Irving was famous among his musicians for dancing along with the music as he conducted. Arnold Goldberg, a tympanist with the City Ballet orchestra who worked under Irving for 30 years, noted in a 1990's interview that he was also a "fantastic" piano player. "Once he played *Liebeslieder Walzer* up at Saratoga [NYCB's summer home]," Mr. Goldberg recalled. "He was on stage, and a very heavy downpour rained in over him, but the dancers danced, and he didn't miss a beat." It seems apt that Irving would have been so devoted to that particular ballet, which portrays a very elegant party of social dancing. "I always used to tell him," Mr. Goldberg said, "he had impeccable rhythm."

"My dear boy," Irving once replied. "I used to be a ballroom dancer."

—M.A.

Dancing and Related Theatrical Professions

Rope Dancing

Alexander Placide (1750–1812) was an eighteenth-century pantomimist and the scion of the Placide theatrical family. He had trained in London with Philip Astley (commonly thought of as the father of the modern circus) and had become, among other things, a virtuoso at rope dancing—that is, at dancing on a tightrope, which was popular in the Colonies and the United States during much of the century. Early American musical theater historian Julian Mates reports that "Boston's Exhibition Room opened, in 1792, with 'Tight and Slack-Rope Performances,' and Rickett's second Philadelphia circus featured tight-rope performers who doubled in pantomime and ballet."

Henry J. Colton was one eyewitness to Placide:

The first time I saw him was at Charleston . . . dancing the tight rope. At that period it was considered a great and graceful feat of address and always drew crowded houses. Placide had with him a pantomime dancer. . . . The preparations for the Dance were always imposing. The attendants, with livery, carried the rope to the center of the pit, where it was duly attached and drawn upon the stage. A palace scene was set for the rope dancing, and a row of wax candles were placed at equal distances near the rope. Placide, habited in a light silk Spanish dress, with silk stockings and pumps and two watch chains, then greatly in fashion, made his appearance amid shouts of applause, Spinacuta playing the clown, with chalked face and parti-colored pants.

—Mates, pp. 165–166

Haute on the Hoof

Classical ballet and the art of dressage emerged in Europe in about the same era, and their maneuvers share some of the same vocabulary, even when the horses are performing in the circus:

> Some of the riding acts still seen in the ring date back to stories of the Napoleonic wars. . . . [I]t is the *haute école* which is recognized as the very highest achievement of circus horsemanship. It is introduced into the ring with the imposing rites accorded to star acts. There is a fanfare of trumpets and the ringmaster and attendants stand in two rows at the ring entrance as the horse and its rider trot in. The act begins with a three-legged gallop, the horse's fourth leg sticking out in a straight line. The horse trots, changes feet and dances in time to the music. Finally, pacing backwards and faster, he rears up on his hind legs while the rider remains immovable.
>
> The *haute école* derives from the days when horses were schooled for war. The terms used in those days for these warlike exercises still survive in the circus ring. The *levade* was the movement in which the horse lifted its rider above the foot-soldier's attack; the *capriole* was the backward kick which disabled him. There were also movements for the tournament, such as the *pirouette* or a *demi-volte*, the return to the attack if an opponent was not unseated at the first onset. These movements were known as *airs*. The *passage* was the final *air*, the horse stepping proudly as it bore its rider to the tournament queen to receive his reward.
>
> François Baucher and James Fillis were the two great exponents and teachers of the circus *haute école*. Baucher revolutionized the theories then in vogue. Having no belief in the intelligence of the horse, his method was to make the horse a machine: a piece of mechanism obedient to the lightest touch. Baucher's circus career ended dramatically and tragically. In 1855, standing in the ring and about to mount his horse, he was crushed by the weight of a chandelier, which fell and smashed to pieces in the circus ring. The horse, having no intelligence, had bounded clear. Baucher was still conscious when an attendant reached his side. In a calm voice he asked to be released from the wreckage, which was pinning him to the ground. He lived for another 18 years, but there is no further mention of his name in circus history.
>
> —Croft-Cooke, pp. 36–37

The Whirlwind and the Ruffled Silence

In 1949, Jean-Louis Barrault—one of the greatest French actors of the twentieth century, genius of the ancient art of mime, and a friend of theater philosopher Antonin Artaud, poet Robert Desnos, artist and theatrical designer Christian Bérard, and choreographer Paul Taylor—published a book of memoirs and ideas that was later translated into English as *Reflections on the The-atre*. Among its poetic observations and original drawings by Bérard, Balthus, and André Masson is this prose poem, "Concerning Mime and Dance":

A theater stage has always made me think of a conjuror's box. A theater stage has always made me think of a mysterious cube, ten meters a side, a sort of dark room where enchantment reigns.

Let us imagine it: the box, the magic room, the cube.

At the moment it is empty, a block of frozen silence, full of potentialities.

Suddenly there is a squall of noise, a sonorous whirlwind. A breath of music has penetrated there, and it turns and turns, up and up, its spirals getting smaller and smaller, like a column of smoke. And from the ground we see a little pyramid of dust rising, turning, whirling round, too, like a top—a potter's wheel gone mad. This little pyramid becomes larger, larger, and takes shape. First, we discern a foot on tiptoe, an ankle, a calf, a stretched knee, a taut thigh, a swirling disc of light tulle, a straight slender body, a vertical neck, two arms horizontal like the beam of a balance, and finally a face with a frozen smile and two eyes seeking some point to fix in a fleeting world:

The dancer is born.

She is born out of the whirlwind of music. If the music becomes slower and dies away, then the vertical projection that is the dancer will melt away like snow in sunshine. The dust, become dancer, will fall to the ground and shrink back into a little heap of ash.

This is Dance—in its simplicity.

Then our magic box becomes ice-bound again, wrapped in our fa-mous silence.

Soon the silence is gently ruffled, as water is rippled by the passing of an invisible fish.

A Mimer is in the offing.

Now he makes his entry into the room, his chest puffed out before him. His movement rolls the air before him like little boats that lift the water with their prows; from either side, two rippling lines form the let-ter V; he brings a faithful eddy in his wake. He stirs the silence; he creates rhythm, first visual, but then we seem to hear a faint echo of music show-ing that music has come into being.

This is Mime.

In the art of mime, the first intimation of music is its echo.

If the mimer ceases to operate, the music dies, the echo fades away, and silence returns. The man is then possessed by the famous ice of our famous silence, like the unhappy Alpine climbers for whom the glacier waits, year after year, to make its own.

Here, in all simplicity, is the difference between mime and dance. (Bar-bara Wall, trans.)

—Barrault, pp. 155–156

Eek!

Boris Kochno:

Schéhérazade was the first true creation of the Ballets Russes, because, except for the dances from the opera *Prince Igor* that Fokine had choreographed for the company in 1909, all the other ballets in Diaghilev's first Paris season were fresh versions of already existing works. . . . *Schéhérazade* was a total success, thanks to the harmonious combination of music, mis-en-scène, and choreography. Bakst's décor and costumes turned theatrical concepts of the period upside-down, and engendered the so-called "Ballets Russes" style. The miming of Ida Rubinstein, Nijinsky's dances, and the ensembles devised by Fokine aroused a degree of interest that was unusual for a dance performance; quite simply, they created a sensation.

Such enthusiasm persuaded Sarah Bernhardt to see the ballet. Already lame, the great tragedienne had herself carried into the theater, but scarcely had the curtain gone up than she was seen to become much overwrought. Laying about her with her cane, she cried, "Let's get out of here! Quickly! . . . I'm afraid. They are all mutes!"

—Kochno, p. 46

Variety

During my vaudeville days, I saw such a variety of acts—well, that's what it was all about. Sometimes people don't even believe me when I describe an act! For example, there was a girl dancer who used to tap dance on toe shoes. And then she invented ball bearings in her toe shoes to turn faster! Gloria Gilbert was her name. . . .

In those days, all the performers wanted to do everything but what they were doing. Acrobats always wanted to be comedians. And they had the least sense of humor of anybody! (Donald O'Connor)

—Frank, p. 149

Dancing and the Movies

The Red Shoes

I am often asked why *The Red Shoes* [1948], of all our films, became such a success in every country of the world. More than a success, it became a legend. Even today, I am constantly meeting men and women who claim that it changed their lives. This is natural enough, for women who were girls at the time, and who were growing up in countries that had been wracked by war. But my friend Ron Kitaj, who was thinking of becoming an art student at the time, has told me the same thing. "It changed my direction," he said. "It gave art a new meaning to me." These are personal reactions, but I think that the real reason why *The Red Shoes* was such a success was that we had all been told for ten years to go out and die for freedom and democracy, for this and for that, and now that the war was over, *The Red Shoes* told us to go and die for art.

—Powell, p. 653

Akira Kurosawa, ca. 1945

During the war [World War II] I had been starved for beauty, so I rushed headlong into the world of traditional Japanese arts as to a feast. I may have been motivated by a desire to escape from the reality around me, but what I managed to learn despite the motive was nevertheless of great value to me. I went to see the Noh for the first time. I read the art theories the great fourteenth-century Noh playwright Zeami left behind him. I read all there was to read about Zeami himself, and I devoured books on the Noh.

I was attracted by the Noh because of the admiration I felt for its unique-ness, part of which may be that its form of expression is so far removed from that of film. At any rate, I took this opportunity to become familiar with the Noh, and I had the pleasure of viewing the performances of the great actors of each school—Kita Roppeita, Umewaka Manzaburo and Sakurama Kintaro.

Among their plays there are many performances I will never forget, but the most memorable of all was Manzaburo's *Hanjo* ("The Lady Han"). It was thundering and raining outside, but while I watched him on the stage I heard nothing of the weather. Then, when he came out on stage again and began the dance of the jo introduction act, the evening sun was suddenly reflected off his form. "Ah, the moonflower has bloomed," I thought, entranced. It was a moment that allowed me to savor to the fullest the play's poetic reference to the moonflower chapter of *The Tale of Genji*. (Audie E. Bock, trans.)

—Kurosawa, pp. 147–148

Kurosawa's *Dreams*

In this late film from 1990, Kurosawa incorporated dances and ceremonial processions derived from Noh into several of the self-contained sections. The most resplendent is the dance for the life-sized dolls of what, in the English-language intertitle, is translated as "The Peach Orchard." The following memoir, by Michiyo Hata, the master of classical Japanese dance who served as the choreographer for *Dreams*, gives a sense of the intensive preparation for the sequence:

The second story, "Peach Garden," was a dream about the doll festival. A young boy brings sweets to his sister and her friends who are celebrating the doll festival. There were supposed to be just enough sweets for each of the girls, but when handing them out he realizes that there is one extra sweet. Puzzled, he looks out into the garden and sees a strange little girl— the spirit of the peach trees—looking back at him. He chases after her, and finds himself in a terraced field of peach trees behind the house, where a large group (60 in all) of life-size dolls are standing, dressed in their gorgeous robes. The dolls say, "We won't ever visit your house again. Your family have cut down all the peach trees. The fallen peach trees are weeping." But one of the princess dolls defends him, saying, "No, this is the good boy, the one who cried when they cut down the trees." The other dolls, having learned the truth, perform a wonderful dance for the boy. When the dance is over they disappear, and all that remain are the sad stumps of the trees.

Mr. Kurosawa wanted the actors' faces to look like actual *hina* dolls, so the main selection of the actors was based mainly on this physical resemblance. Most of the actors chosen were from the *Nijuki-kai*, Kurosawa's cherished team of 20 people who appear in all of his movies. Some of the cast, therefore, had no dancing experience at all, and we held a month of intensive lessons for them.

This turned out to be effective, and the day of the shooting went smoothly, finishing up at about 1:00 in the afternoon. The location was a hillside in Kirigaoka, Midori Ward, Yokohama. It had been rented the year before, cut into layered terraces like the stand used to display the dolls, and grass was planted over it. We came back six months later, and cameras were set up on the opposing bank, facing the hill.

It rained the day before shooting, and I watched anxiously as the actors climbed to their places, holding their long trailing scarlet robes, praying that they would not muddy their costumes.

The actors were concentrating so strongly that they may not have noticed it, but the final scene, when a blizzard of peach blossoms rains down, was so beautiful that it seemed otherworldly. I will never forget that scene, as several cranes dumped huge quantities of peach petals all at once; it was like, truly, a dream. I repeated "Thank you, thank you" over and over again in my heart, filled with gratitude that Mr. Kurosawa had granted me the privilege of experiencing this moment.

I picked up some of the blossoms and there were many different colors—nearly white pink, pale pink, medium pink, and deep pink—and different sizes, too, so that they fell so beautifully and naturally.

—Hata, pp. 98–99

Balanchine's Kurosawa

In 1963, George Balanchine cast Allegra Kent and Edward Villella as the leads in a new ballet, *Bugaku*. In the following passage, Kent tells how she prepared for her role:

One of Balanchine's inspirations for *Bugaku* was the gagaku, a group of male Japanese dancers and musicians who performed ancient dances on a raised platform. Lincoln Kirstein had invited them over to open every program in the 1959 season. The mesmeric movements and sound of the gagaku took one back to feudal times in Japan, and Mr. B cast Eddie as a samurai warrior for his new work. As I watched Eddie dance this role, I thought he resembled Toshiro Mifune in action. Had Mr. B. seen *Rashomon*? In a role even more erotic than my part in *The Seven Deadly Sins*, I was cast as a Japanese creature having an arranged, first-time sexual experience, a ceremonial coupling. Was I a wife, a concubine, or something else? It didn't seem to matter. The ritual was the important thing. The ballet opens in a formal setting and proceeds toward a ceremony that sanctions the physical. After the couple's physical consummation in the sensual pas de deux, our translucent trains return in the arms of our attendants, and we go back to courtly manners, back to formality. The ballet presents the two sides of courtship—the mannered and the sexual, the classic and romantic.

I had understood immediately how I was going to study for the role. I wanted to portray something of the look, beauty, and mystery of Japanese women, particularly as I remembered them from two Kurosawa films,

Throne of Blood, a version of *Macbeth*, which I had seen in Japan, and *Rashomon*, the movie that had startled the entire film industry. My objective was not Lady Macbeth Japanese-style, only some intangible quality that would evoke the haunting aura of this ancient culture. For refreshment I invited Mimi Paul, my understudy, to come to the movies with me so we could slip into a different world and century with the huge images of make-believe. The Japanese words were sounds and tones I didn't understand, so they became extra music. I decided that more should happen in the eyes and body and less on the face, that a perfectly simple ritualistic movement could be rich with currents under the surface, as the famous Noh puppets illustrated. Liquid movements were a favorite with me because of my love for the water, so I tried to contrast the fluid with the sudden, and the straightforward with the sidewinding. The music for *Bugaku* sounded like movie music, so I decided to accent a dramatic sound with a dramatic move, as Hollywood would do. It was the time to be obvious.

—Kent, *Once*, pp. 179–180

Jean Renoir and *The River*

After reading a laudatory review in *The New Yorker* of Rumer Godden's 1949 novel, *The River*, set in India, the great director Jean Renoir decided that here was a story that could open the doors of Hollywood for him, and he decided to make a film of it, on location. For the character of the shy and complicated half-Indian girl Melanie, Renoir chose the young, gorgeous Bharata Natyam dancer Radha Sriram, a woman who, still today, is considered by dancers and dance critics in India to be among the country's most beautiful and dignified performers. Her fantasy wedding dance as a goddess is one of the film's highlights. Renoir remembers how she came to be cast in the picture:

It was in the holy city of Benares that we made the acquaintance of Radha, the dancer. We had met her future husband, Raymond Burnier, at the home of Christine Bossennec, the French cultural attachée in Calcutta, who had asked me to give a lecture at the École Française. Raymond invited us to spend Christmas with him at his palatial residence in Benares. He had a passion for India, was thinking of being converted to Hinduism, and wore his hair in a pigtail in the Hindu fashion. What caused him to hesitate was the fact that, not having been born of a high caste, he could be accepted only as an "untouchable." It was at his home that I met Alain Daniélou, the musicologist with such a wide knowledge of India.

Radha introduced me to the dance called "Katakali" and in general to the music of the province of Madras, where she lived. Her father was president of the Theosophical Society [of which Burnier, herself, is now president]. Claude [J. R.'s nephew] and I were so charmed by her personality after three or four days in her company that we suggested she should play the part of Melanie. [Kenneth] McEldowney [the film's producer] at first took fright, thinking that the idea was madness: Radha's beauty was of a kind not easily intelligible to Western eyes. But we took him to a dance session which overcame his objections. These preliminaries were accomplished in Raymond Burnier's home under the friendly eye of an enormous bird, a crane named Syphon, which was extremely gluttonous.

—Renoir, p. 255

A-Pic, B-Pic

Musicals were always my most favorite thing in the world. I was such a movie fan as a child, and I actually had a clipping service for all my favorite stars! I absolutely adored Ginger Rogers and always wished I could dance like she did. I loved Donald O'Connor, The Nicholas Brothers, Gene Nelson, and, of course, I adored Bill Robinson. Absolutely adored him! He'd always come up to me at the studio, and every time, he'd do a little step and I would mimic his step. Then I'd give him another one. And he'd say, "Oh, I'd give anything in the world if I could get to dance with you in a picture." I said, "Mr. Robinson, that's never going to happen. You make A pictures and I make B's, and I guess you belong to Shirley Temple." But he said, "Well we could always dream, can't we." I said, "Yes, sir. That's what life is made of." (Jane Withers)

—Frank, p. 166

The Umbrella Test

Stephen M. Silverman's *Dancing on the Ceiling*, a study of the life and career of Stanley Donen—dancer, director, and maker of some of most joyful and treasured movie musicals ever to emerge from Hollywood—is one of the most engaging and intelligent books on theatrical dancing ever published. Donen's contributions to *Anchors Aweigh*, *On the Town*, and *Singin' in the Rain* (all with Gene Kelly) and *Royal Wedding* and *Funny Face* (with Fred Astaire) were crucial to why these pictures speak to audiences internationally and across generations. In "Heaven!," the chapter on *Funny Face* (1957), for example, one finds the following paragraph from an interview that Silverman conducted with the photographer Richard Avedon, whose career served as the inspiration for the script and who worked closely with Donen and his team on the look of the movie. Here, Avedon speaks about his reverence for Astaire and his reservations about another male musical star of the 1950s, Gene Kelly. Regardless of whether readers agree with Avedon's conclusion, the sharp intelligence of his argument gives tremendous insight into the styles of both dancers and represents the exacting connoisseurship that informs the book—and Donen's work:

Fred taught me a step," said Avedon, "because I said I can't let this experience be over without my learning something. He taught me the most wonderful Fred Astaire-like step, with an umbrella. It was a complete throwaway; it was almost invisible. It was in the way he walked. As he moved along, he bounced the umbrella on the floor to the beat and then he grabbed it. It was effortless and invisible. As a matter of fact, a few years later I was photographing Gene Kelly and told him that Fred Astaire had taught me this trick with an umbrella. And Kelly said, "Oh, I'll teach you one," and he did, and the two tricks with an umbrella in some way define the difference between Fred Astaire and Gene Kelly, and, in my view, demonstrate who is the greater of the artists. With Gene Kelly, he threw the umbrella way up into the air, then he moved to catch it, very slowly, grabbing it behind his back.

It was a big, grandstand play, about nothing.

—Silverman, p. 241

Twin Peaks

The two hardest things I ever did in my life . . . childbirth and *Singin' in the Rain*. (Debbie Reynolds)

—Tractenberg, unpaginated

"Gene Kelly, My Sore Eyes Look to You"

From a column by Kena Herod, dance critic of *Maisonneuve*, the Canadian magazine of arts and ideas:

My daughter is a huge Gene Kelly fan. Well, as much as any three-year-old can be. Like so many parents today, I have resorted to the electronic babysitter: about a year ago, with a deadline looming and a restless toddler, I desperately scanned our movie collection and plopped my well-worn copy of *Singin' in the Rain* into the VCR. It was love at first sight. Since then, Vivienne has moved on to *An American in Paris* and *On the Town*. Ask her what she wants to do after she gets home from daycare and her answer inevitably is, "I want Gene Kelly, please." And which of the three movies to choose is a matter of serious deliberation.

—Herod, unpaginated

Injuries, Maladies, Misfortunes, and Cures

One Day It's Kicks, Then It's Kicks in the Shins

When Marius Petipa, the nineteenth-century choreographer who master-minded *Swan Lake* and *The Sleeping Beauty*, was sixteen, he was hired as *premier danseur* and ballet master in Nantes. His first season went well, and he produced three ballets. He picks up the story in his memoirs:

> I was happy in this position and remained a second season, but misfortune fell upon me: on stage, dancing, I broke my shinbone and spent six weeks in bed. There I came to know how the majority of impresarios treat the actors whom they exploit. At the end of the month, I gave my mother power of attorney to receive my salary, but although I had broken my leg during the fulfillment of my duty on stage, the director still refused to make any payment, on the basis of the conditions of my contract. What to do? How to get the second month's salary from them? I still could not use my leg, but I had to take part in the performance. I devised a new Spanish *pas*, in which, with my hands, I showed another dancer how to work the feet, and myself appeared, accompanying the *pas* with castanets. The management found itself legally defeated, and with a change of heart paid all my salary for the second month. But the job with these gentlemen did not appeal to me any more, and with pleasure I set out for New York, with my father. We took a sailing ship, and crossed the ocean in exactly 22 days.

Unfortunately, New York added insult to injury and blew its chance to be-come the home of the young man who would go on to change the course of ballet forever in Russia. As Petipa recounts:

Sad was our acquaintance with the United States, where an impresario, a certain Lecomte, had brought us promising mountains of gold, and where we soon found that we had fallen into the hands of an interna-tional adventurer.

My father was engaged as ballet master, I as *premier danseur*, and we appeared within five days of our arrival in New York. The opening took place with some kind of play and ballet; the first performance had full box office receipts, bits of which fell into our hands in the form of an insignificant advance. A week passed, the receipts were good, but they paid us only half of the salary due, and after the second week they cyni-cally, categorically, explained that there was no money and they couldn't pay us, but asked us to be patient. We waited patiently for the third and fourth weeks, but then the impertinence of the swindler-impresario passed all bounds, which circumstance, together with the danger of catching yellow fever, then raging there, obliged my father to escape from this, for us, inhospitable city. (Helen Whittaker, trans.)

—Petipa, *Russian*, pp. 8–9

51 Years

Over the past millennium, the impulse to dance has often led to diagnoses of insanity in the dancer, as well as severe versions of exorcism and punish-ment on religious grounds in both Europe and, from its earliest Massachu-setts settlements, the United States. On March 17, 2005, *The New York Times* published the obituary of a woman named Opal Petty, who had died in her native Texas a week prior. Opal Petty was eighty-six years old at her death, of natural causes. For fifty-one years of her life—from the age of sixteen—she had been incarcerated in a mental institution for having flouted her family of rigorously devoted Baptists by going out dancing. Her original diagnosis of schizophrenia was never reviewed in all those years (her lawyers claimed that, in fact, she had suffered "at worst" from psychotic depression), and, eventually, she succumbed to a condition called "institutional syndrome," which apparently caused permanent damage to her personality. According to the testimony of a psychiatrist during a trial brought by Ms. Petty's rela-tives against the Texas Department of Mental Health and Mental Retarda-tion in 1989, both her institutional records and the physician's own examination of her convinced him that her psychotic symptoms at the age of sixteen "quickly subsided, and . . . she should have been released."

Ms. Petty is mentioned here as a representative for countless other women whose desire to dance brought them imprisonment, torture, and death.

—Lehmann-Haupt

Fire, Fire Burning Bright

As early as the fifth century B.C., there existed in Greece the so-called orpheotelestae, . . . itinerant healers, who offered to dance around the sick, not infrequently in the form of a ring-dance. They pretended that thus they could cure all diseases, even mental disease. . . .

During the Middle Ages, according to a 14th-century manuscript, there existed a dance with flaming torches around a newborn child; it was supposed to protect the child against evil spirits, especially against maladies which were thought to be induced by demoniac possession.

—Backman, pp. 5–6

Devil Dancers: Rangoon, Burma, March 4, 1892

The most singular of all Burmese customs is perhaps the employment of dancing as a sovereign medicine. We know that faith will work wonders; and it is quite possible that the Natzò or devil dance does, in some cases, cure such an abjectly credulous subject as the Burman is in regard to things supernatural. A Burmese physician, when his nostrums fail to take effect, will gravely attribute the disorder to malice on the part of an evil spirit, and to exorcise the demon he will order that it shall dance. As the grievously sick patient is incapable of submitting to this ordeal, a professional dancing woman—called the wife of the Natzò—is engaged; and she dances to the sound of musical instruments, working herself into a frenzy until she becomes infuriated. The incoherent words she utters whilst in this state are interpreted by the physician as an answer from the Natzò himself, and if the patient recovers, the physician is looked upon as a great wizard indeed. Should, however, the sufferer die in spite of the dance, then the physician acquits himself from blame by declaring that the power of the Natzò has been such that no mortal could overcome.

—*Dancing*, p. 137

Ghost Dance

Associated with murders and a massacre, in 1890–91, by U.S. soldiers of some three hundred Native American men, women, and children, including the legendary chief Sitting Bull (who had bested Custer at Little Bighorn), the Ghost Dance of Native America evolved from a prophetic belief that, with its practice (in the words of Dick Fool Bull), "the earth will roll up like a blanket with all the bad white man's stuff, the fences and railroads and mines and telegraph poles; and underneath will be our old-young Indian earth with all our relatives come to life again"; and, also, the decimated buffalo would return to life. For its tribal practitioners, the dance was a grand gesture toward heavenly peace. Its actual procedure has been described by Melissa Amen:

The dance was to last for five days and four nights and would occur every six weeks. Before and after the dance, participants were required to bathe. Preliminary painting and dressing for the dance would take about two hours. After this was done, the leaders of the dance, usually four men, would gather in a circle. They would face inward and sing the opening song. The song was repeated as the dancers begin moving slowly in the shuffle step from right to left. They go in that direction because it follows the course of the sun. Different songs are sung throughout the dance, including a special, closing song. These songs vary amongst the different tribes, but, in one tribe, they are the same for each performance of the dance. Unlike most other Native American dances, no drums or instruments accompany the Ghost Dance. The rhythm of the chanting is all that guides the dancers' steps.

As the songs are sung by the leaders, more people join in the circle. Although led by men only, everyone, including women and children, participate in the dance. Each song begins slowly and then rises in volume and speed each time it is sung. By the time the song is repeated for the fourth time, it is loud and fast. The next song [begins] slowly and with each repetition [speeds] up. Throughout the dance, the people fell into trances. Most claim that in these trances they see their dead relatives, and this gives them, and the people they share their stories with, the strength to continue the dance.

The historian Trudy Griffin-Pierce also notes that the dancers "wore special clothing that was supposed to have supernatural power and to be bulletproof. Ideally, such garments were similar to those they had worn before white contact and were made of buckskin painted with visionary Ghost Dance designs. However, they often had to use cloth in place of buckskin, which was becoming more difficult to obtain."

Both of these chroniclers—and many others—have written very affectingly of the massacre at Wounded Knee, when it became clear to both Native Americans and their oppressors that the only peace available in this world would be on the terms of the whites. Shortly before, Sitting Bull and fourteen other individuals had been killed when soldiers came to arrest him, mistakenly thinking that he was the leader of the Ghost Dance movement that so alarmed the white authorities. Griffin-Pierce, referring to that December 1890 event, offers a succinct account of the next one:

The last glimmer of hope offered by the Ghost Dance was extinguished when an even greater tragedy occurred later that same month. White authorities had grown increasingly nervous at the frenzied spread of the Ghost Dance and the warlike look of the protective shirts. When the Minneconjou Sioux, led by Big Foot, journeyed to collect rations, the authorities intercepted the travelers and took them to Wounded Knee Creek. There the people began a Ghost Dance. When one Indian fired a

concealed gun, panicked soldiers opened fire. . . . The Wounded Knee
massacre broke their spirit: by 1891, armed Sioux resistance had ended.
—Amen, unpaginated; Griffin-Pierce, pp. 89–91

Choreomania

Dance epidemics—in which hundreds, even thousands of people joined in
bouts of continuous dancing, sometimes from city to city—have been
chronicled in Europe from the seventh century. E. Louis Backman, a scholar
of medieval music, discussed the origins of the phenomenon at length in his
remarkable book, *Religious Dances*. Below is his brief overview and a description of one such epidemic of dancers, called choreomaniacs: the Dance at
Kölbigk, in Saxony, in 1021. Many famous legends are, in some way, legacies
of choreomaniac epidemics. Among them are the tale of the Pied Piper of
Hamelin, who, in revenge on the townspeople for not paying him to free
the town of rats, piped their children into a mountain; later literary stories
are the Grimm Brothers' "Snow White," in which a character is forced to
wear an iron boot heated red-hot; or Hans Christian Andersen's tale "The
Red Shoes," about a girl who is forced by a pair of mysterious dancing shoes
to dance herself to death.

One of the most unusual and remarkable phenomena of the Middle Ages,
either from a medical or a religious standpoint, was the so-called Dance
Epidemic. Crowds of people, great or small, seemed suddenly to be smitten with a wild fury of dancing, and professed to be suffering great ago-
nies while so engaged. Often they danced themselves to death.
Occasionally these epidemics affected many thousands of people, and they
gave the impression of being very infectious. . . .The commonest belief
was that it was a question of phenomena of an hysterical kind, nervous
disturbances, mental disease, and especially fraud. It is obvious that in
olden days these dancers were held to have been possessed by evil spirits.
. . . It must be stated here that the victims of these dance epidemics were
seriously affected by physical disease and mental confusion; they suffered
from convulsions and violent pains, and not seldom succumbed entirely
to this horrible illness. . . .

In 1074, Abbot Hartwig commanded one of his monks, Lambert of
Hersfeld by name, to write the history of the monastery of Hersfeld, including therein the miracle dance at Kölbigk in 1021. Lambert himself
had not witnessed the event, but he heard the story of it from a certain
Othbert, who had himself taken part in the famous Christmas Dance, and
now 23 years later, when he told Lambert about it, was still suffering
from nervous tremors. In gratitude for his release from great pain, he had
devoted himself to his work as a lay servant of the monastery.

It was Christmas Eve in Kölbigk, and, outside the church dedicated to
St. Magnus the Martyr, there had gathered 15 men and three women,

among them a son and a daughter of the priest who was to play such a fateful part of the story. Instead of attending the Christmas mass, they were led by the wiles of the Devil to perform a dance in the churchyard, or, according to another account, in the porch of the church itself. Othbert leading, they clasped each other's hands and began their mad dance, following him round and round. Without ceasing for an instant, they danced on, stamping on the ground, leaping into the air and clapping their hands. As they danced, they sang, and this was the song:

> Bovo rode through the dark green forest
> With him he bore the fair Mersvinden
> Why do we stay? Why don't we follow?

Bovo and Mersvinden are two of the dancers. [The scholar E.] Schröder calls this an epic song in ballad form. Presumably the dance was of the kind where the participants form a circle, and, in the center, one couple dances while the others sing the song; they also clap their hands and jump in the air. With the chorus or refrain they perform the actual ring-dance, probably stamping and leaping wildly at this stage also. In short, it must have been a type of dance closely akin to the group we learned earlier to recognize as characteristically popular ecclesiastical dances.

The dancing and singing disturbed the priest at mass. He went out and bade them cease, or rather to come inside the church and attend the service. They refused to listen and continued to dance and sing and brawl. Once more the priest warned them, and then [he] bade his son John [to] try to pull his sister away from the ring. John tried, he caught hold of his sister's arm, but it came away in his hand. At this he returned to the church and showed his father what had happened. The arm was thereafter preserved in the church as a kind of votive offering, and King Henry II had it mounted and set with fine workmanship in memory of a great miracle. But the priest went out a third time, solemnly excommunicated the dancers, and commanded, in the name of God and St. Magnus, that they should not cease from dancing for one whole year. When the year came to an end, the ban of excommunication was raised by the Bishop of Cologne. After six months, they had tramped down the soil until they were knee-deep in the ground, and after another six months they were hip-deep. During all this time [they] had neither eaten nor slept, and their clothes were still undamaged. When the ban was lifted, they were brought into church, and before St Magnus' altar once again admitted to the community of Christian people. They then fell into a deep sleep, which lasted for three days. When they awoke, the three women died, also one of the men, named John. The survivors returned home but suffered for the rest of their lives from tremors and nervous twitches in their limbs. One version only has nothing to say of these tremors; it merely recounts that when the men woke up they were looked after by friends or relations, and washed and clothed, although they resisted this. Schröder says that this is the oldest and probably the most accurate version.

—Backman, pp. 174–175

He Didn't Dance

> Old Dr. Gray was at the dance,
> When Ethel said, with merry glance,
> "Doctor, don't you dance the lancers?"
> "No, my dear, I lance the dancers."

—*Dancing*, p. 236

Agnes de Mille's Bow

Agnes de Mille had staged *Fall River Legend* and *Rodeo* (and created ballets *Logger's Clog* and *Summer*) for Boston Ballet for a complete evening of de Mille. After experiencing a stroke that had paralyzed her arm, this indomitable woman, once so full of fire, could now only speak slowly.

On being brought into the studio in her wheelchair, Ms. de Mille told the company that a stewardess on her flight had asked, "Can I help you, Grandmother?" She had replied, "Grandmother? Wait 'till you see me in one hour yelling at those Boston Ballet dancers!" Her stroke had not taken her sense of humor.

At the end of the performance, she stood up for the first time in order to take a bow onstage. Once the curtain came down, she motioned to get the wheelchair off stage. As she stood, concerned people tried to hold her up; she demanded they back off. The curtain went up and she was standing alone as she took her bow. The entire company was in tears. She didn't want to be seen in a wheelchair. She wanted to be seen as Agnes de Mille. (Ron Cunningham)

—Hite, interview

The Ultimate Cure for a Cold

Ballerina and choreographer Ruthanna Boris remembers this home remedy that dancers of the ceaselessly touring Ballet Russe de Monte Carlo used when they had to perform "while lots of stuff streamed out of the nose during pirouettes":

— Set out several sets of nightwear.
— Prepare your bed to be ready to jump into.
— Draw a bath so hot that you can barely tolerate it.
— While the bath is running, prepare a mixture of hot water, lemon, honey, and your favorite hard liquor. (The alcohol can be eliminated; however, she says that the Ballet Russe dancers preferred Jack Daniels.)

— Set the drink on the edge of the tub.
— Get into the bath, and, while you lie there until your skin puck-
  ers, slowly sip the entire drink.
— When you get out of the bath, wrap yourself in a big towel. Do
  not attempt to dry yourself off completely. Instead, throw on the
  first set of nightclothes and jump into bed.
— Soon, you will begin to sweat profusely. Throw off the first set of
  nightclothes and get into the second set.

Continue this process throughout the night, until you've run out of nightclothes.

In the morning, you'll find that "you're either cured, or you're dead."

—Aloff, interview

On Partnering and Partnerships

To Be Asked

Possibly the most romantic moment of partnering on the dance floor in literature occurs in *War and Peace*, when the teenaged Natásha Rostóv attends her first ball on New Year's Eve of 1810. Two men there hold her fate in their hands—the doomed prince with whom she will fall desperately in love, and the "buffoon" who loves her silently and whom she will ultimately marry:

> Suddenly everybody stirred, began talking, and pressed forward and then back, and between the two rows, which separated, the Emperor entered to the sounds of music that had immediately struck up. Behind him walked his host and hostess. He walked in rapidly, bowing to right and left as if anxious to get the first moments of the reception over. The band played the polonaise in vogue at that time. The men began to choose partners and take their places for the polonaise.
>
> More than half the ladies already had partners and were taking up, or preparing to take up, their positions for the polonaise. Natásha felt that she would be left with her mother and Sónya among a minority of women who crowded near the wall, not having been invited to dance. She stood with her slender arms hanging down, her scarcely defined bosom rising and falling regularly, and with bated breath and glittering, frightened eyes gazed straight before her, evidently prepared for the height of joy or misery. She was not concerned about the Emperor or any of those great people whom Perónskaya was pointing out—she had but one thought: "Is it possible no one will ask me, that I shall not be among the first to dance? Is it

possible that not one of all these men will notice me? They do not even seem to see me, or if they do they look as if they were saying, 'Ah, she's not the one I'm after, so it's not worth looking at her!' No, it's impossible," she thought. "They must know how I long to dance, how splendidly I dance, and how they would enjoy dancing with me."

The strains of the polonaise, which had continued for a considerable time, had begun to sound like a sad reminiscence in Natásha's ears. She wanted to cry. Prince Andrew with a lady passed by, evidently not recognizing them. The handsome Anatole was smilingly talking to a partner on his arm and looked at Natásha as one looks at a wall. Borís passed them twice and each time turned away. Berg and his wife, who were not dancing, came up to them.

At last the Emperor stopped beside his last partner (he had danced with three), and the music ceased. A worried aide-de-camp ran up to the Rostóvs requesting them to stand further back, though, as it was, they were already close to the wall, and from the gallery resounded the distinct, precise, enticingly rhythmical strains of a waltz. An aide-de-camp, the master of ceremonies, went up to Countess Bezúkhova and asked her to dance. Natásha gazed at them and was ready to cry because it was not she who was dancing the first turn of the waltz.

Prince Andrew was watching the women who were breathlessly longing to be asked to dance.

Pierre came up to him and caught him by the arm.

"You always dance. I have a protégée, the young Rostóva, here. Ask her," he said. (Louise and Aylmer Maude, trans.)

—Tolstoy, pp. 239–240

Painting the Town Rose

In her remarkable history, *Black Dance: From 1619 to Today*, Lynne Fauley Emery, a scholar of African American dance in the United States, has isolated this electrifying description by the novelist Claude McKay (1890–1948) of a couple dancing at the Congo Club in Harlem during the 1920s as an example of that decade's "Black Renaissance, the literary awakening of the Negro writer":

They danced, Rose and the boy. Oh, they danced! An exercise of rhythmical exactness for two. There was no motion she made that he did not imitate. They reared and pranced together, smacking palm against palm, working knee between knee, grinning with real joy. They shimmied, breast to breast, bent themselves far back and shimmied again. Lifting high her short skirt and showing her green bloomers, Rose kicked . . . , the boy kicked even with her. They were right there together neither going beyond the other.

—Emery, p. 222; McKay, p. 93

Getting to Know You (in 1892)

A contemporary draws attention to the mumbled form of introduction which takes place at dances. How many couples waltz round the ballroom with only the vaguest notion of their respective names, in consequence of the slipshod manner in which their hostess has performed the farcical ceremony which custom and Society demands. Not long since, the writer asserts, a dancing girl was thus left in ignorance of her partner's name; and though a series of circumstances subsequently brought them together several times, in not one instance was the young lady able to ascertain her admirer's cognomen. For it was quite evident that he was considerably smitten; and though she felt inclined that way herself, the rules of propriety forbade her questioning him as to his patronymic. It was getting really serious—ten minutes in the conservatory had done its deadly work, and still she only knew him as George—when, in consultation with her pal, or pal-ess, she exclaimed, "Why, just suppose if his name were Brown?" "Or Buggins," chimed in her friend, who was in the know. And, curiously enough, Buggins it was. And now, Buggins she is.

—*Dancing*, p. 88

Antony Tudor Meets Nora Kaye

The ballerina Nora Kaye was Tudor's most inspiring and devoted muse in America—the dancer for whom he made, as first among many roles, the part of Hagar in his landmark ballet *Pillar of Fire*:

The very first time I saw her was in a class. She was a girl who hit my attention. She was very strange. She had a drive. I remember the dance studio being very long and narrow. This one girl managed to keep getting right in front of where I was sitting. I thought this was rather pushing things a little, and I carefully evaded my eyes from her. It was as though I were never looking at her. Then, at one point, she settled again, right in front of me, and did five or six pirouettes on *pointe*, which I had never seen before. Of course, I made believe I didn't see it, and Nora stomped out of the class and into the dressing room. I think she swore she would never work for that so-and-so Englishman, ever. Meanwhile, I put her on the list for my next day's rehearsal call. She came in like a lamb, and, from then on, I had no trouble with her.

—Gruen, pp. 262–263

Haymaker

One of the most memorable duets that Fred Astaire choreographed for himself and Ginger Rogers was "Let's Face the Music and Dance," in the 1936 picture *Follow the Fleet*. Rogers wore a shimmering dress, fitted to make her look like a figurine; in the hems of the sleeves were weights to help them keep their shape while Rogers was in motion. At one point in the number, she turns and . . . , well, let Astaire historian John Mueller tell it:

> As Rogers spins in front of Astaire in this maneuver, her weighted sleeves pick up quite a bit of momentum. On the first take of this dance, Astaire forgot to get out of the way and was hit on the jaw and eye by a flying sleeve. "I kept on dancing," he recalls, "although somewhat maimed." At the end, Astaire was asked about the take: "I replied that I didn't remember anything about the take—that I had been knocked groggy in the first round." To compensate, they did some 20 more takes that day. The rushes the next morning showed the first take to be perfect, and so that is the one preserved on the finished film.
>
> —Mueller, page 98, n.

Manhandled

Cyd Charisse, on how her husband could tell at the end of the day whether she had been working with Gene Kelly or Fred Astaire: "If I was black and blue, it was Gene. And if it was Fred, I didn't have a scratch."

—Tractenberg, unpaginated

It Will Be Fine . . . Oops!

During the 1930s and 1940s, Eleanor Powell (1912–1982) was widely considered to be the first lady of tap in Hollywood. "One of the all-time great dancing gals," Fred Astaire wrote of her in his autobiography, *Steps in Time*. "She really knocked out a tap dance in a class by herself."

Powell and Astaire were paired in one movie, *Broadway Melody of 1940*. Although their styles, as Powell herself was the first to admit, were polar opposites ("Fred dances on the off-beat and mostly on the foot, while I am always on-beat and get most of my taps from my heel"), they co-choreographed a series of duets, including the spectacular nine-minute number to Cole Porter's "Begin the Beguine," that crystallize what two outstanding pros with different approaches can achieve when they work at it. And they worked hard: Powell's biographer, Alice B. Levin, quotes an interview that Powell gave to historian of musicals Miles Kreuger, to the effect that Astaire and Powell spent three weeks of rehearsal on their arms alone! ("So they would be right together.")

Yes, *Broadway Melody of 1940* was a movie where, in the breathless words of a reporter for *Action*, "Eleanor Powell [dances] her head off in a series of production numbers." Powell also danced a duet with George Murphy—"Between You and Me"—which *Action*, a magazine for film directors, described as "ending with swirling, partnered spin-outs, a galloping tap pattern scooting the breadth of the stage." Levin explains that, in one rehearsal, she almost danced off some other things, too:

> Of primary importance were the sets on which Eleanor was to dance. They had to be constructed to accommodate her and allow her the proper mobility. On occasion, she was not consulted during their preparation—with potentially disastrous results. For the "Between You and Me" duet, Eleanor realized during rehearsal that a ramp on which she and George Murphy were to slide was much too high for them to successfully carry out the number. Arnold Gillespie, the film's technical expert, disagreed, telling Eleanor, "No, it is not. Watch me do it. It will be fine." She observed on the sidelines while Gillespie promptly injured an ankle. The adjustment was made.
>
> —Levin, pp. 66–71

Coach

> I wasn't allowed to dance in Hollywood for about a year and a half. I had been a dancer, but nobody would give me a job to dance. But when I did, I danced with the greatest. I did two pictures with Eleanor Powell, three with Judy Garland, one with Shirley Temple, one with Kelly, one with Astaire. You can imagine my nerve; first number I did with Eleanor Powell I said, "All your numbers look alike. Let's make them all look different." So she said, "Great." What was I doing? I did turns like a hockey player. You can imagine me trying to teach her how to do hockey turns! (George Murphy)
>
> —Frank, p. 56

Strange Things Happen

In 1978, Jonathan Cott—a writer on literature and the performing arts and also a frequent contributor to *Rolling Stone*—conducted the first of two "talks" with George Balanchine. (The second took place in 1982.) They may well be the most surprising, revealing, and humorous—if not the most logically organized—conversations on record with the choreographer. What follows is one interchange about partnering from 1978:

> COTT: It's strange, though—when I see your pas de deux—especially those in *Agon, Stravinsky Violin Concerto, Duo Concertant, Pithoprakta*, I pay less attention, finally, to the fact that there's a man and a woman dancing, but rather start thinking of things like identity, personality, separation, reflections, duplications.
>
> BALANCHINE: That's right. Some people, though, see in these pas de deux only pure man-woman relationships: "The woman didn't have any guts, the man wasn't sexy enough." This isn't my business. And what you're

saying is absolutely right. Strange things happen. In the Webern [*Episodes*] pas de deux, for example, it's like a roof . . . raindrops on a crystal roof.

—Kirstein, *Portrait*, p. 138

Mr. and Ms. God

A [New York] City Ballet follower once named Balanchine's emblematic pairing of [Suzanne] Farrell and [Peter] Martins in *Chaconne* as "Mr. and Ms God." The irony of reflecting today on this witticism was lost on few Balanchine watchers, in view of the fact that Farrell's stagings were presented in Washington [D.C.], rather than in New York, because Mr. God had dismissed Ms God from City Ballet's artistic family in 1993. Officially, Martins's action came for budgetary reasons. More probably, it came because Farrell was characterized in print as being unhappy about her exclusion from the process of preparing Balanchine's ballets at the company he founded, especially in its large-scale 1993 Balanchine Celebration, as well as being dismayed at the ways in which this work was being done by Martins and his staff. Farrell's efforts in Washington continued to honor Balanchine's principles, while Martins's actions in New York further tarnish his status as Mr. God.

—Greskovic, p. 52

The Girl in the Red Velvet Swing

The lusciously beautiful Evelyn Nesbit (1884–1967) has been impersonated in such movies as the one starring Joan Collins that gives this anecdote its title and in the musical *Ragtime*, where her character, played by Elizabeth MacCracken, was part of a subplot. The events that occasioned Nesbit's notoriety took place when she was still a teenager, whose deflowering by and subsequent year-long affair with the magisterial and hedonistic Beaux-Arts architect Stanford White led her violently jealous husband, Harry K. Thaw, the son of a coal and railroad baron (as well as a sadist who beat Nesbit with a dog whip), to shoot White dead in the roof theater of the old Madison Square Garden, in 1906. Born in a small town in Pennsylvania, Nesbit had begun quite young to support her family as an artists' model, which, on moving to New York, she continued to do (with modeling stints for, among others, Charles Dana Gibson) before becoming a Florodora Girl on Broadway. After two sensational murder trials of Thaw—the first produced a hung jury; the second, in which Nesbit testified, produced a verdict of innocent by reason of insanity—Nesbit gained her divorce from him in 1915. That same year, she teamed up with Virgil James Montani, who went by the stage name of Jack Clifford, in a vaudeville act that ballroom-dance historian Julie Malnig characterizes as "sumptuous" and one of the most lucrative ballroom-dancing acts ever to play at the vaudeville theater owned by Oscar Hammerstein:

Billed as "Evelyn Nesbit and Jack Clifford in their Original Songs and Dances," the team wove exhibition ballroom numbers in between flirtatious songs and extravagant costume changes.

Their vaudeville act during the 1915-16 season typically opened with the romantic song duet "Tumble in Love" (or as one reporter called it, "a duet built about a rustic bench"), followed by a solo song by Nesbit. The act then shifted quickly to full stage, with Nesbit appearing before plush purple curtains, attired in an elegant orange gown with fur trimming. She and Clifford next performed two ballroom specialties, which they called the Evelyn Fox Trot and the Clifford Walk. The act concluded with their signature dance, an acrobatic whirlwind, in which Nesbit swung in mid-air with arms around her partner's neck.

Most critics concurred with the *New York Star* reviewer who called Nesbit and Clifford's act "a great display of talent and wardrobe." By 1917 they had begun to add flirtatious pantomime to their basic format: in a full-stage setting, Clifford mimed a monkey cavorting in a coconut tree while Nesbit sang to him. The act continued with a song-duet, followed by the usual whirlwind finish. The enormous success of the Nesbit-Clifford act can be attributed to their sense of showmanship, as well as their swift timing, elegant sets, and attire. The exhibition ballroom numbers functioned largely as specialties designed to accent the dancers and their talents.

Alas, the success didn't last long. Nesbit married Montani-Clifford in 1916; however, he abandoned her two years later. She tried to make a go of it on her own in various other show-business jobs but without much success; in 1926, she attempted suicide after losing a job as a dancer at the Moulin Rouge café in Chicago. She finally received a divorce in 1933. Her one child, Russell William Thaw (1910–2002), of whom she wrote affectionately in her memoirs, became an aviator and also sometimes appeared in movies.

At the end of her long life, Nesbit is reported to have said that "Stanny" was the only man she ever really loved.

—Malnig, pp. 59–60; *Wikipedia*; Lessard, passim.

Tradition! Tradition!

As a teenager, the French-speaking writer Tété-Michel Kpomassie—born in Togo, in 1941—one day dropped into The Evangelical Bookshop in his hometown of Lomé and fell into an illustrated volume called *The Eskimos from Greenland to Alaska* by one Dr. Robert Gessain. He bought it, and, by the next day, he had not only finished reading it but had made up his mind to travel to the Arctic to find the Eskimos himself. And over the next decade or so, that's exactly what he did, slowly working his way, first up the coast of Africa, to France, and then to Greenland, where he got as far north as Upernavik, about two thirds up the western coast of the country. *An African in Greenland*, Kpomassie's memoir of his unique odyssey—now considered a classic story of multiculturalism in practice—was first published in 1981, in Paris. The English translation was first published in 1983.

In a section on a village's celebration of its first glimpse of the sun early in January, after months of winter darkness, Kpomassie recounts his remembrance of "the most curious of Greenland celebrations" that he encountered: a dance, held in the town hall, to which no youngsters were admitted—only adult males and their wives:

> For the first time I saw coffee being served in a village hall during a dance. The women were no longer separated from the men, as they usually were, but sitting with them. I felt out of place, with everybody paired off from the start. After midnight, with great uproar and loud singing, and faces pouring with sweat, people began to exchange wives. I had read that those present at these public wife-swappings practiced what was referred to as "dowsing the lamps," but that didn't happen on this occasion. You just saw a man get up and go sit beside another couple. He talked for a few moments, then simply left the hall with the other man's wife. Sometimes this happened while the other partner was dancing. . . . Though the husbands relieved of their mates in this way gave the impression of not being too upset, it looked to me as if most of the women, if you watched closely, were only half willing. Still, like the co-wives in my native land, they seemed resigned to an age-old tradition. (James Kirkup, trans.)
>
> —Kpomassie, pp. 231–232

Casting Boronskaya

In developing the international hit movie *The Red Shoes* (1948), the co-creators Michael Powell and Emeric Pressburger began with the story, by Pressburger. Then Powell went out to find the living people who would embody the characters. The following is an account of how he came to cast the part of the "other" ballerina in the picture, a character named Irina Boronskaya:

> The part of Irina called for an impressive young dancer, a beauty, a good-humored, lazy slut, destined to become the wife of a rich, easy-going racehorse owner, by whom she would have three children. No more and no less.
>
> By now, I was so convinced of my good luck that I reckoned she would turn up, and she did—in a French film starring Louis Jouvet. There she was, sluttish and lovely, 20 years old, a face to dream about, skin like the petal of a rose, eyes like twin moons, sprawling all over M. Jouvet's bed, and apparently a dancer as well, or at any rate she danced or seemed to dance in the film, none of which I remember. What a dish! I ordered it to be brought to London. She arrived with a young man as beautiful and as

remarkable as she was—her husband, Edmond Audran, the grandson of the poet. He was the most beautiful man I have ever seen. He looked and moved like a deer, and was tall and slim with broad shoulders. Kindness and friendliness radiated from him. The word that describes him best is "lovable." He was about 24. These two beautiful human beings faced me expectantly in a hotel room. I was already more in love with Edmond than with Monique, which was how he referred to his wife, although her professional name was Ludmilla Tcherina. Her mother was French, her father a Russian general.

The part of Irina might have been written for the girl, but I asked her a few questions for politeness' sake. She and Edmond had met as ballet students, and had got married a year ago ("but we were dancing together long before that"), and now they were touring Europe as a team, going wherever engagements were offered to them. I asked them if they could get free from these engagements, and they answered with alacrity that they could. I described the part, and told her she could have it subject to agreement over money.

Edmond had been watching me closely and now spoke up. "Excuse me, Mr. Powell. What makes you so sure Monique can play this part, and in English? She speaks no English."

I said: "She can learn English. And I have offered her the part because I think she can do it, and because she appeals to me physically."

Monique giggled. Edmond made a very French face. "Ohhhhh!"

I said: "I can't work with women on any other terms."

"But if she is ugly?"

"Even an ugly woman has something attractive about her for some men."

He still looked quizzically at me. I knew that he liked me, so I said: "You'll come with her, won't you?" They looked at each other. I said: "Expenses paid, of course."

They looked at me, they looked at each other. It was touching to see them. Then we all burst out laughing, and were friends until the end of Edmond's short life.

—Powell, pp. 644–645

The Scarcity of Dancing Men

Why are there so few dancing men? This question may be heard every day from the lips of anxious hostesses and pleasure-seeking young damsels, and indeed, not without good cause, as besides the London drawing rooms there is ample proof of the state of affairs elsewhere as well. One contemporary, for instance, relates how the Cheltenham Christmas Ball revealed the usual nakedness of the land in the matter of men. There used to be a disrespectful proverb that at Cheltenham balls there were 600 women and about 16 men. Things are not quite as bad as that, for men are swept in from all parts on the eve of a ball, so as to supplement

the rather poor show of hobbledehoys and retired colonels who constitute the "men" of Cheltenham. It cannot be said that Cheltenham does
not labor zealously to attract the male element during the season, for there
was a Golf Club Ball, there is a New Year's Ball, and there are to be a
Flower Ball, a New Club Ball, a Ladies' Ball, a Bachelors' Ball, and a
Town and Country Ball in the course of the season. . . .

When men care at all about dancing, they are more fond of it even than
girls, and seldom miss a single ball they have the opportunity of going to;
in fact, there is more than one instance where young men have given up
everything else for the pleasure of dancing every night during a whole
week perhaps, but these exceptions are few and far between; the average
society man, though he may be passionately fond of cricket, golf and football, finds dancing too much trouble for him. This seems an absolute
contradiction till we enquire deeper in the subject, and the influences
under which young men have grown up and developed into manhood.
We will take Eton and Harrow for examples, as all the other schools, from
the most important down to those of small country places, follow as near
as possible the standard put down there as "the thing" for young gentlemen to do or to avoid. In both those schools, football and cricket are
compulsory recreations; dancing, of course, is entirely wanting in the program. Here we find, then, the strange anomaly peculiar to English education that football, which, even by its warmest champions, is conceded to
have a tendency towards developing brutal instincts, is made compulsory,
where dancing that teaches refinement, grace, and good manners is almost tabooed. A natural consequence of this is that the boys think nothing of dancing, which is good enough for the girls but much too effeminate
for them, the future lords of creation; and as they despise the girls because they cannot play football, so they despise dancing because the girls
can do it, and they can not. With these prejudices they go through their
school and perhaps even remain faithful to them during the years they
spend at the University, but nature will take her revenge upon the hard-
ened sinner, and punish him for his high and mightiness. Sooner or later
he would be delighted if he could only dance as girls do, but then he
discovers the difficulty. (1893)

—*Dancing*, p. 231

Beelzebub at the Ball

In *Moving Lessons*, a study of Margaret H'Doubler's introduction of dance
into the curricula of U.S. higher education in the early twentieth century,
Janice Ross discusses cultural attitudes toward dance and women in the period of H'Doubler's youth, some of which might have accounted for a scarcity of men on the dancing floor in this country. *Where Satan Sows His
Seed: Plain Talks on the Amusements of Fashionable Society*, by Milan Bertrand
Williams (mentioned below), was published in Chicago in 1896.

The evangelist M. B. Williams, while decrying the dance as "unspiritual" and "immoral," says, "It remains a physical necessity for men to attend brothels," and hence they surely will not be able to rein themselves in at dances. "Are there then no circumstances under which the modern dance is justifiable?" Williams asks in his treatise (actually a collection of three sermons against theater, dance, and drink). "A young man might dance with his grandmother," he answers sarcastically, "if she was not rheumatic."

—Ross, p. 49

Ph.D.

During the early 1950s, the Argentinian milonguero and tango choreographer Juan Carlos Copes (b. 1931) was planning to pursue a career in electronic engineering when, out of 300 entrants, he won a big dance contest. So much for engineering. Copes went on to become one of Argentina's greatest proponents of the tango and its related dances, the milonga and the tango waltz. For most of his career, his partner was Maria Nieves [Rego]—the two were married for a time—and it was Copes and Nieves who astonished the United States in the 1980s in the hit revue *Tango Argentino*, much of which Copes choreographed. Copes has also been featured in movies, such as Carlos Saura's *Tango* and Wong Kar-Wai's *Happy Together*.

In my club (late forties and fifties), one side of the dance floor was called "the capital," the other side was called "the provinces." The girls from the provinces were on one side, the girls from the capital were on the other. We, the *milongueros*, were in the center of the floor. We observed the following ritual: the beginner—for example, myself—had to dance with girl number 1, then girl number 2, and so on. The girls from the provinces were ranked from 1 to 50, the girls from the capital were ranked from 50 to 100. The girls from the capital were prettier; they all went accompanied by their mothers. The girls from the provinces went by themselves (they were somehow unprotected). But I had to dance with the number 1 first. The *milongueros* watched you and would either approve of you or not. This was an unwritten law. This was the university: I got my Ph.D. as *milonguero*.

—Collier, p. 152

Even the Cowgirl Gets the Blues

It was 1980, and we (Canada's Royal Winnipeg Ballet) were performing at Sadler's Wells in London. After dancing the lead role of the Cowgirl in Agnes de Mille's *Rodeo*, I was summoned into the presence of Sir Anton Dolin, who had been in the audience. Without so much as a "How do you do?," he blurted, "Agnes didn't OK you for that role, I know!" His tone was playful, even mischievous, without the slightest accusation.

Completely comfortable, I responded, "And how do you know that, Sir?" He said, "Because you're far too pretty. Agnes would never permit it." He kindly added that he thought I'd done a marvelous job, but he was nevertheless going to "tell" on me.

And so he did. My presence was demanded in New York City on the final day of that year. The summons was accompanied by the threat that if I did not appear, the role would be denied me. My session with Miss de Mille was an afternoon to remember. Within the first ten minutes, she pronounced me a "natural actress." From there, however, everything went rapidly down hill. I had cautioned myself to be utterly respectful and thoroughly professional. It took great effort to be calm in her presence, but I succeeded, and so well, in fact, that shortly she misconstrued my calm demeanor for self-confidence. She said, "You think very highly of yourself, don't you?" I swallowed, counted to ten, and responded, "No, Miss de Mille. In fact, I am so in awe of you that I am trying very hard to be as mature and professional as possible." This answer infuriated her further, no doubt because it was delivered with the same, stammer-free calm. We were now working on the moment in the ballet when the Cowgirl finds herself rejected, partnerless for the square dance. Miss de Mille raised her voice. "When I danced this, I cried here. So cry!" I asked for one moment, permitted myself to feel the full horror of the moment, and, as I executed the scene, dutifully cried.

After two hours, Agnes de Mille pronounced that I could never dance the Cowgirl again. Arnold Spohr, then the director of the RWB, eventually convinced her otherwise. Bless his heart. It was my favorite role. (Julie Whittaker)

—Hite, interview

A Mark, a Yen, a Buck, or a Pound

Will You Command Me to Use My Legs?

Few productions of Shakespeare's *Henry IV, Part II* (Act V, scene 5, ll. 116 ff) actually end the play where Shakespeare did: with a direct address to the audience by "a Dancer," who expresses the hope that the paying customers received full measure for the price of admission:

> Epilogue:
> *Spoken by a* Dancer.
> First my fear; then my courtesy; last my speech. My fear is, your displeasure; my courtesy, my duty; and my speech, to beg your pardons. If you look for a good speech now, you undo me: for what I have to say is of my own making; and what indeed I should say will, I doubt, prove my own marring. But to the purpose, and so to the venture. Be it known to you, as it is very well, I was lately here in the end of a displeasing play, to pray your patience for it and to promise you a better. I meant indeed to pay you with this; which, if like an ill venture it come unluckily home, I break, and you, my gentle creditors, lose. Here I promised you I would be and here I commit my body to your mercies: bate me some and I will pay you some and, as most debtors do, promise you infinitely.
> If my tongue cannot entreat you to acquit me, will you command me to use my legs? And yet that were but light payment, to dance out of your debt. But a good conscience will make any possible satisfaction, and so would I. All the gentlewomen here have forgiven me: if the gentlemen will not, then the gentlemen do not agree with the gentlewomen, which was never seen before in such an assembly.

One word more, I beseech you. If you be not too much cloyed with fat meat, our humble author will continue the story, with Sir John in it, and make you merry with fair Katharine of France: where, for anything I know, Falstaff shall die of a sweat, unless already a' be killed with your hard opinions; for Oldcastle died a martyr, and this is not the man. My tongue is weary; when my legs are too, I will bid you good night: and so kneel down before you; but, indeed, to pray for the queen.

—Shakespeare

By the Numbers

Mathilde Kschessinska (1872–1971) was prima ballerina assoluta at the Maryinsky until she and her family had to flee during the Revolution, eventually making their way to Paris. Apart from her virtuosity as a pirouettist, her ebullient stage personality, her gifts for acting, and her association with the ballets of Marius Petipa, in which she often starred, among the many offstage details for which Kschessinska is remembered are her youthful affair with the tsarevich who would become Czar Nicholas II and the treasury of jewels he bestowed on her. Kschessinska was often disparaged for wearing her jewelry on stage, even for the role of Esmeralda, a poor street dancer; however, she was hardly the first European ballerina to wear personal jewelry in performance. And, as she recounts below, in an excerpt from her charming memoir, translated into English as *Dancing in Petersburg*, even Serge Diaghilev, the standard bearer of high taste in the art of ballet, didn't attempt to dissuade her from wearing her jewels when he invited her to perform with his Ballets Russes in London in 1911 and in London, Vienna, Budapest, and Monte Carlo in 1912:

For my first performance Diaghilev advised me to appear in the pas de deux from *The Sleeping Beauty*, partnered by Nijinsky. I was very fond of this pas de deux, but in a new town and before a strange audience I should have preferred a more effective number. However, since I was sure that Diaghilev knew London better than I did, I followed his advice. He, himself, chose me a very beautiful blue costume, and together we discussed the question of the jewels I was to wear.

My diamonds and other precious stones were so valuable that they raised delicate problems. On the advice of Agathon Fabergé, the famous jeweller's son, who was also one of my great friends, I had entrusted the dispatch of my jewels to his firm, the London branch looking after them until my arrival. Two catalogues were made, and each piece of jewellery was numbered: I had only to know the numbers of the jewels I needed every evening, without giving further details. At the appointed hour an official of the firm, who was also a detective, brought them to me in my dressing-room and prevented any unauthorized person from entering; when the performance was over, he took the jewels away again.

—Kschessinska, p. 133

Thanks!

In the winter of 1994, a young Danish dancer told me the mime behind Danish curtain calls, as he had been taught it. First, the dancer raises both arms to, and looks up at, the patrons in the balcony. He then drops the left arm to his side and pulls the right arm in to his chest, hand over heart, as he humbly bows: "Thank you for appreciating my art." Then he lifts his head slightly and smiles, while raising both arms chest high and spreading them to take in the people in the Royal Theatre's most expensive seats, the orchestra's first four rows: "And thank you for paying." (Alexandra Tomalonis)

On a Silver Tray

Xenia Zarina, a ballet dancer born in Brussels and trained in Europe and the United States, traveled to India, Southeast Asia, and Japan prior to World War II to study and observe the classic dance traditions of each region. Below is her report of a performance in Cambodia, in which, as according to tradition, all the parts, including those of male characters, are taken by women. Although it has been abbreviated here, Zarina's full description is well worth seeking out in a library:

It was King Sisowath Monivong's birthday, and my brightest hope was to materialize: I was invited to the palace to see the King's dancers perform that evening. The palace walls and gardens were all charmingly illuminated. The upturning roofs and spires of all the buildings within the palace enclosure, outlined in small electric lights, looked like so many Christmas trees or a fairy city at night, so fantastic and dainty an effect they made against the dark sky. . . .

Presently the King, followed by the French Resident and Madame, his wife, and courtiers and other French and Cambodian officials came in and took their places. The guests all rose and bowed to their host, the King. The musicians then played the Cambodian national anthem and the Marseillaise. The Marseillaise, played on Cambodian instruments, sounded very well indeed, although more celestial than martial. The King and Cambodian courtiers wore the ceremonial costume: a purple silk sampot draped into trousers, and a tailored coat of white in European cut, with decorations and signia set with rubies, emeralds, and diamonds. . . .

When all were seated, the King gave friendly nods to those guests whom he recognized, sitting opposite; then refreshments were passed by servitors: tea, bonbons, and delicious petit fours. The orchestra began to play, and suddenly the floor between us and the King was filled with the most exquisite creatures imaginable. They were aglow with gold and little mirrors that flashed lights; the air was filled with the perfume of champaka flowers hanging from their golden mokots (headdresses) and from the jasmine-flower bracelets on their wrists. The features of their white-painted faces were dainty, and their expressions of expressionlessness were fascinating. . . . The "impersonal" faces were each alive with individuality—with a light that shone from within.

Attendant on the dancers, according to ancient tradition, are two old women. They represent "guardians" and pick up fallen jewels, straighten costumes, and make themselves useful in other ways during the dance. . . .

There was a love-scene on one bed-table enacted by a prince and a princess. According to tradition, the "princess," with dainty gestures and little screams, rejected the amorous advances of the "prince." The King was especially delighted with the girl, a real beauty, who played the part of the prince. He watched her, constantly smiling, and many times during the ballet beckoned to one of the two guardians, who came hurrying across the dance floor, crouching amid the dancers as inconspicuously as possible, to the King, where she knelt before His Majesty with her hands in Anjali. The King then handed her a package of money, indicating the dancer on whom he wished to bestow it. The old woman would place it on a silver tray, and crouching again inconspicuously among the dancers, would kneel before the chosen one, proffering the tray and the present. The dancer, with no sign of recognition other than a lowering of the eyes to rest for a brief second upon the offering, danced straight on. The old attendant then carried the tray and package to the exit door where the dancer would claim it after the ballet. The "princess" received such awards twice; two secondary dancers, once each; but I lost count of the kingly favors to his favorite, the "prince." The ballet lasted about two hours and was by far the most beautiful Cambodian dancing I had seen.

—Zarina, pp. 71–72

Gold Rush

Ann Miller has been quoted as saying that, when she worked in Hollywood, she knew four outstanding tap coaches there: Nick Castle, Louis DaPron, Hermes Pan (who collaborated with Fred Astaire), and Willie Covan. Covan (1897–1988)—a born dancer with a highly-oxygenated enthusiasm about his work—coached Miller, Judy Garland, Mickey Rooney, and Eleanor Powell. A member of an African American two-couple act called "The Four Covans" as a young man, Willie was a tap translator-inventor, among other things. (Iver Cooper, himself the inventor of a dance notation system, has written a precise description of how, as early as 1917, Covan was ringing changes on a step from Russian and Ukrainian dance, which Russians call "the coffee grinder" and tappers call "Around the World": "You squat on one leg and scythe the other leg around in a circle, transferring weight briefly to your hands as the scything leg comes around behind." Covan "fancied it up, eventually arriving at a double 'Around the World,' i.e., alternating the scything leg, with NO hands.")

Covan also had a most adventuresome life. By the age of six he was performing in minstrel shows; and around 1908, he and his brother, Dewey,
were touring the West in a show headed up by a Canadian-Indian singer
called *Cosie Smith and Her Six Pickaninnies*. And the Wild West it seems to
have been, as Covan remembered it in Rusty Frank's *Tap!* (a treasury of tap
memoirs with a memorable story on every page):

We played a town in Montana called Roundup. It was a real cowboy
town. Those fellows in their chaps with their guns, bringin' in horses—
this was the real West. They had never seen coloreds before. But, the
cowboys didn't care nuthin' about no prejudice. They loved the dancin'!
They'd encourage us, "yeah, come on, dance!" So after the show, a white
boy who lived in Roundup comes backstage. He was a youngster, must
have been about seventeen years old. He seen us, and he loved us! Brought
us peanuts and Cracker Jacks backstage. Say, he was crazy about us! So he
asked us, "What are you doin' after the show?" We were just gonna go
home, so we said, "Nuthin', why?" He said, "You wanna make some
money?" We say, "Yeah!" He said, "Well, I can take you to a place where
you can make some money." He had one of them old Fords, and we all
piled in.

Now, the theater was right in town. But this place must have been
seven miles out of town. We were fryin' out there, and he said, "you see
them lights out there? That's where we're goin'." It was, well, I guess
you would call it a saloon. They was gamblin' in there, carryin' on,
shootin' craps. A real Western saloon. We went in there and went up to
the bartender. He said, "What do you do?" We said, "We sing and we
dance." So we sang "Sweet Adeline." And then all the cowboys gathered
in a circle around us and we danced, and we picked up that money and
stuffed it in our pockets! We kept dancin'. They kept throwin' money!
Some of those old cowboys got so excited and were havin' so much fun
that they just picked up their guns and started shootin' around our feet!
But we weren't afraid. We just kept dancin' and singin' and pickin' up
that money. Our pockets were bulging with coins. We were flyin'! We
were a hit!

When we couldn't pick up any more money, we went outside to count
all those coins. That white boy asked us if we made any money. We said,
"Oh, yeah! We made a lot of money. Our pockets are full of pennies. We
probably made five or ten dollars—each!" Which was a lot of money in
those days. So, he said, "Take it out of your pockets and count it." I think
he was excited as we were! We began taking the coins out. And you know
what? It wasn't no pennies they was throwin' at us. It was gold! Gold
coins! We each had pockets full of gold coins! It turned out there was a
gold rush on there. But we didn't know that, we was just kids. And now
we was rich! We made eleven hundred dollars!

—Frank, pp. 25–26

Of Payrolls and Perks

The following is drawn from the memoirs of John Ebers, who, between 1821 and 1827, served as the manager of the King's Theater in The Haymarket, London—an opera house with a busy calendar of opera and ballet performances:

The Ballet department comprises a first and second Ballet-Master and the following principal performers—

First Male Dancer (at present)	Mons. Albert.
Second Do.	Mons. Gosselin.
Third Do.	– D'Aumont.
First Female Dancers,	Made. Anatole.
	Mlle. Brocard,
	Made. Le Compte.
	Mlle. Louisa.
Second Do.	Mlles. Copère

— La Vasseur.
— Angelica.
— O'Brien.
— Leilaire.

The Corps de Ballet, comprising the dancers of inferior rank, consists of 16 men and the like number of women.

Connected with the business of the stage are the
    Scene Painter and his Assistants.
    Property Man.
    Head Tailor.
    Head Mantua-maker.
    Wardrobe Keeper.
    Draper for the Men.
    Do. For the Ladies.

The dresses are, at least in the estimation of foreigners, whether in the opera or ballet, a subject of great moment, and of frequent disagreement, as every singer or dancer has an almost invincible abhorrence of sparing the treasury by making use of any dresses already in the wardrobe, however excellent, every one choosing to exercise his own taste in the adaptation of his garb.

The dresses naturally introduce the dressing-rooms, the regulation of which, as established by the usage of the theater, [is] amusingly adapted to the rank of the performers. A prima donna is entitled to a separate dressing-room, with a sofa and six wax candles; a seconda donna, a dressing-room, without a sofa, and two wax-candles. The same principle obtains with the chief male performers, and with the first and second dancers of both sexes. Ludicrous as it may seem, these marks of precedency are insisted upon with the greatest exactness. Madame Vestris went beyond all others, and furnished herself with two additional candles; and one night, there not being, by some inadvertency, candles enough in the house, she stood on the stage behind the curtain and refused to dress for her part until the required number of lights was obtained.

—Ebers, pp. 369–372

Dancers, Rehearsal Studio, Musicians, Designer, Publicist, Theater

Money is time. It's a fluid that converts into time. (Christopher Caines, choreographer)

—Aloff, interview

Respectable

Rodolpho Guglielmi was a young, blazing-eyed Castellanetan immigrant to the United States who was self-trained as a tango dancer in New York dance halls and cafés, where he functioned, in the lingo of the period, as a "gigolo." In 1917, he became involved in a rather delicate legal situation with one of his dancing companions and found himself arrested by New York's Finest on the charge of "Misdemeanor, white slave investigation." Reluctant to be classified as an undesirable alien, he decided that the better part of valor was to leave town. And so, for 75 dollars a week and traveling expenses, he joined the cast of a musical comedy called *The Masked Model*, which planned to perform its way West across the country to San Francisco. By Omaha, audiences were so small that the show closed, and each cast member was given a one-way day-coach ticket back to New York. Guglielmi decided to exhange his for a ticket to San Francisco, where, happily, he was hired to dance in the chorus line of a show called *Nobody Home*. While with that show, Guglielmi met a young movie actor named Norman Kerry at the Palace bar, to whom Guglielmi confided that *Nobody Home* was scheduled to close in three weeks, and he was worried that he hadn't lined up any jobs for after the closing. Kerry, however, sold him on the idea that Hollywood was burgeoning with opportunities for young actors, and Guglielmi—who believed in his own talent now, having been congratulated on his dancing in *Nobody Home* by Bryan Foy, of the headliner act Eddie Foy and the Seven Little Foys—moved to Los Angeles on the strength of Kerry's enthusiasm. Guglielmi soon got a bit part in a picture but was just as quickly pounding the pavement again. One late afternoon, he found himself, along with a population his biographer Irving Shulman describes as "every other unemployed actor in Los Angeles," ruminating on his bleak future:

No matter how sanguine he attempted to be about his situation, no matter what reserves of Latin optimism he drew upon, his prospects in the picture business seemed dismal. Life had become a begging for favors from arrogant little men, accepting handouts, cadging drinks and living off the free-lunch counter. These indignities convinced him he would have to turn again to dancing if he wished to obtain even a small measure of personal respectability.

By 1920, having weathered more bit parts and disappointments in his career and off stage, Rodolpho Guglielmi burst onto movie screens across America as a star in the movie *The Four Horseman of the Apocalypse*. His new name: Rudolph Valentino.

—Shulman, p. 122

A Dubious but High-Hearted and Courageous Venture

For purposes of summary, so far as ballet in our time in the Western Hemisphere is concerned, it would be well to remember that, late in 1933, to the St. James Theatre in New York—a playhouse of the Broadway type that was by coincidence a decade later to serve as the long-time home of the musical comedy *Oklahoma!*—there came, almost unsung and unheralded, a European ballet organization known as Colonel de Basil's Ballet Russe de Monte Carlo. At one of its performances, the gross receipts totaled $48.

Late in 1949, this time to the Metropolitan Opera House in New York, came, widely heralded, the Sadler's Wells Ballet of London. Practically unknown to the Western Hemisphere, after four weeks in New York and five of touring the hinterland, it gathered some $500,000 from the sale of tickets.

In 1933, such meager support as ballet had came from a handful of people composed of those who knew from experience what ballet was, a few who were sufficiently curious to wish to investigate, and a tiny, hysterical fringe of idolators from whom stalwart men flinched.

In 1956, the enormous audience that storms the doors may fairly be described as a cross-section of the American public.

In 1933, ballet was a highly speculative, dubious, but high-hearted and courageous venture, looked upon skeptically and, since it seemed something foreign to the temper and taste of the American people, generally regarded as being without a future. Today there is certainly no question about its popularity; any fear there may be for its survival springs from other sources than its public appeal. (1956)

—Deakin, pp. 184–185

Overtime for Margot Fonteyn

During one of the seasons of The Royal Ballet at the Metropolitan Opera House in New York, Jasper Johns and I were to visit Margot one afternoon in the apartment where she was staying with her family. I arrived early, and Margot, greeting me warmly, asked if I would mind waiting a few minutes until Jasper came. "No, not at all." She left the room, and I sat, gradually becoming aware of a conversation taking place in another room. The voices were loud enough for me to make out that it was concerning the approaching wedding of Margot's stepdaughter. There were references to various necessities for such an event and the costs. After further discussion, Margot said, in that clear voice: "Well, I'll just do another *Swan Lake*." (Merce Cunningham)

—Macaulay, p. 21

From the Spectacular to the Suds

May 1989. The final program of my first season as a principal dancer with the Fort Worth Ballet was entitled "A Russian Evening." Although the ballet I was most prominently featured in was danced to a selection of Brahms' waltzes, the theme was continued by the presence of Alexander Toradze— a Russian national and former Van Cliburn competition winner—who played the score from the apron of the stage.

To honor Mr. Toradze, Van Cliburn had arranged for our closing-night cast party to be held at his mansion. The house, itself, being a spectacular Tudor-styled pile of brick, it evokes nothing of Texas but would be right at home in the English countryside, that is, if the countryside had valet parking.

After being ushered inside, thankful that I had parked my Hyundai myself, I was met by Anne Bass [patron of the company], who steered me off to go find Van and Alexander.

Alex saw me coming and pushed his way through a group of Ft. Worth luminaries who had pinned him in at one of the many pianos in the house (one in every room except the kitchen and baths, in fact). After making sure I had a glass of Champagne and a plate of canapés, Alex pulled me over to meet Van.

For the next few minutes, I was praised about as effusively as possible by two men of the kind of artistic stature that I could hardly dream of attaining; Van Cliburn used the word "genius" more than once. Alexander kept insisting that there had to be some Russian blood in me somewhere, because the dramatic component of my dancing could only be Russian.

Anyway, the rest of the night was more of the same: expensive Champagne, expensive tidbits on crackers, over-the-top praise from people rich, famous, or both.

I left that party feeling about as high and mighty as I ever have in my life. Such a beautiful, wonderful feeling of satisfaction with the world and my position therein. A feeling that wasn't even completely dispelled when I punched in on my summer job less than 24 hours later—washing dishes in a greasy spoon at three bucks an hour! (Benjamin Bowman)

—Hite, interview

Sets and Stagecraft

An Idyll and a Storm

Legend has it that the most spectacular, beautiful, and refined theatrical effects ever produced for the ballet were devised in nineteenth-century Russia, at the czar's various theaters (notably the Maryinsky in St. Petersburg) and estates, where hundreds of men drawn from various branches of Russia's armed forces would be commandeered to help achieve the spectacle. Whether the effects are, indeed, supreme in dance history—the scenic designs for some seventeenth-century court ballets in Continental Europe were also elaborate and refined—they are certainly in the running.

The following stories are told by the ballerina Tamara Karsavina (1885–1978) in her memoir, *Theatre Street*. The first describes her participation, as a student at the Imperial Theater School, in an outdoor performance-ceremony at Peterhof, a summer palace. The second describes the scene of a great storm and shipwreck in the ballet *Le Corsaire*, in which Karsavina danced the lead of Medora as a member of the Maryinsky company. Many of the earlier Maryinsky spectacles were designed by Andrei Roller (1805–91); Karsavina does not specify who was responsible for these.

> In the late spring a Command Performance was given at Peterhof on the occasion of the state visit of the German Emperor. An open-air performance of the ballet *Peleus* had been elaborately prepared. Another spectacle was in readiness to be given at the Theatre in case of a wet evening. On the morning of the performance the news from the Observatory was reassuring, and it was decided to give the ballet. The spot chosen for the performance was a small island on the Peterhof lake. On this island an amphitheatre had been built backed by ruins, constructed in a previous reign, and reminiscent of a picture by Hubert Robert. The stage backed on to the lake, which stretched level with it as far as the eye could see. On

a tiny islet out on the lake a high rock had been built up, with a cave of Vulcan in the center. As the curtain rose, Vulcan, in his forge, was hammering the armour destined to be worn by Peleus. The inside of his cave was weirdly lit; sparks flew from under his hammer. The elements played their part in the general effect: summer lightning from time to time lit the sky, and a faint rumbling of far-away thunder was heard during this scene. The prologue finished with the appearance of Mars and Venus, with their suite on top of the rock. Peleus, kneeling, received his armour and befeathered helmet from the god's hands. Rosy light now flooded the stage, and Thetis surrounded by nymphs was seen gliding over the water. This beautiful illusion had been effected by a simple device—a raft with a mirror surface. Another effective entrance was that of Venus, throned high on a gilt barque and attended by cupids, pleasures, laughters, and nymphs. I was one of the cupids. We embarked some way off on the other side of the island behind the amphitheatre, and for a time drifted out of sight. At a given signal, the barge, hung with garlands of flowers, sailed into sight and landed Venus and her cortège on the stage. The arrival of the barge was well timed with the music; the whole of the performance went without a hitch. The transparent stillness of a "white night" cast a spell of unreality all round, that curious sense of detachment from time and place. A more wonderful setting for the fête could hardly have been imagined, and the spectacle would have been fit for the Court of the Roi Soleil, himself. One thing, however, worried the performers a good deal. Owing to the damp night air, all our elaborately curled wigs got somewhat disheveled, but it could hardly have been called a serious drawback to the effect of the whole.

—Karsavina, pp. 82–83

The last act [of Le Corsaire] did not require any dancing or histrionic skill, but was ever such fun for me. The whole of the scene represents a choppy sea. Under painted canvas hired sailors run on all fours. A storm breaks, and the sailors run on two legs. At the back, the Corsair's caravel pitches and rolls over a trap-door. Birbanto, leading a mutiny, treacherously attacks Conrad, and is killed by a pistol shot. Medora, still in tarlatans, now looks through a telescope, now prays on her knees.

What the stage directions were I never quite knew, but we took them to be ad libitum, and, in the heat of make-believe, rather overacted this scene and played at shipwreck like excited children. Guerdt shouted orders through the megaphone; when the caravel split and sank in two tidy halves, my female attendants and I screamed. But screams, cannon, megaphone, and orchestra were all drowned by the thunder and howling wind. The rebellious corsairs all perished with the ship, Guerdt and I, creeping low and making swimming movements, reached the wings. There I hastily put on a white chemise and let down my hair preparatory to appearing on a crag now jutting out of a quickly pacified sea. Up there, arms raised

to thank Heaven for landing us on a desert rock, we struck the final group
of the apotheosis.

—Karsavina, pp. 183–184

Pillow Walks

Merce Cunningham's 1968 masterpiece, *RainForest*, whose set, by Andy
Warhol, consists of silver pillows ballooning at various heights, drew on the
choreographer's memories of rain forests he knew from his youth in the
Pacific Northwest. "You have all this stuff around and above you," Cunningham told interviewer Robert Tracy. "You always have the sense of something over your head, and damp and wetness and lots of greenery underfoot,
and above you dripping." The set for *RainForest* is one of the most magical
ever to appear in a Cunningham work, because the pillows become a softly
glamorous abstraction of the real rain forests the choreographer had in mind
when he made the dance. Cunningham's dances don't usually offer such an
organic connection between the choreography and sets, which, like the musical scores, tend to be commissions that the designers work on in isolation
and that aren't brought together with the dancing until the first performance.
But, as Cunningham explains below, in *RainForest* he took an unusually active part in selecting the set. At the time, the painter Jasper Johns was in
charge of set design for the Cunningham company:

> I saw Andy Warhol's pillows at the first exhibition of them in New York.
> Andy called them "Silver Clouds." I thought they were wonderful. There
> was something engaging about them. Later, when I was beginning to work
> on a dance, it occurred to me it would be marvelous to have them on
> stage because of their extraordinary quality. I spoke to Jasper Johns about
> it, and I can't remember whether Jasper asked Andy or I did. We said,
> "Would it be all right to use them as a set?" and Andy said, in his own way,
> "Oh, sure. Great! Wonderful."
>
> Right from the start when I first saw them I thought they would be
> remarkable in a stage space because they fill the space, but they are not
> heavy. They are also animated. They can move. Sometimes they don't
> [laughter], but they can. The first time we did the dance *RainForest* was at
> Buffalo, New York, and that was a fairly small stage. Jasper was there, and
> he placed them, saying, "It shouldn't look like a bubble bath." [laughter]
> We didn't use any colored lights because that would have made it seem
> like a disco.

Cunningham also essentially designed the costumes for *RainForest* (leotards
and tights that have been gashed, so that the dancers' skin shows through),
another atypical aspect of the work:

> I don't think Andy was interested in costumes. He thought we should be
> nude. That wasn't practical, so Jasper and I talked about it, and I had this

idea of torn flesh—like when the skin gets hit by vines in a rain forest. Scratched. If one lives in that environment, it is something one would be used to. Jasper did the original cutting on the costumes while the dancers wore them.

—Tracy, "Bicycle," p. 57

Big Pictures

Real Stars in Real Skies

Some modern scholars have suggested that the dance may be the oldest of all the arts of man. The Greeks, being a people of great intellectual curiosity, also speculated upon the antiquity of the art, and upon how it all began. Lucian is one of the ancient writers who trace dancing all the way back to the time of the creation of the universe and the appearance of Eros, god of love. These writers, observing the rhythmical movements of the planets in the sky, regard them as constituting a cosmic dance. It is interesting in this connection that Urania, divine patroness of astronomy, was also one of the Muses, patronesses of the dance. Libanius, following Lucian, elaborates on the idea of a dance of heavenly bodies, but speaks also of the gods as "fathers of the dance"; they inspire men to assume various characterizations in their dances, he says, even as the gods assume shapes and bodies of all sorts in their divine activities. He implies that the Muses, too, who habitually dance "with soft feet" on Mount Helicon, had a share in the creation of the dance. Another writer attributes the invention of the dance to the Muse Polyhymnia; and the Muse Terpsichore, whose particular province is the graceful art, and whose very name means "joy in the dance," is also associated closely with its early development.

—Lawler, pp. 12–13

All in the Family

10 February 1640 was the birthday of Madame Royale, the Duchess Christina of Savoy, sister of Louis XIII and widow of the Duke Victor Amadeus I. That year it was celebrated at the castle of Chambéry by a ballet entitled *Hercules and Love*, invented by her counselor and devoted friend, Count

Filippo Aglié. There is a marvelous pictorial record of this princely spectacle, as indeed of all Savoy fêtes for over 20 years, preserved in a series of
volumes written and illuminated by one Tommaso Borgonio. In the ballet, Duchess Christina saw her own son, the little Duke Charles Emman-
uel, play the part of Love attired in a wonderful costume of cloth of gold
and silver, with diminutive wings sprouting from his shoulders, an absurd bunch of multi-colored ostrich plumes on his head, and clutching a
tiny bow and arrow. Not only did she have the delight of seeing her son
dance for her, but her 11-year-old daughter arrived later in the ballet in a
ship, along with other court ladies dressed as Cypriots, having voyaged
from that island, the haven of Love, to pay tribute to the Duchess and
offer her greetings on her birthday.

—Strong, p. 3

The Art of Being Itself

From a review by Edwin Denby of a New York season by the Ballet Russe de
Monte Carlo, in the November–December 1941 issue of *Modern Music*:

The ultimate, inexcusable worst in local stage design was the third
première, *The Magic Swan*, an act resurrected out of *Swan Lake* (Petipa-
Tchaikovsky). There seemed to be some unhappy misunderstanding in
this production about what constitutes classic dancing. Such fine dancers
as Mladova, Rostova, in fact a whole string of soloists of both sexes, appeared as smooth and languid as ballroom performers. And then, exactly
on this subject, *Magic Swan* brought a magnificent revelation: Toumanova
in her pas de deux and finale with Eglevsky. Her classicism doesn't express any emotion; it is passionately just itself. Her incredibly swift tiny
battements on the ankle are somehow magnified so that the moment fills
the whole opera house. There is no being nice to the audience; there is
no letting go of them either. When she dances it is a matter of life and
death. Dancing can be other things than this, but I don't see how it can be
any greater. . . .

—Denby, *Dance Writings*, p. 81

Pinnacle of Achievement

Iris Morley:

Among students in the graduating class of the Bolshoi, it is not uncommon to see the classic parts danced with a good deal more attack than
feeling. However, if a dancer is talented and properly trained, a stage of
physical perfection is reached in the early twenties, when the body becomes an instrument for expressing the most subtle moods of music or
drama, and every achievement appears quite effortless.

I saw this happen in the young Plisetskaya when she was about 21 and danced *Les Sylphides* as if to the romantic manner born, a materialization of the Chopin music, and also in Kondratov when he was about 27. I think it true to say that male dancers usually reach this stage later than female ones, and it is something which progressively becomes richer and deeper up to the age of about 40. Finally, on the pinnacle of achievement we see Semyonova dancing *Swan Lake* or Ulanova *Giselle*.

—Manchester, p. 30

Unforgettable

Galina Ulanova (1910–1998), the twentieth-century Bolshoi ballerina whose very name has become a byword for spirituality and integrity in Russian ballet, was trained in Leningrad at what is now called the Vaganova School, from which Ulanova graduated on March 18, 1928. Each March 18, to commemorate that momentous occasion, the Galina Ulanova Foundation puts on a special program at the Bolshoi Theater. The programming for the evening looks back to its inspiration, presents awards to outstanding working artists of the current generation, and looks forward to young dancers currently on the threshold of a career. In 2005, Clement Crisp, the dance critic for London's *Financial Times*, traveled to Moscow to attend the Ulanova event. It was, for him, a moment of deep personal significance: "I know that the opening night of the Bolshoi season in London in 1956, which showed us Ulanova's Juliet, is the most important, most tremendous of all the thousands of evenings I have sat watching dance of every kind," Crisp wrote in his report. However, he also observed that, for the Russian people, Ulanova's importance went beyond the theater:

Perhaps the most touching tribute of all came when Vladimir Vasiliev spoke of a letter Ulanova received during the [Second World] war from "Soldier Alexander Dorogush": "Dear Galina Sergeyevna: a photograph of you in *Swan Lake* stands on the table in our dug-out. The photograph bears the traces of fascist bullets. We found it in a village from which, two days ago, we ousted the enemy. Now, every day, we place flowers before your photograph." Another letter, from a terribly wounded soldier, said: "I survived only because I had your unforgettable images stored in my memory." No other tribute to Ulanova's significance, or the dignity of her art, is needed.

—Crisp

An Instantaneous String of Firecrackers

Dance critic Arlene Croce:

So far, if I'd had to give my scalp for one ticket, I'd have given it for *Les Patineurs*. In this transcendent Baryshnikov performance (which, alas

for the scalpers, he gave exactly twice), one didn't have to wait around
for him to dance. Each appearance was an instantaneous string of fire-
crackers, a flaring up of incalculable human energy in its most elegant
form. The Ashton ballet, thirty-eight years old, is still a model of construction. The central role is so well designed that a dancer can get by
on neat execution alone. Baryshnikov embellished it like a bel-canto
tenor, and as often happens, he made the choreography look as if he had
invented or at the least inspired it. A now famous Baryshnikovism, the
split tour-jeté, looked right for the first time in the context of this ballet
about ice skaters, and Baryshnikov produced the step as none of his
imitators so far have done—coming out of a double air turn. Curiously,
in the performance I saw (the second of the two), the role had none of
the brash extrovert character that is associated with it. It had instead a
sense of spiritual dissociation, as if the Green Skater's isolation were to
be attributed to his genius. He—the "character" as Baryshnikov assumed
it—suggested a boy who builds dynamos in his attic; he had that kind of
tragic happiness.

—Croce, pp. 81–82

"I Love Life!"

As a child, I knew I had one great possession: my body. It was little and
quick. I lived within it. I looked out of it with my eyes, my irises, and that
was also my name, Iris—like the flower, like the rainbow, and like my
eyes. I'd wake up in the morning, excited, ready to go out and look at the
world. Breakfast would only slow me down. I wanted to leap into the
empty lots outside our windows just as soon as I could and see what had
happened overnight. I'd say to my mother, "I love life!" As an adult, I met
people who talked passionately about their new Rolls-Royce. But that
isn't a real possession. All we actually have is our body and its muscles
that allow us to be under our own power, to glide in the water, to roll
down a hill, and to jump into someone's arms. (Allegra Kent [née Iris
Cohen])

—Kent, *Once*, p. xi

Brilliantly in the Darkness of the Night

The Japanese novelist and diarist Lady Murasaki (born ca. 973), author of
The Tale of Genji, served, in her widowhood, as a lady-in-waiting during Japan's
Heian era, a time of comparative political stability and cultural efflorescence.
It was also a period of extensive diary-keeping by women at court, whose
writing exhibited a highly developed literary style that was marked by nu-
ance, delicate reporting, and exquisite irony. (Sei Shonegan, author of *The
Pillow Book*, was one of Lady Murasaki's contemporaries.) The following
anecdote from Lady Murasaki's diary concerns a group of young girls (about

ten years of age) who attended the four "Gosechi dancers," who performed for the emperor during an annual four-day festival. This passage reports on the ceremonial entrance at court of the dancers, each the daughter of a nobleman and each of whom was accompanied by some ten little attendants:

The Gosechi dancers arrived on the twentieth. Her Majesty presented her adviser Sanemari with dresses for his dancer. She also gave Kanetaka, Adviser of the Right, the cord pendants that he had requested. We took the opportunity to give them both some incense in a set of boxes with artificial plum branches attached as decoration, to spur on their rivalry. I knew full well how hard the young dancers had prepared this year in comparison to normal years, when things were usually done in such a hurry, so, as they entered the glare of the torches that lined the standing screen opposite Her Majesty's rooms on the east side—they were more exposed than they would have been in broad daylight—all I could think of was what a dreadful ordeal it must be for them. The same misfortune had been visited on us as well, of course, but at least we had been spared the torches and the direct stares of the senior courtiers, for we had been surrounded by curtains to ward off the curious. In general, however, we must have presented a similar spectacle. I shudder to recall it.

The ladies in attendance on Narito's dancer wore brocade jackets that stood out brilliantly, even in the darkness of the night. They wore so many layers they seemed to have difficulty in moving, so the senior courtiers did what they could to help them. His Majesty came over to watch from our side of the building, and his Excellency stole over as well and stood to the north of the sliding door; this was rather inconvenient, since it meant we could not do exactly as we wished.

The attendants for Nakakiyo's dancer were all chosen to be exactly the same height and were pronounced to be every bit as magnificent and splendid as their rivals. Those in the Adviser of the Right's party had arranged everything perfectly; they even included two cleaning maids, whose very stiffness made them seem a little provincial, bringing a smile to everyone's lips.

Last in line was the party belonging to Adviser Sanemari. Perhaps I was imagining things, but they all appeared particularly well dressed. There were ten attendants. The hems of their robes cascaded out from beneath the blinds, which had been lowered in the outer gallery. The effect was not ostentatious: on the contrary, they looked extremely attractive in the glow of the lights. (Richard Bowring, trans.)

—Murasaki, pp. 37–38

More than Flesh

Many editors have put together collections of poems related to dance. Perhaps the best anthology—*The Dance, the Dancer, and the Poem*—was compiled by the poet Jack Anderson, who for several decades has also contributed dance reviews and essays to *The New York Times* and authored books on the-atrical dancing, notably *The One and Only: The Ballet Russe de Monte Carlo*. Anderson's bouquet of dance poetry, published as a monograph by the periodical *Dance Perspectives*, includes this delicate and thoughtful poem on ballet by the English novelist Thomas Hardy (1840–1928), better known for his dour fictional masterpieces than for his theatergoing:

The Ballet
>They crush together—a rustling heap of flesh—
>>Of more than flesh, a heap of souls; and then
>>>They part, enmesh
>>>And crush together again,
>>Like the pink petals of a too sanguine rose
>>>Frightened shut just when it blows.

>>Though all alike in their tinsel livery,
>>And indistinguishable at a sweeping glance,
>>>They muster, maybe,
>>>As lives wide in irrelevance;
>>A world of her own has each one underneath,
>>>Detached as a sword from its sheath.

>>Daughters, wives, mistresses; honest or false, sold, bought;
>>Hearts of all sizes; gay, fond, gushing, or penned,
>>>Various in thought
>>>Of lover, rival, friend,
>>Links in a one-pulsed chain, all showing one smile,
>>>Yet severed so many a mile!

—Anderson, p. 12

Champagne

Edwin Denby:

Agon, a ballet composed by Igor Stravinsky in his personal twelve-tone style, choreographed by George Balanchine, and danced by the New York City Ballet, was given an enormous ovation last winter by the opening night audience. The balcony stood up shouting and whistling when the choreographer took his bow. Downstairs, people came out into the lobby, their eyes bright as if the piece had been Champagne. Marcel Duchamp, the painter, said he felt the way he had after the opening of *Le Sacre*. At later performances, *Agon* continued to be vehemently applauded. Some people said the ballet set their teeth on edge. The dancers showed nothing but coolness and brilliantly high spirits.

—Denby, *Dance Writings*, p. 459

The Greatest Tribute

Two of the most impressive moments I ever remember in the theater in connection with the dance were linked with Anna Pavlova. The first was at the old Trocadero in Paris, a building now pulled down. This huge concert hall was packed from floor to ceiling with an audience of at least 4,000 people for a Pavlova evening, and after she had danced *Le Cygne* she was given the greatest tribute that a performer can receive—those three or four seconds of perfect and complete silence—silence in which the proverbial pin could have been heard had it dropped—before the tumultuous applause broke out. She danced *Le Cygne* three times that night. (Philip J. S. Richardson)

—Franks, p. 67

Shangri-La

Ballet is a "never never land" of make believe—to be enjoyed by those fortunate enough to be initiated. Let us never destroy that Shangri-La, lest we disturb the immortal spirit that must be sleeping there. (Laurent Novikov)

—Franks, p. 97

Of Taste and Rhythm

Let us endeavor to sing *purely* and to dance *beautifully*. (Patricia N. McAndrew, trans.)

—Bournonville, *My Theater Life*, p. 136

"Oh God. What Is Going to Happen?"

Glen Tetley, who went on to become a choreographer, danced for Martha Graham between 1956 and 1958. He created the role of the Stranger (i.e., the Serpent) in her *Embattled Garden*:

Embattled Garden was in pieces when I stepped into rehearsal. Martha would come in, get into the choreography, but then there would be a block. She would leave it. Often we would be called for 7 o'clock, after evening class, to be ready for an 8 o'clock rehearsal. Martha would come by maybe 9:30 or 10 o'clock, and she would stand at the back and lean against the wall. She would say, "All right, start."

I remember one evening she came in and she was in street clothes, immaculately dressed. I was up in the Noguchi "tree of knowledge"—actually a large phallus, I discovered, when we were in the theater and I went out front and saw it from a distance. It faced a platform in the stylized form of a pelvis. Martha had me jump from this tree. She had me jumping from what seemed like an enormous height. Yuriko was combing her hair, and I would grab Yuriko and pull her into a runaway rape. Martha yelled, "Stop! Stop!" She looked at me, "Get up into your tree." And she said to Yuriko, "I will be Eve. Give me the comb." Martha said to me, "You jump out of the tree and you embrace me. You don't kiss me on the cheek, you kiss me here, on the chest," slapping herself between her breasts. I thought, "Oh God. What is going to happen?" I had never physically touched Martha. So the music started. She was in her beautiful tailored dress and her famous bun. I thought to myself, "Here goes everything." I jumped out of the tree, and I ran over and grabbed Martha, pulling her into the movement. Martha grabbed me like a tiger, pushing herself against me. It was all very ecstatic and spasmodic, and I remember her whole bun falling out and her hair falling down. Finally she stood up, completely flushed, and she said, "*That* is the Garden of Eden."

—Tracy, *Goddess*, pp. 260–261

Incomparable

Despite clerical bans on dancing that go back over 1,000 years, Hungary has enjoyed a long, vigorous, and inventive tradition of social dancing among the general population, courtiers, and, notably, warriors. The pride and prowess of the steps in many dances indicate their origins in folk dancing by men. In *Dances of Hungary*, the illustrator George Buday notes that "one of the earliest references to dancing is by the monk of St. Gall, the chronicler Ekkehard, who describes Hungarian soldiers who fought near Lake Constance as dancing 'jubilant with joy' before their leaders." During the sixteenth and seventeenth centuries, Buday explains, the most popular Hungarian folk dance was the Hajdutánc, described by traveling English physician Edward Brown, who witnessed it in 1669, as a dance with unsheathed swords, whose owners were "clashing the same, turning, winding, elevating, and depressing their bodies with strong and active motions . . . singing withal unto their measures." (Buday also writes that "we learn from records of the great peasant revolution in 1514 . . . of the shocking end of the revolutionary leader, burnt to death by the barbaric nobles who forced his comrades to dance the Hajdutánc round their dying chief.")

Buday goes on to describe wedding dances, work dances, and also the eighteenth-century Verbunkós or Verbunks—"recruiting dances" for the French wars—which were performed by hussars, who would go into a village, hoist a flag, and begin to dance in a circle, alternating slow figures with fast ones. Villagers who were attracted by the dancing and general jollity to enlist would join the circle, and the dancing would continue as long as it took to muster the required number of recruits. "The national introduction of the Verbunk coincided with the revival of national literature and aspirations," Buday writes, "and soon Hungarian musicians were composing music for it, while foreign composers such as Haydn, Beethoven, Berlioz, and Brahms fell captive to its rhythm."

In his memoirs, Berlioz records how he fell in love with Hungarian dancing during two balls he attended while visiting Pesht in 1846:

> I have not seen anything to compare with these balls: on the one hand the
> incredible luxury of them, on the other the brilliantly exotic native cos-
> tumes and the proud beauty of the Magyar race. The dances are quite un-
> like anything seen in the rest of Europe. Our chilly French quadrilles are
> almost unknown; the mazurka, the tarsalgo, the keringo, and the czardas
> reign joyously supreme. The czardas in particular, a polished version of the
> rustic dance which Hungarian peasants perform with such wonderful aban-
> don and energy, seemed in high aristocratic favor, notwithstanding the fears
> expressed in a newspaper article by an ill-omened critic, who claimed that
> the attitudes and movements of the czardas were a trifle indecorous, liken-
> ing them—erroneously, in my opinion—to the irregularities of that un-
> mentionable dance lately banned by the Paris police [possibly the can-can].
> Imagine the reception he must have got when he showed his face at the ball
> after the article appeared! One can just picture the barrage of protests, the
> splendid eyes flashing in indignant scorn. (David Cairns, trans.)
>   —Buday, pp.7–19; Berlioz, pp. 418–419

An Instantaneous and Agreeable Act of Life

But the pleasure of dance does not lie in its analysis, though one might
sometimes be led to think otherwise. Dancing is a lively human activity,
which, by its very nature, is part of all of us, spectators and performers
alike. It's not the discussion, it's the doing and seeing—of whatever kind.
As an adolescent I took lessons in various forms of ballroom. But my
teacher insisted there was not such a thing as just "tap"; there was "the
waltz clog," "the southern soft shoes," "the buck and wing," and all were
different, and she would proceed to show us how they were different.
The rhythm in each case was the inflecting force that gave each particular
dance its style and color. The tempo for a slower dance, for instance,
allowed for a certain weight and swing and stopping of the arms that wasn't
indicated in a faster dance. These lessons eventually led to performances
in various halls as the entertainers for local events and finally a short and
intoxicating "vaudeville tour." I remember one of these situations when
we (there were four of us) stood huddled and cold in a sort of closet that
was the lone dressing room, behind the tiny platform that was the stage
this time, and our teacher was in the front of the hall making last-minute
preparations. Finally, she hurried back, took one look at the four of us,
and smiled and said, "All right, kids, we haven't any make-up, so bite your
lips and pinch your cheeks, and you're on." It was a kind of theater energy and devotion she radiated. This was a devotion to dancing as an instantaneous and agreeable act of life. All my subsequent involvements
with dancers who were concerned with dance as a conveyor of social

message or to be used as a testing ground for psychological types have not succeeded in destroying that feeling Mrs. Barrett gave me that dance is most deeply concerned with each single instant as it comes along, and its life and vigor and attraction lie in just that singleness. It is as accurate and impermanent as breathing. (Merce Cunningham, 1952)

—Vaughan, p. 87

Hopsichordist

Dance critic Tobi Tobias:

Savion Glover is more than the greatest tap dancer of his generation. He's a phenomenon—as a technician, an inventor, and a compelling presence. He's been going from strength to strength since he was, at 12, the tap dance kid. His latest project, *Classical Savion*, has him strutting his stuff to music by Vivaldi, Bach, Bartók, and Mendelssohn, with Astor Piazzolla thrown in for seasoning. Then, just in case you were missing tap's more conventional accompaniment, Glover offers that as a finale, integrating the classical musicians—young enthusiastic academy virtuosi led by Robert Sadin—into the suave proceedings of his familiar partners, The Otherz, a handful of jazzmen who couldn't be more mellow.

The stage provides Glover with a wide, miked wooden platform, the musicians ranged in curving tiers behind it, as if to hold the dancer in their embrace. Looking a decade younger than his 31 years, Glover enters wearing formal black evening jacket and trousers with a cantaloupe-colored shirt (untucked, unbuttoned at the neck and cuffs) and a black bow tie (untied). The costume suggests a rebellious guy who's fully aware of the grown-up dress code for concert performance and complies, all the while adamantly reasserting his own identity. His luxurious dreads are caught up in a low pony tail; he sports a beard that makes you think Abraham Lincoln.

In the course of what may be the longest vigorous solo stint in Western dance history, he'll shed the jacket so that you can watch the shirt darken as it soaks up his sweat. In the course of the show, he'll change the shirt a couple of times to a fresh one of a different hue, leaving the subsequent shirts open to reveal a white singlet, adding a bead necklace—all this a gradual return to the image of a slouchy street kid. Eventually he dances clutching his water bottle in one hand and, in the other, the black hand towel with which he mops his face. In the wake of his movement, the towel flares like a quietly menacing flag.

Like his costume, his stage demeanor slowly and inexorably reverts to a state that seems natural to his identity. Glover used to be a glum, deeply introverted performer. His refusal to make eye contact with his audience looked, to viewers expecting an ingratiating entertainer, both neurotic and hostile. He's lightened up some in the last couple of years. He's learned to smile, and his smile is delicious if still somewhat surreptitious. A quarter of

the way through the program, though, he begins to lose his apparent re-
solve to look his public in the face. Performing to an excerpt from Bach's
Brandenburg concerti, he dances largely with his back to the audience, as
if he were directing his efforts to the harpsichordist positioned upstage,
or in profile, eyes averted from the house. Maybe it's time, I'm thinking,
to quit asking him for something different. The fierce inward focus of his
dancing suggests that he's delving deep into himself, and it's not our love
he's after but the achievement of ecstasy. Let him be; after all, he does
take us along with him.

Now for what really counts—the dancing. Here's what I notice most:
energy (which seems to be part physical, part passion); control (tap is,
among other things, a balancing act); a rhythmic acuity operating at genius level; a sly wit. Glover can, and often does, make a big ferocious
sound, savage and blunt, the noise of a bad boy in the throes of a singu-
larly destructive tantrum. At other loud moments he becomes a one-man
artillery attack, all lethal precision. He juxtaposes his Orange Alert work
with cascades of slow lustrous tapping (sensuousness in the abstract) or a
tiny, quiet babble of taps that might come from small animals or even
insects busily at work on a spring morning. Sometimes he rides the music; sometimes he becomes one of the instruments in the ensemble; sometimes he converts the score into a concerto in which he alternately plays
solo and blends back seamlessly into the group.

He's his own choreographer, of course, and his invention is wide-rang-
ing and seemingly inexhaustible. I can't count the number of things I
hear (and see) Glover's feet accomplish that I've never been privy to before. The improvisatory air of everything he does is invigorating, and the
conversation his feet conduct with the floor is probably the most fascinating dialogue I'll hear all year.

—Tobias, "Going"

Lies in the Service of Artistic Truth

Paul Taylor:

I grew up watching for the telling movement, both animals' and humans',
as I suppose, but have never known for sure, all children do. To see a
truth, you also have to spot a lie. I eventually appreciated the artistry of a
movement lie—the guilty tail wagging, the overly steady gaze, the phony
humility of drooping shoulders and caved-in chest, the decorative-look-
ing little shuffles of pretended pain, the heavy, monumental dances of
mock happiness. It is said that the body doesn't lie, but this is wishful
thinking. All earthly creatures do it, only some more artfully than others.
It's just a matter of degree. And although there is much to admire in the
beauty of natural movement, much to derive from a pedestrian's smallest
gesture, the most communicative dances, in my opinion, are those based
on physical truths that in the making have been transformed for the stage
into believability by the artistry of calculated lies.

—Taylor, p. 31

Powers

Lincoln Kirstein:

But tell me about it," she begged. "Tell me all about it. Who is this Russian? Are the dances his?"

"Diaghilev?" asked Roger. She nodded. Why I don't know much about him. Of course he has a curious reputation."

"So you said." She looked at him. "What sort of a reputation?"

"Well, he never has any money, and yet from year to year he goes on and gives the ballet and commissions painters and musicians and they seem to work for him."

"Well, that seems very shrewd," said Christine. "Don't they ever get paid?"

"Why, sometimes they do I guess, but not very much. But often if you have a ballet done by Diaghilev it makes your name."

"Well, I think that's fine," said Christine. "What's the matter with that?"

"Nothing," said Roger. "He's got very strong personal connections with everybody that works for him. I mean they work well because they like him."

"I see," she said, "one of those men who devours people's talent."

"Not at all," said Roger, "he makes them use it in the best way. Or at least he can get them to work better for him than for anyone else."

"Just because they like him," asked Christine.

"I guess that's as good reason as any," said Roger. "Sometimes they happen to be used up. They go out like a light. But it was marvelous while it lasted."

"And he has power to destroy people?" asked Christine.

"More than that. He creates them."

—Kirstein, *Flesh*, pp. 152–153

The Tree of Dance

When I was a child, I heard about a kind of enormous water lily—it was called Victoria Regina—that opens only once every hundred years. It's like wax, and everything is in there, everything lives . . . by itself, and it doesn't tell anybody anything. It goes to sleep and then comes back again. It doesn't say: "Look at me, now I'm going to wake up, I'm going to jump. . . . Look, Ma, I'm dancing!" But if you happen to be around, and are ready, you'll probably see something.

It's like the time capsule with everything in it. Or like the seed that, when you plant it, becomes an enormous tree with leaves and fruit. Everything was in that little seed, and so everything can open. The tree of dance is like that. It just takes a long, long time to blossom. (George Balanchine)

—Kirstein, *Portrait*, p. 140

Afterword:
A Note on Anecdotes
as Ingredients of
Dance History

Here are some stories you won't find in this book:

Scenarist-poet A asks impresario B what he wants in the theater, and B replies, "Astonish me!" (a command that has had a baleful effect on subsequent generations of experimentalists who were not making dances for impresario B). Choreographer C likes to tell his dancers, "Don't think; do" (which has been consistently and even perversely misinterpreted ever since). Mutually envious ballerinas D and E (and/or their mothers, D' and E') put ground glass in one another's toe shoes. Choreographer F succumbs to alcoholism. One day, choreographer G gets his comeuppance from the Broadway cast he had been screaming at when he backs up during a stage rehearsal to the edge of the orchestra pit, no one tells him how close he is to the edge, and he falls in. Ballerina H, one of the twentieth century's outstanding Giselles, literally goes mad in her hotel room. Choreographer I makes dancers cry during rehearsals. As for the revelation about choreographer J and the melon, fuhgeddaboudid! These and similar anecdotes, now so famous in the dance world (and, in some cases, the wider world as well) that they have more or less reduced their subjects to caricature only, you can find on your own. If you have any interest in dance, you've already supplied all the names above. And if dancing isn't your meat, then you won't miss them.

Anecdotes, like gossip—and, sometimes, the two seem indistinguishable—are varieties of history. Once considered minor varieties, they have, in our era, been elevated to major sources of news. However, their reporting is frequently suspect as unreliable, and the first element in them to breed skepticism is the tidy punch line: they have come to be identified exclusively with jokes. And yet, the term "anecdote" has two dictionary definitions. One is a humorous story; the other is something unpublished, or, by extension, secret.

For most readers outside dance, the history of dance itself is what seems to be the secret, and I was guided by that in putting together this collection. I resisted including anecdotes or apothegms whose only point was the easy laugh; or the smirking delights of schaudenfreude, the pleasure at another's misfortune; or the celebration of celebrity for its own sake. Instead, I tried to choose entries that would, even in a tiny way, contribute to a dancer's sense of identity as part of a lineage, that would treat the subjects as real people rather than icons, and that emphasized firsthand experience. Once these were amassed, my principal reason for including something was that I liked it: this is a very personal book, and its bibliography is far from scholarly. Indeed, it does not represent even a tenth of the sources I consulted for this anthology. In poking around libraries, interviewing colleagues (and, in the case of several anecdotes, relying on interviews by Emily Hite), and keeping my ears open over fifteen years, I've gathered a library's worth of possible stories. There is plenty of room for someone else to research a collection of dance anecdotes that does not overlap this one by a single entry.

Most of the entries in this collection have narratives, although not all. A few passages by historians and critics are included. If the subjects were still on the scene, I chose stories that I wouldn't be embarrassed or disheartened to hand to them personally to read. This cuts out the more vicious or lubricious possibilities, and I encountered a number of them in my research. When in doubt about including something, I considered whether I'd want to tell the story myself to someone I cared for—not a very sophisticated yardstick, admittedly, yet an honest representation of my feelings about dance, which has given me countless hours of wonderment and pleasure.

The news that stays news in these stories and sayings isn't necessarily a factual account of a particular situation, although sometimes the anecdotes do feel as if they can be trusted in that way. More important, though, is whether they provide some insight into a way of thinking and acting. I wanted a collection of stories that, regardless of their value as reporting, contain an element of the motivation to go on dancing, when there is every reason in the world to stop. They tend to be telling, rather than exclusively amusing. And what they disclose, sometimes directly, sometimes elliptically or mysteriously, sometimes with cheer, often with a latent sadness, is the dancer's inevitable battle with the effects of passing time on the body. For a dancer, who always faces the prospect of two deaths—the first being retirement, frequently at an age when his or her nondancing agemates are just starting their life's work—there is never enough time.

Consider the following example, related by dance historian Don McDonagh some years ago in conversation:

"One day, the Argentinian choreographer Hector Zaraspe was in a plane, flying to take a job. While en route, he decided to brush up on the fingering of his castanet routines—sans castanets. Putting his hands under the airline blanket during the long trip, he began to go through the motions. Eventually, he became aware that the stranger in the next seat kept staring at his lap.

"Zaraspe could not resist. Turning to the dumbfounded observer, he said, 'It is more difficult with castanets.'"

Even though the story has been polished into a neat joke, it retains the ring of truth. The classic confusion of dancing and sex on which the anecdote turns is both silly and flattering, although, in other times and places, similar misunderstandings have had much graver results. What makes the confusion charming here is the discrepancy between the dancer's work and the observer's perception of play—which is, of course, exactly the effect that the work of rehearsing is supposed to produce. What could have been a moment of blushing embarrassment has been transformed by Zaraspe's quick riposte, by his exercise of wit, into a grace note about technique.

Now, consider this anecdote, also about castanets. It is attributed to Antonia Rosa Mercé y Luque (1888–1936), the aristocratically avant-garde and widely admired twentieth-century exponent of Spanish dancing, called "La Argentina" for her country of birth, whose castanet technique was considered practically Mozartean:

"When I was little, barely five, I constantly heard castanets in my parents' house, as they taught dance lessons. This anti-musical sound irritated me to the point where I hid in the farthest room of the house to escape its echo. There, I practiced my girlish fingers on a pair of little castanets that my father had given me. I was forcing myself unconsciously (since, at that age, one doesn't reason) to get sounds out of that instrument, sounds that would not hurt my ears like the others. Those were my beginnings in the art I now practice, and I can very well say that the liking I took to my castanets followed my dislike of the castanets of others."

This story isn't funny in the sense of a joke with a punch line, although the image of the little girl running away from the sound of battering castanets in order to build her own musical world has a certain wry charm that borders on the amusing. Still, to me, the significant difference between the anecdotes of Zaraspe and La Argentina is that the first is situational and generic, that is, it distinguishes the art the dancer practices from other, nonartistic behavior, while the second is essential and defining of a particular artist. However, because this second kind of anecdote is offered as an element in the construction of an individual's artistic identity, one asks harder questions of it than one does of the first kind. Is La Argentina's story true in the sense that each of its details could be fact-checked? And, does the issue of whether it is reported as the event it describes actually happened *matter* to the story's value as a tool to help readers in 2006 understand the perspective of an artist a century before? Mercé's most recent biographer, Ninotchka Bennahum, who quotes the story in *Antonia Mercé "La Argentina": Flamenco and the Avant Garde* (pp. 31–32), notes that the anecdote's original souce is a 1932 interview in a London newspaper. At this distance from both Mercé and her British interviewer, we have no way of independently testing whether the story of the five-year-old is a fully verifiable account of what happened when the dancer was little; or if it was a memory constructed in adulthood by Mercé from fragments of other memories, used to justify the dancer's mature aesthetic standards; or if it was a displacement to a dance context of Mercé's private or possibly suppressed memories of the human cacophony in her childhood, from which she sought escape in art.

Still, we can tell from it indisputably *what* her aesthetic standards were. Mercé's details about trying to flee castanet-playing that was "anti-musical" and loudly echoing, and her insistence that her own castanet technique was developed in direct opposition to these characteristics, serve as clues to her concern for pianissimo effects, for legato, for elegance, for a holistic expression that is closer to singing than to shouting, and to her crisp, exacting approach to individual pitches, that is, to a sound-world without overtones. Happily, these can, indeed, be verified independently. One way is through the writings of critics and other observers of La Argentina's performances. The Russian émigré André Levinson, for instance, who was a devotee of the dancer—to the extent that he wanted to travel with her—wrote of her in 1928, in *Theatre Arts Monthly*, that "Her rhythmic sense is marvelous. Her castanets show such a variety of *timbres* that they grow almost vocal, and such an intensity of expression—impatience, defiance, triumph—that they are not merely a voice, but speech."

A second kind of verification comes from the actual hands of the dancer. Two 78 r.p.m. recordings of her castanet-playing from the 1930s are held by The New York Public Library of the Performing Arts at Lincoln Center, and they might be compared with Alicia de la Rocha performing Albeniz or Mozart. One can also hear recordings of Mercé's castanet-playing (possibly the same recordings) at the library in a videotape of the 1977 *Admiring "La Argentina"*—an unnerving yet persuasively earnest solo of female impersonation in homage to Mercé by Japanese Butoh dancer Kazuo Ono, who performed it internationally, including several times in New York, when he was in his eighties. Ono had seen La Argentina perform some fifty years before he choreographed the work, and he was forever changed by the impact of her beauty in motion and the finesse of her craftsmanship as both a dancer and a musician. During a question-and-answer period following his last New York appearance at the Japan Society—when, aged ninety-two, he was no longer performing the rather arduous evening-length solo (although he did open that last evening with a number in which he impersonated Elvis Presley)—I asked Ono how he obtained the castanet recordings he had used in *Admiring*. He answered that he had sought out Mercé's family after her death, and that they had given them to him. He had held onto them all those decades as private sources of inspiration before making them available to the public through his solo homage.

A dance critic cannot overstress the significance of Ono's generosity, stimulated by his experience as a member of another dancer's audience and fueled

by decades of that obsession we call, generally, balletomania. Long memories and unswerving loyalties are the stuff of which dance traditions are made.
The cross-cultural dimension here is also significant. Butoh is about as far
removed from the classical techniques of La Argentina as it is possible to get:
expressionist, deeply internalized, and visceral, it was developed in the late
1950s and 1960s by an iconoclast named Tatsumi Hijikata as a rebellion against
theatrical traditions, and it retains an element of the fury that erupted in his
generation in Japan over the effects of the hydrogen bombs that the Allies
had dropped during the Second World War. Its unmetered, intensely theatrical images—which can be exhausting, even sickening, to follow for audience members who are unprepared for them—can pack a terrible punch, as
they tend to be impulsive, glacial in their transformations, and accented by
highly stylized choreography for bodily parts and processes usually left under wraps. Butoh makes the id concrete; it is inimical to classicism (or entertainment) of any stripe. And yet, not only was Ono, one of Butoh's earliest
adherents, the gentleman who revived the reputation of La Argentina on an
international scale for several generations of dancers and audiences to whom
she was a name only (if they knew her name at all), but Hijikata himself also
served as the stage director for the show. The history of dance is filled with
such dramatic, unpredictable, and generous multicultural associations and
encounters. Another one of the missions of this book is to showcase examples of them.

Dance history comprises much more than the attempts of professional
dance historians to piece together, analyze, induce the cultural environments
of, and interpret the stories of dancers, choreographers, dances, and related
subjects. It begins with the memories, muscular and cognitive, of the dancers themselves in the studio and on stage. As the dance critic Martha Ullman
West has observed, dancers, first and foremost, constitute the living archive
of dance. As performers, they are sometimes compared to musical instruments; however, the closer analogy would be to computers with souls. They
are expected to learn and retain choreography which the choreographer,
deeply engaged in the creative process, actually might not remember—and
not only their own parts. Sometimes they are required to learn other parts as
well, in case the casting needs to shift around suddenly. (Occasionally, they
have to do this backward, from a position in mirror-image to the action.)
Or, as for dancers working with Jerome Robbins, they might be asked to
learn three or four versions of a dance, which they are expected to reproduce on demand in rehearsal, so the choreographer can choose among them.
And sometimes, in emergencies, a dancer will be forced to learn choreography on stage, in the midst of a performance, as a partner or the surrounding
ensemble whisper the last-minute substitute through the steps.

Frequently, the dancers also contribute to the act of creation. For example,
a choreographer making a dance may ask the cast to supply movement phrases
they improvise on the spot, which the choreographer then shapes, edits, and
otherwise absorbs into his or her own imaginative product. Sometimes,

dancers even supply more-or-less finished choreography for entire portions of a dance, as James Truitte choreographed the male solo "I Want to Be Ready" in the middle of Alvin Ailey's *Revelations*; although the principal choreographer—who developed the concept, chose the music, perhaps taught and/or developed the dance technique being employed, and provided the imaginative weather for the dancer's contribution—is (properly) given principal credit. As for the classroom, regardless of whether one is speaking of theatrical dance, folk dance, or dancing that is religious or ceremonial, the learning process is more or less the same: the dancer learns through imitation of experienced and trusted practitioners and through corrections by teachers and mentors. Dancers never stop practicing and learning; and theatrical dancers never stop attending class. As the body changes and technique is acquired or erodes, there is always something new to be learned, and there is always some aspect of the dancer's physicality or concentration that requires work to maintain.

Some dancers—such as Frederic Franklin, a star for twenty years with the Ballet Russe de Monte Carlo (and who, in his early nineties at this writing, still actively coaches as well as performs pantomime roles); or Yuriko Kikuchi, who enjoyed a fifty-year association with the Martha Graham Dance Company as a star dancer, a teacher, a stager, and a coach (and who, now in her mid-eighties, continues to stage and coach Graham's dances)—are renowned for their near-photographic memories of steps and details of approach to performance. Across the globe, the leading theatrical families who practice the tradition of Kabuki theater in Japan make decisions about new productions of old plays, in which dancing figures prominently, based on production notebooks kept by their ancestors. Some of those notebooks are centuries old. Notebooks, letters, journals, reports, notation systems of choreography, souvenir books, newspaper cuttings, still photographs, artists' drawings (such as those made by Abraham Walkowitz of Isadora Duncan or those by Valentina Gross of Vaslav Nijinsky's staging of *Le Sacre du printemps*): such ephemera are also the stuff of dance history, before one even turns to films and videos. Press releases can be critical, too: in New York, for instance, the press releases of Jonathan Slaff, who oversees downtown dance events, or of the World Music Institute, which imports many dancers from Asia, Latin America, and the Middle East, can be better written, more knowledgeable, and more reliable than reviews.

Sometimes, dance historians will focus on what may seem, from outside the field, like minutiae, because tiny details can matter tremendously in the practice of dancing, as they can in living. And nowhere are details more important than in class and rehearsal. Indeed, anecdotes about how dancers learn and practice the vocabulary of classical ballet, alone—collected here in the sections "Coaches and Teachers" and "The Rehearsal Room"—could fill several volumes. The studio is not only where dancers spend the better part of their waking hours: it is also where they can experiment, work to improve, create, observe their peers. How dancers conduct themselves in the studio, their degrees of self-discipline (or indiscipline), can tell quite a lot about their attitudes toward dancing as an art and a profession and will sometimes go very far to explain the personality of a given company on stage. And how dancers conduct themselves backstage and in the wings during performance—the places of highest anxiety, where many people tend to let off steam—indicate how much they've been holding back elsewhere. In the time I've researched this book, I've found that anecdotes from backstage can be deeply bitter and cruel, as well as very funny: it's a place for extremes, as the late actor Tony Randall, once a student of Martha Graham, captured to the cuticles in this memory:

"On Broadway, the 'gypsies' today are fabulous. Every one of them has a technique that's stunning. But they have a mentality that knows they are never going any higher in their work. They become sarcastic and bitter and invidious. I did a musical, *Oh, Captain*, in 1958. Alexandra Danilova, the Ballet Russe star, was in it. The chorus gypsies, the men especially, were all good, but within a week after we opened the show they just passively went through a performance. They would talk onstage to each other and over the actors' lines. They could not be disciplined because they didn't care. They would be late for entrances and knew nothing but their own stuff. They had stopped learning after they signed a contract.

"Danilova, however, would stand in the wings transfixed, and she had been around for about fifty years! She had only one scene in the show, but her discipline and training allowed her to renew herself at each performance. She had intelligence, taste, elegance, and was present in the sense of being involved at each performance.

"Martha was like that." (Marian Horosko, *Martha Graham: The Evolution of Her Dance Theory and Training*, pp. 99–100)

Dancing ultimately is not very amusing from the inside. The performing careers of dancers are typically brutish and frequently short; many are quite nasty as well. Even superstars—Pavlova, Nijinsky, Duncan, Graham, Balanchine, Fonteyn, Nureyev, Baryshnikov, Danilova (as she recounted in her memoir, *Choura*)—undergo suffering almost unimaginable to a nondancer. Given the potential for serious injury; the small (sometimes absent) financial compensation; the need to evacuate one's entire life of everything else in earliest youth; the lack of a tangible product of which one can say, "That's my work: that's what I do"; the low esteem in which dance has been held vis-à-vis other professions; and the ruinously homogenizing effects of globalization on ancient practices worldwide, it's a continual amazement that the more exacting traditions have not gone the way of lacemaking and linotyping. Indeed, in certain parts of Africa, Asia, and Southeast Asia, there are dance traditions today whose master practitioners, in their seventies or eighties, have almost no artistic progeny, in part because younger generations consider the traditions antique and irrelevant to their lives and in part because the cost of keeping them going at their highest, labor-intensive and offstage life-denying level—and they aren't worth doing professionally except at that level—is prohibitive.

Great artists make for great stories. Nevertheless, some of the best dance anecdotes in my opinion are about individuals you may never have heard of. In terms of literary style and depth of reliable reporting, the finest single anecdote I can recommend in print by a dancer is Agnes de Mille's word-portrait of Carmelita Maracci, the California virtuosa of classical ballet and Spanish dancing and an early teacher of ballerinas Cynthia Gregory and Allegra Kent, as well as of de Mille herself. Kent has written in her own memoir, *Once a Dancer . . .* , about Maracci with fondness and poignancy. However, de Mille's unflinching and somewhat forensic analysis of Maracci's jaw-dropping technique is far from fond. It functions as a sort of bear-trap for Maracci's dance effects, essentially pinioning her to the floor: the prose reads as a declaration of triumph in some struggle between de Mille and Maracci that is not actually discussed. Even so, de Mille seems to reanimate this bygone figure as if the page were a window through which one were watching her; and in that reanimation, the author confers a kind of gift on her subject, too. Maracci, a dancer of nearly freakish physical genius, also possessed a personality that tripped her up in her professional dealings; between that and sheer bad luck, she never enjoyed a performing career on the scale of her abilities. Apart from the passages about her in a couple of de Mille's memoirs, in Kent's, and in a few other remembrances, she has become a footnote to American dance. Yet de Mille's exasperation and competitiveness—prompted, perhaps, by jealousy of Maracci's abilities, perhaps by rage at Maracci's arrogance—ultimately prove beneficial on the page. In its wedding of literary tension with reportorial realism, the following paragraph from de Mille's memoir *Dance to the Piper* restores to life a figure who was clearly a phenomenon:

> I had heard about Maracci from many sources, but the first time I saw her was when I went to class at the Perry Studio on Highland Avenue. She was dressed in a little knitted bathing suit and she sat upright on the edge of her chair, her insteps, the most beautiful feet in the ballet world, crossed precisely before her. She was smoking. She had tiny hands and long, quick fingers, the nails extravagantly long for castanet playing. She was very small, doll-like, and compact. Her black hair was nailed, Spanish style, in a knot at the back of her head. I have said she was doll-like, but there was no hint of prettiness in the face. She had rather the head of a precocious monkey or a wicked marionette. Under the bald, hard, round forehead, the eyes opened large and were flecked with yellow lights reminiscent of Graham's. The large mouth, peeled back from strong teeth, was aggressive and mobile. It was an angry little head, proud, taut, and passionate—the head of a Spanish Gypsy. She always held it curved in as though there were a bit in the mouth, the cords of her neck jutting out in strong, vertical lines. She looked under flickering lids as though she were about to bolt. Her voice rang out in flat, Southwestern speech. (She had been born in Montevideo of Italian-German parentage, but she talked like a housewife in Bakersfield.) "Oh my goodness," she said, in washday Bakersfield impatience, "show some gumption! You look like limp lettuce leaves. What do you think you're doing?" And with this she threw her cigarette down and ground it out on the studio floor under the toe of her pink satin slipper. "Now, let's get going!" Up came the chest, the spine tautened. Her neck and head assumed the tension of accumulated force

which is a dancer's preparation. The long arms moved to fourth position, her knees galvanized, and she was off on cold legs, without a *plié* or an excuse-me, in a series of the most astonishing *chaîné* pirouettes one could ask for, revolving as fast as the eye could follow, as smooth as silk unwinding from a spool. Her lungs were filled with smoke, her thighs relaxed from sitting down. She stopped in arabesque, erect like a T-square, the straight supporting leg planted on its delicate point, the structure of her body balanced and counterbalanced, sinew against bone against height against sinew hung in the air, tension counterbalanced on tension. And the lovely, tense foot was adequate to all, attaching itself to the bare floor and permitting the body to branch and flower above. She posed there on one point, in defiance of gravity, until her knee got tired, and then, and only then, she allowed her heel to touch ground. She had remained immobile, in full flight, for about twelve seconds.

"Glory be to God," I said.

"Well!" said Carmelita, with a throaty chuckle. "That was pretty good. I think I'll have another smoke on that one. Now, how about some of you trying?"

There are a few purely humorous entries here, then, but not too many. A collection of dance anecdotes made up solely of funny stories would be more than heartless: it would profoundly misrepresent the spiritual or ecstatic motivation that inspires all dancers at some point in their lives, regardless of whether the context is religious or commercial and of whether they are "nice people" offstage. And it would misrepresent as well the daunting physical realities and emotional tensions that are attendant on the production of dancing as an art, an entertainment, or a prayer.

Finally, in selecting the anecdotes and apothegms, I wanted to draw the reader's attention to some of the many worthy dance histories and memoirs that are no longer in print. If you like an entry, you might consult the title of its source in the full bibliography that follows this note and track down the book: where there's one good story, there are likely to be others.

Be prepared, though, for many of them to be galvanized—like the dances themselves—by the L-word (love: often unrequited), or by untimely death, or by renunciation in pursuit of impossible ideals. Although the word "romance" is no longer considered even viable parlance, apart from its usage to indicate a literary genre, the most haunting stories about dance and dancers, especially those of classical ballet, contain at least an indispensable touch of it. The effect is often most powerful when dancing as a craft or as an image of an ideal is in the foreground, that is, when the writing tries, as exactingly as possible, to recreate some aspect of dance as either a body of knowledge or, as in the scene of Natasha at her first ball in *War and Peace*, an emblem of the yearning for joy, perfection, beauty—all those words whose definitions we feel we know, even though it's nearly impossible to pin them down.

A brilliant example of how dance technique can acquire the luster of poetry is the following passage by John Updike from his short story "The Bulgarian Poetess," collected in *Bech: A Book* (1970). Set in a Russian ballet studio, it offers a description of one closely observed technical practice called "spotting," a term for the way a dancer focuses her vision and uses her head during a multiple pirouette, in order to keep from getting dizzy. Updike presents it in apposition to the tendency of his nondancing protagonist to lose his emotional balance, to fall in love with women in dizzying succession:

> Men traveling alone develop a romantic vertigo. Bech had already fallen in love with a freckled embassy wife in Prague, a buck-toothed chanteuse in Rumania, a stolid Mongolian sculptress in Kazakhstan. In the Tretyakov Gallery he had fallen in love with a recumbent statue, and at the Moscow Ballet School with an entire roomful of girls. Entering the room, he had been struck by the aroma, tenderly acrid, of young female sweat. Sixteen and seventeen, wearing patchy practice suits, the girls were twirling so strenuously their slippers were unraveling. Demure student faces crowned the unconscious insolence of their bodies. The room was doubled in depth by a floor-to-ceiling mirror. Bech was seated on a bench at its base. Staring above his head, each girl watched herself with frowning eyes frozen, for an instant in the turn, by the imperious delay and snap of her head. Bech tried to remember the lines of Rilke that expressed it, this snap and delay: *did not the drawing remain / that the dark stroke of your eyebrow / swiftly wrote on the wall of its own turning?* At one point the teacher, a shapeless old Ukrainian lady with gold canines, a *prima* of the thirties, had arisen and cried something translated to Bech as, "No, no, the arms free, *free!*" And in demonstration she had executed a rapid series of pirouettes with such proud effortlessness that all the girls, standing this way and that like deer along the wall, had applauded. Bech had loved them for that. In all his loves, there was an urge to rescue.

The heart of Updike's description—"the imperious delay and snap of her head"—is a pristine rendering of what a dancer does as she spots during a turn; Updike's analysis of spotting as a two-part action is right on the mark. And his association of that action with the lines from Rilke endows the physicality of the moment with a suggestion of the long-range poetic ideals that the dancers and their teacher are striving to serve. Furthermore, despite the old saying that "love is blind," in the case of Updike's Bech, the act of falling in love is clarifying, focusing, just as the pirouettes require the dancers to focus. Updike made up Bech's story, but he did not make up Bech's world: he translated it responsibly and, I think, eloquently. As an anecdote, it doesn't matter that this is embedded in a work of fiction, since the exactitude of its rendering, its moral dimension, is pure fact.

—Mindy Aloff
Brooklyn, New York

Bibliography

Acocella, Joan. *Mark Morris* [galleys]. New York: Farrar, Straus and Giroux, 1993.

——— (ed.). *The Diary of Vaslav Nijinsky: Unexpurgated Edition.* Kyril FitzLyon (trans.). New York: Farrar, Straus and Giroux, 1999.

Albert, Gennady. *Alexander Pushkin: Master Teacher of Dance.* Antonina W. Bouis (trans.). New York Public Library, 2001.

Aloff, Mindy. *Russian Journal: June 16–July 3, 1983.* Unpublished.

Amen, Melissa. "The Native American Ghost Dances." *Dr. Quinn Times* (on line): www.thedqtimes.com/pages/castpages/other/Indian%20Customs/ghostdances.htm.

Andersen, Hans Christian. *The Fairytale of My Life: An Autobiography.* Translator unidentified. London: Paddington Press, 1868, 1975.

Anderson, Jack (ed.). *The Dance, the Dancer, and the Poem: An Anthology of Twentieth-Century Dance Poems. Dance Perspectives* 52 (Winter 1972).

Aroldingen, Karin von. "Cooking with Balanchine: Three from the Sea and Two Celebrations." *Ballet Review* 32, no. 2 (Summer 2004).

Backman, E. Louis. *Religious Dances in the Christian Church and in Popular Medicine.* E. Classen (trans.). London: George Allen & Unwin, 1952.

Banes, Sally. *Writing Dancing in the Age of Postmodernism.* Middletown, Conn.: Wesleyan/New England Press, 1984.

Barrault, Jean-Louis. *Reflections on the Theatre.* Barbara Wall (trans.). London: Rockliff, 1951.

Beaumont, Cyril W. *The Complete Book of Ballets.* New York: Grosset & Dunlap, 1938.

Behrman, S. N. *People in a Diary: A Memoir.* Boston: Little, Brown, 1972.

Benchley, Robert. *Benchley at the Theatre: Dramatic Criticism 1920–1940.* Charles Getchell (ed.). Ipswich, Mass.: Ipswich Press, 1985.

Bennahum, Ninotchka Devorah. *Antonia Mercé "La Argentina": Flamenco and the Avant Garde.* Middletown, Conn.: Wesleyan/New England Press, 2000.

Berlioz, Hector. *The Memoirs*. David Cairns (ed. and trans.). New York: Alfred A. Knopf, 2002.

Bird, Dorothy, and Joyce Greenberg. *Bird's Eye View: Dancing with Martha Graham and on Broadway*. Pittsburgh, Penn.: University of Pittsburgh Press, 1997.

Blair, Fredrika. *Isadora: Portrait of the Artist as a Woman*. New York: McGraw-Hill, 1986.

Bournonville, August. *Letters on Dance and Choreography*. Knud Arne Jürgensen (trans. and annot.). London: Dance Books, 1999.

———. *My Theater Life*. Patricia N. McAndrew (trans.). Middletown, Conn.: Wesleyan University Press, 1979.

Brewer, Ebenezer Cobham. *Dictionary of Phrase and Fable, Giving the Derivation, Source, or Origin of Common Phrases, Allusions, and Words That Have a Tale to Tell*. www.Bartleby.com, 2000. Originally published by Henry Altemus, 1898.

Buckle, Richard. *In Search of Diaghilev*. London: Sidgwick and Jackson, 1955.

Buckle, Richard, in collaboration with John Taras. *George Balanchine: Ballet Master*. New York: Random House, 1988.

Buday, George. *Dances of Hungary*. Violet Alford (ed.). London: Chanticleer Press, 1950.

Burns, George. *The Most of George Burns*. New York: Galahad Books, 1991.

Carmer, Carl. *Stars Fell on Alabama*. Cyrus LeRoy Baldridge (illus.). New York: Blue Ribbon Books, 1934, 1940.

Casanova, Giacomo. *History of My Life*. Willard R. Trask (trans.). Baltimore, Md.: Johns Hopkins University Press, 1996, 1997.

Castle, Irene. *Castles in the Air*. As told to Bob and Wanda Duncan. New York: Doubleday, 1958.

Cavett, Dick. *The Dick Cavett Show*. Taped June 19, 1981; aired November 23, 1981. Audio transcribed by Patricia Meja.

Céline, Louis-Ferdinand. *Ballets without Music, without Dancers, without Anything*. Thomas and Carol Christensen (trans.). Los Angeles: Green Integer Press, 1999.

Cohen, Selma Jeanne (ed.). *The Modern Dance: Seven Statements of Belief*. Middletown, Conn.: Wesleyan University Press, 1973.

Colette. *"Mitsou" and "Music-Hall Sidelights."* Raymond Postgate and Anne-Marie Callimachi (trans.). New York: Farrar, Straus and Giroux, 1957.

Collier, Simon, Artemis Cooper, María Susana Azzi, and Richard Martin. *¡Tango! The Dance, the Song, the Story*. London: Thames and Hudson, 1993.

Copland, Aaron, and Vivian Perlis. *Copland: Since 1943*. New York: St. Martin's Griffin, 1989.

Craig, Edward. *Gordon Craig*. New York: Alfred A. Knopf, 1968.

Crisp, Clement. "Homage to Galina Ulanova, Bolshoi Theatre, Moscow." *Financial Times* (London), May 20, 2005.

Croce, Arlene. *Writing in the Dark, Dancing in the* New Yorker: *An Arlene Croce Reader*. New York: Farrar, Straus and Giroux, 2000.

Croft-Cooke, Rupert, and W. S. Meadmore. *The Sawdust Ring.* London[?]: Odhams Press, T.551.Q., [194–?].

Dancing: A Journal Devoted to the Terpsichorean Art, Physical Culture, and Fashionable Entertainments. London: June 8, 1891, to May 1893. Reprinted, Toronto: Press of Terpsichore, 1984.

Daneman, Meredith. *Margot Fonteyn: A Life.* New York: Viking, 2004.

de Cossart, Michael. *Ida Rubinstein: A Theatrical Life.* Liverpool, England: Liverpool University Press, 1987.

de Jong, Bettie. Interview by Alan Olshun. Web site, Paul Taylor Dance Company (www.ptdc.org).

De Mari, Terry (ed.). *Reminiscences II of Ballets Russes Dancers: Ballets Russes Celebration, The Legacy; New Orleans—June 2000.* Privately published, n.d.

de Mille, Agnes. *Dance to the Piper: Memoirs of the Ballet.* London: Columbus Books, 1987. First edition: Boston: Little, Brown-Atlantic Monthly Press Book, 1952.

Deakin, Irving. *At the Ballet: A Guide to Enjoyment.* New York: Thomas Nelson, 1956.

Delarue, Allison (ed.) *Fanny Elssler in America.* With introduction and notes by the editor. New York: Dance Horizons, 1976.

Denby, Edwin. *Dance Writings.* Robert Cornfield and William MacKay (eds.). New York: Alfred A. Knopf, 1987.

———. *Dancers, Buildings and People in the Streets.* New York: Popular Library, 1965.

Dickens, Charles. *American Notes.* Greenwich, Conn.: Fawcett, 1961.

———. *Sketches by Boz: Illustrative of Every-day Life and Every-day People.* With 41 illustrations by George Cruickshank. London: Mandarin/Octopus Publishing Group, 1991.

———. *A Tale of Two Cities.* New York: Penguin Books, 1970.

Duncan, Irma. *Duncan Dancer.* Middletown, Conn.: Wesleyan University Press, 1965, 1966.

Duncan, Isadora. *The Art of the Dance.* Sheldon Cheney (ed.). New York: Theatre Arts Books, 1928, 1969.

———. *My Life.* New York: Liveright, 1955.

Ebers, John. *Seven Years of the King's Theatre.* New York: Benjamin Blom, 1969.

Emery, Lynne Fauley. *Black Dance: From 1619 to Today.* 2nd rev. ed., with a new chapter by Dr. Brenda Dixon-Stowell; foreword by Katherine Dunham. Princeton, N.J.: Princeton Book Company/Dance Horizons, 1988.

Encyclopedia Britannica. 1911. Volume V. www.encyclopedia.jrank.org.

Farrell, Suzanne, and Toni Bentley. *Holding onto the Air: An Autobiography.* New York: Summit Books, 1990. Reprinted, Gainesville: University Press of Florida, 2002.

Frank, Rusty E. *Tap! The Greatest Tap Dance Stars and Their Stories 1900–1955.* Boston: Da Capo, 1994.

Franks, A. H. (ed.). *Pavlova: A Collection of Memoirs.* New York: Da Capo, ca. 1979. Reprint of *Pavlova, a Biography* (ed. A. H. Franks, in collaboration with members of the Pavlova Commemoration Committee). London, 1956.

García Lorca, Federico. *In Search of Duende*. Christopher Maurer (ed. and trans.). New York: New Directions, 1998.

Gautier, Théophile. *Gautier on Dance*. Ivor Guest (ed. and trans.). London: Dance Books, 1986.

Gershunoff, Max, and Leon Van Dyke. *It's Not All Song and Dance: A Life behind the Scenes in the Performing Arts*. Pompton Plains, N.J.: Limelight Editions, 2005.

Geva, Tamara. *Split Seconds: A Remembrance*. New York: Limelight Editions, 1972.

Glover, Savion, and Bruce Weber. *Savion: My Life in Tap*. New York: William Morrow, 2000.

Goethe, Johann Wolfgang von. *Wilhelm Meister's Apprenticeship*. Thomas Carlyle (trans.). With a new introduction by Franz Schoenberner and illustrations by William Sharp. New York: Heritage Press, 1959.

Gordon, Beate Sirota. *The Only Woman in the Room: A Memoir*. Tokyo: Kodansha International, 1997.

Gorer, Geoffrey. *Africa Dances*. Revised with a new introduction by the author. London: John Lehmann, 1949.

Gottfried, Martin. *All His Jazz: The Life and Death of Bob Fosse*. Cambridge, Mass.: Da Capo, 1998. Originally published 1990.

Gottlieb, Robert A. *George Balanchine:The Ballet Maker*. New York: HarperCollins, 2004.

Graham, Martha. *Blood Memory*. New York: Doubleday, 1991.

Gregory, John (ed.), and André Eglevsky (co-ed.). *Heritage of a Ballet Master, Nicolas Legat*. Brooklyn, N.Y.: Dance Horizons, 1977.

Greskovic, Robert. "Washington, D.C., Report." *Dance International* 23, no. 4 (Winter 1995/96).

Griffin-Pierce, Trudy. *The Encyclopedia of Native America*. New York: Viking, 1995.

Grody, Svetlana McLee, and Dorothy Daniels Lister. *Conversations with Choreographers*. Portsmouth, N.H.: Heinemann, 1996.

Gruen, John. *The Private World of Ballet*. New York: Penguin Books, 1976.

Guest, Ivor. *Victorian Ballet Girl*. London: Adam and Charles Black, 1957.

Halford, Aubrey S., and Giovanna Halford. *The Kabuki Handbook: A Guide to Understanding and Appreciation, with Summaries of Favorite Plays, Explanatory Notes, and Illustrations*. North Clarendon, Vt.: Charles E. Tuttle, 1956.

Hata, Michiyo. *Tradition and Creativity in Japanese Dance*. New York: Weatherhill, 2001.

Herod, Kena. "Gene Kelly, My Sore Eyes Look to You: An Expatriate American Considers an American Dancer and Icon." *Maisonneuve*, "The Dance Scene," January 18, 2005. www.maisonneuve.org.

Holmes, Olive (ed.). *Motion Arrested: Dance Reviews of H. T. Parker*. Middletown, Conn.: Wesleyan University Press, 1982.

Homberger, Eric. *The Visual Atlas of New York City: A Celebration of Nearly 400 Years of New York City's History.* Alice Hudson (cartographic consultant). New York: Henry Holt, 1994.

Horosko, Marian. *Martha Graham: The Evolution of Her Dance Theory and Training.* Gainesville: University Press of Florida, 1991, 2002.

Humphrey, Doris. *Doris Humphrey: An Artist First.* An autobiography, edited and completed by Selma Jeanne Cohen. Middletown, Conn.: Wesleyan University Press, 1972.

Jackson, George. "Beyond Technique: A Master Class with Katherine Dunham." *Dance View Times* 3, no. 16 (April 25, 2005). www.danceview times.com.

Jenyns, Soame. *The Art of Dancing: A Poem in Three Cantos* (1729 edition). Ann Cottis (ed.). London: Dance Books: 1978.

Jones, Bill T., with Peggy Gillespie. *Last Night on Earth.* New York: Pantheon Books, 1995.

Jowitt, Deborah. "Bella Lewitsky [*sic*]—Some Memories and a Greeting." House program, Brooklyn Academy of Music, October 1971, pp. 5–7.

———. *Time and the Dancing Image.* New York: William Morrow, 1988.

Karsavina, Tamara. *Theatre Street: The Reminiscences of Tamara Karsavina.* London: Constable, 1930. Revised and enlarged, 1948.

Kawakatsu, Ken-Ichi. *Kimono.* Japanese Travel Bureau, 1962.

Kent, Allegra. *Once a Dancer . . .* New York: St. Martin's, 1997.

———. "To Toss or Not to Toss." *Dance Magazine* (January 2005).

Kinkeldey, Otto. *A Jewish Dancing Master of the Renaissance: Guglielmo Ebreo.* A. S. Friedus Memorial Volume, 1929. Reprinted, Brooklyn, N.Y.: Dance Horizons, 1972.

Kirkland, Gelsey, with Greg Lawrence. *Dancing on My Grave.* New York: Jove Books, 1987. Originally published, New York: Doubleday, 1986.

Kirstein, Lincoln. *By With To & From: A Lincoln Kirstein Reader.* Nicholas Jenkins (ed.). New York: Farrar, Straus and Giroux, 1991.

———. *Flesh Is Heir.* New York: Popular Library, 1932, 1975, 1977.

——— (ed.). *Portrait of Mr. B: Photographs of George Balanchine with an Essay by Lincoln Kirstein.* New York: Ballet Society/Viking: 1984.

Klein, Marcus, and Robert Pack. *Short Stories: Classic, Modern, Contemporary.* Boston: Little, Brown, 1967.

Kochno, Boris. *Diaghilev and the Ballets Russes.* Adrienne Foulke (trans.). New York: Harper and Row, 1970.

Kpomassie, Tété-Michel. *An African in Greenland.* James Kirkup (trans.). New York: New York Review of Books, 2001.

Kschessinska, Mathilde (H.S.H. The Princess Romanovsky-Krassinsky). *Dancing in Petersburg: The Memoirs of Kschessinska.* Arnold Haskell (trans.). New York: Da Capo Press, 1972. Reprint of 1961 edition published by Doubleday.

Kurosawa, Akira. *Something Like an Autobiography.* Audie E. Bock (trans.). New York: Vintage, 1982.

Lacotte, Pierre. "Marie Taglioni: Inspired Ballerina." In *Marie Taglioni: La Sylphide*. Paris: Editions Mario Bois, 1980.

Lawler, Lillian B. *The Dance in Ancient Greece*. Middletown, Conn.: Wesleyan University Press, 1964.

Lehmann-Haupt, Christopher. "Opal Petty, 86, Patient Held 51 Years Involuntarily in Texas, Dies." *New York Times*, March 17, 2005, late edition—final, Section C, p. 15.

Lemon, Ralph. *Geography: Art/Race/Exile*. Middletown, Conn.: Wesleyan/New England Press, 2000.

Lessard, Suzannah. *The Architect of Desire: Beauty and Danger in the Stanford White Family*. New York: Trafalgar Square, 1996.

Lesschaeve, Jacqueline. *The Dancer and the Dance: Merce Cunningham in Conversation with Jacqueline Lesschaeve*. New York: M. Boyars/Scribner Book Companies, 1985.

Lesser, Wendy. *The Amateur: An Independent Life of Letters*. New York: Pantheon Books, 1999.

Levin, Alice B. *Eleanor Powell: First Lady of Dance*. Potomac, Md.: Empire, 1997.

Macaulay, Alastair (ed.). *The Fonteyn Phenomenon: Proceedings of the 1999 Conference of the Royal Academy of Dancing*. (Manuscript.)

Makarova, Natalia. *A Dance Autobiography*. New York: Alfred A. Knopf, 1979.

Malnig, Julie. *Dancing till Dawn: A Century of Exhibition Ballroom Dance*. New York: New York University Press, 1995.

Manchester, P. W., and Iris Morley. *The Rose and the Star: Ballet in England and Russia Compared*. London: Victor Gollancz, 1949.

Mates, Julian. *The American Musical Stage before 1800*. Rutgers, N.J.: Rutgers University Press, 1962.

McCabe, John. *Cagney*. New York: Carroll & Graf, 1997.

McKay, Claude. *Home to Harlem*. New York: Harper and Brothers, 1928.

McKinley, Jesse. "Fierstein as Tevye: Sounds Crazy, No?" *New York Times*, January 2, 2005, Section 2, p. 5.

Migel, Parmenia. *Pablo Picasso Designs for "The Three-Cornered Hat" (Le Tricorne)*. New York: Dover Publications in association with the Stravinsky-Diaghilev Foundation, 1978.

Montaigne, Michel de. *The Essays*. M. A. Screech (trans. and ed.). London: Allen Lane/Penguin Press, 1987, 1991. Originally published Stanford, Calif.: Stanford University Press, 1957.

Moore, Lillian. *Artists of the Dance*. New York: Thomas Y. Crowell, 1938. Reprinted, Brooklyn, N.Y.: Dance Horizons, 1975.

Morgan, Barbara. *Martha Graham: Sixteen Dances in Photographs*. Dobbs Ferry, N.Y.: Morgan & Morgan, 1941, 1980.

Mozart, Wolfgang Amadeus. *Mozart's Letters, Mozart's Life*. Robert Spaethling (ed. and trans.). New York: W.W. Norton, 2000.

Mueller, John. *Astaire Dancing: The Musical Films*. New York: Alfred A. Knopf, 1985.

Murasaki Shikibu. *The Diary of Lady Murasaki*. Richard Bowring (ed. and trans., and with an introduction and notes). New York: Penguin, 1996.

Nathan, Hans. *Dan Emmett and the Rise of Early Negro Minstrelsy*. Norman: University of Oklahoma Press, 1962.

Newman, Barbara. *Striking a Balance: Dancers Talk about Dancing*. New York: Houghton Mifflin, 1981. Revised edition: Pompton Plains, N.J.: Limelight Editions, 1992.

Noverre, Jean Georges. *Letters on Dancing and Ballets* (trans. Cyril W. Beaumont from the revised and enlarged edition, published in St. Petersburg in 1803). Brooklyn, N.Y.: Dance Horizons, 1968.

Parker, Derek. *Nijinsky: God of the Dance*. London: Equation, 1988.

Pearlman, Ellen. *Tibetan Sacred Dance: A Journey into the Religious and Folk Traditions*. Rochester, Vt.: Inner Traditions, 2002.

Petipa, Marius. *The Diaries*. Lynn Garafola (ed. and trans.). *Studies in Dance History: Journal of the Society of Dance History Scholars* 3, no. 1 (Spring 1992).

———. *Russian Ballet Master: The Memoirs*. Lillian Moore (ed.; trans. Helen Whittaker). London: Dance Books, 1958.

Phillips, Tom. "Bang! That's Balanchine: A Conversation with Susan Pilarre." *DanceView: A Quarterly Review of Dance* 22, no. 1 (Winter 2005).

Plisetskaya, Maya. *I, Maya Plisetskaya*. New Haven, Conn.: Yale University Press, 2001.

Powell, Michael. *A Life in Movies: An Autobiography*. London: Faber and Faber, 2000. (Originally published 1986.)

Proust, Marcel. *Remembrance of Things Past*. Vol. I: *Swann's Way*. C. K. Scott Moncrieff (trans.). New York: Vintage Books, 1970.

Pushkin, Alexander. *Eugene Onegin*. John Bayley (trans.). London: Penguin Classics, 1977, 1981.

Rambert, Marie. *Quicksilver: An Autobiography*. London: Macmillan, 1972.

Renoir, Jean. *My Life and My Films*. Norman Denny (trans.). New York: Atheneum, 1974. Reprinted by Da Capo Press, undated.

Reynolds, Nancy. *Repertory in Review: 40 Years of the New York City Ballet*. New York: Dial Press, 1977.

Ross, Janice. *Moving Lessons: Margaret H'Doubler and the Beginning of Dance in American Education*. Madison: University of Wisconsin Press, 2000.

Sachs, Curt. *World History of Dance*. Bessie Schönberg (trans.). New York: W.W. Norton, 1937.

St. Denis, Ruth. *An Unfinished Life: An Autobiography*. New York: Harper and Brothers, 1939.

Schneider, Ilya Ilyich. *Isadora Duncan: The Russian Years*. David Magarshack (trans.). New York: Harcourt, Brace & World, 1968.

Scholl, Tim. *"Sleeping Beauty": Legend in Progress*. New Haven, Conn.: Yale University Press, 2004.

Seymour, Bruce. *Lola Montez: A Life*. New Haven, Conn.: Yale University Press, 1996.

Shakespeare, William. *The Complete Works: Arranged in Their Chronological Order.* W.G. Clark and W. Aldis Wright (eds.). New York: Nelson Doubleday, [1939?].

Shearer, Moira. *Balletmaster: A Dancer's View of George Balanchine.* London: Sidgwick & Jackson, 1986.

Shulman, Irving. *Valentino.* New York: Trident Press, 1967.

Siegel, Marcia B. *Watching the Dance Go By.* Boston: Houghton Mifflin, 1977.

Silverman, Stephen M. *Dancing on the Ceiling: Stanley Donen and His Movies.* New York: Alfred A. Knopf, 1996.

Slonimsky, Yuri. *Writings on Lev Ivanov with a biography of Ivanov in excerpts from M. Borisoglebsky.* Anatole Chujoy (ed. and trans.). *Dance Perspectives* 2 (Spring 1959).

Starr, Sandra Leonard. *Joseph Cornell and the Ballet.* New York: Castelli-Feigen-Corcoran, 1983.

Steegmuller, Francis. *Jean Cocteau: A Biography.* Boston: Little, Brown, 1970.

Strong, Roy. *Splendor at Court: Renaissance Spectacle and the Theater of Power.* New York: Houghton Mifflin, 1973.

Swift, Mary Grace. *A Loftier Flight: The Life and Accomplishments of Charles-Louis Didelot, Balletmaster.* Middletown, Conn.: Wesleyan University Press, 1974.

Tallchief, Maria, with Larry Kaplan. *Maria Tallchief: America's Prima Ballerina.* New York: Henry Holt, 1997.

Taper, Bernard. *Balanchine: A Biography, with a New Epilogue.* Berkeley: University of California Press, 1996.

Taylor, Paul. *Private Domain: An Autobiography.* Pittsburgh: University of Pittsburgh Press, 1999. Originally published, New York: Alfred A. Knopf, 1987.

Tobias, Tobi. "Ballet Galore Week #5. New York City Ballet: Ivesiana." *ArtsJournal.com: The Daily Digest of Arts, Culture and Ideas* www.arts journal.com/tobias). Posted May 31, 2004.

———. "Going to the Wood" (*Classical Savion*). *ArtsJournal.com: The Daily Digest of Arts, Culture and Ideas* (www.artsjournal.com/tobias). Posted January 9, 2005.

Tolstoy, Leo. *War and Peace.* Louise and Aylmer Maude (trans.). New York: Oxford University Press, 1922; New York: Pocket Books, 1968.

Tracy, Robert. "Bicycle in the Sky: Merce Cunningham on Décor." *Ballet Review* (Fall 1992).

———. *Goddess: Martha Graham's Dancers Remember.* New York: Limelight Editions, 1997.

Tractenberg, Robert (writer, producer, director). *Gene Kelly: Anatomy of a Dancer.* PBS: American Masters, 2002.

Updike, John. *Bech: A Book.* New York: Alfred A. Knopf, 1970.

Van Vechten, Carl. *Parties: Scenes from Contemporary Life.* New York: Alfred A. Knopf, 1930.

Vaughan, David. *Merce Cunningham: 50 Years.* New York: Aperture, 1997.

Warrack, John. *Tchaikovsky Ballet Music.* Seattle: University of Washington Press, 1979. First published in 1979 by the British Broadcasting Company.

Wayburn, Ned. *The Art of Stage Dancing.* New York: Belvedere/Chelsea House, 1980. Originally published as *The Art of Stage Dancing: The Story of a Beautiful and Profitable Profession, a Manual of Stage-Craft.* New York: The Ned Wayburn Studios of Stage Dancing, ca. 1925.

Welty, Eudora. *One Writer's Beginnings.* New York: Library of America, 1998.

Wikipedia, the free encyclopedia. http://en.wikipedia.org/wiki/EvelynNesbit.

Zafran, Eric M., with Eugene Gaddis and Susan Hood. *Ballets Russes to Balanchine.* Hartford, Conn.: Wadsworth Atheneum Museum of Art, 2004.

Zarina, Xenia. *Classic Dances of the Orient.* New York: Crown Publishers, 1967.

Zellmer, David. *The Spectator: A World War II Bomber Pilot's Journal of the Artist as Warrior.* New York: Praeger, 1999.

Interviews and Conversations

Mindy Aloff: Ruthanna Boris, Joy Williams Brown, Christopher Caines, David Daniel, Arnold Goldberg, Alastair Macaulay, Don McDonagh, Alexandra Tomalonis, David Vaughan.

Emily Hite: Benjamin Bowman (written comment), Ron Cunningham, Yvonne Mounsey, Julie Whittaker (written comment).

Acknowledgments

There were two models for this collection: the well-known anthology of ballet stories from the eighteenth through the early twentieth century, *A Miscellany for Dancers*, compiled and translated by Cyril W. Beaumont; and an anthology of literary extracts from many countries and from antiquity through modern times called *The Bed or the Clinophile's Vade Mecum*, by Cecil and Margery Gray, "decorated" by Michael Ayrton. I restrained my impulses to raid them in the hope that readers would seek them out.

The contract for *Dance Anecdotes* was signed in 1988. Among the things that have happened since is that Sheldon Meyer, the commissioning editor at Oxford University Press, retired. And yet he did not give up on this project. Every so often he would call to see how I was doing, and when I was ready to deliver the manuscript, he asked to edit it, which he did with dispatch and grace. There would be no book without him: "thanks-you" is a placeholder phrase for gratitude I don't know how to articulate.

Furthermore, the rest of the kind and highly capable staff from Oxford who worked with me personally to shepherd this volume to completion have made the publishing experience a joy: Joellyn Ausanka, Ellen Chodosh, Betsy DeJesu, Woody Gilmartin, Patterson Lamb, Kathleen Lynch, Elda Rotor, Laura Stickney, Cybele Tom. I also thank Mary I. P. Bergin-Cartwright, of the Oxford office in England.

When I signed on with Oxford, I had no agent and no resources. The lawyer Neal Gantcher agreed to look at the contract for a fee that approached charity. My ancient knees offer him a curtsy.

A much-appreciated 1987 award from the Whiting Writers Foundation and a 1990 fellowship from The John Simon Guggenheim Memorial Foundation permitted me to begin my research here.

It took a village to bring this book into being. Here is a partial list of the individuals who contributed directly to this project in one way or another—by suggesting anecdotes, by offering help or advice, by serving as liaisons, or by giving personal permission for their words or those of writers whom they represent to be published. I began to write little paragraphs for the close friends and colleagues of long standing among them but decided to try to thank them in other ways. Suffice it to say publicly that I am forever in their debt: Joan Acocella, Bjorn Amelan (Bill T. Jones/Arnie Zane Dance Company), Verity Andrews (Reading University Library), Karin von Aroldingen, Meredith M. Babb (University Press of Florida), John Bayley, Ruthanna Boris, Benjamin Bowman, Joy Williams Brown, Christopher Caines, Mary Cargill, Dick Cavett, Mary Cochran (Barnard College), the late Selma Jeanne Cohen, Robert Cornfield (estate of Edwin Denby), Arlene Croce, Merce Cunningham, Ron Cunningham, the late David Daniel, George Dorris, Judy Englander, John Esten, Suzanne Farrell, Harvey Fierstein, Jessica Fjeld (James Atlas Books), Rusty E. Frank, Doug Fullerton, Lynn Garafola, Rachel Gershman (Ellen Jacobs Associates), Katie Glasner (Barnard College), William W. Gifford, Beate Sirota Gordon, Robert A. Gottlieb, Maxine Groffsky, John Gruen, Kena Herod, Barbara Horgan (The George Balanchine Trust), Marilyn Hunt, Jock Ireland, George Jackson, Nicholas Jenkins (estate of Lincoln Kirstein), Charliss Jennings, Bettie de Jong, Deborah Jowitt, Allegra Kent, Yuriko Kikuchi, Brenda King (Yale University Press), Pierre Lacotte, Russell Lee, Laura Leivick, Wendy Lesser, Julie Malnig, Patricia N. McAndrew, Don McDonagh, Yvonne Mounsey, Barbara Newman, Alan Olshan (Paul Taylor Dance Company), Paul Parish, Tom Phillips, Susan Pilarre, Susan Reiter, Nancy Reynolds, the late Brian Rushton, Janet Soares (Barnard College), Thelma Schoonmaker (Mrs. Michael Powell), Suki Schorer, Valda Setterfield, Lynn Seymour, Stephen M. Silverman, Jonathan Slaff, the late Susan Sontag, Lauren Sweeney (William Morris Agency), Suzanna Tamminen (Wesleyan University Press), Paul Taylor, Ghislaine Thesmar, Tobi Tobias, Alexandra Tomalonis, David Vaughan, Julie Whittaker, Martha Ullman West, Fiona Williams (Berlin Associates), the late David Zellmer and his family, Lauren Zeranski (James Atlas Books), and George Zournas (Theatre Arts Books). To Alastair Macaulay, who made available a treasury of anecdotes concerning Margot Fonteyn, including a beautiful one of his own, I tender a special thank-you. Grateful acknowledgment is also made to Atlas Books/ HarperCollins for permission to reprint from *George Balanchine: The Ballet Maker* by Robert Gottlieb, Copyright © 2004 by Robert Gottlieb.

Richard Bailey and Kevin Jones, who packed my library for a move in the midst of this book's completion, cannot be sufficiently praised for their understanding and compassion.

At 7th Avenue Copy in Park Slope, Brooklyn, Eddie Dobson, Sherry-Ann Griffith, and Win Komian performed miracles of timely photocopying. At the UPS Store on Seventh Avenue, Donald and Bobby offered patient assistance with my efforts to print out the manuscript. Over the years, I've had occasion to messenger portions of this book myself or to ferry other relevant books on an emergency basis. I should like to thank the excellent dispatchers and the reliable, charming drivers of Cheer's Car Service for seventeen years of courteous and often funny rides under tough driving conditions.

If I've forgotten the name of anyone who should have been included, I apologize heartily for any oversights. I also apologize in advance for any errors of fact or intellectual peculiarities in the book, which are mine, alone.

Several libraries were crucial, and I thank the institutions from the bottom of my heart: the Harvard Theatre Collection, the libraries of Barnard College and Columbia University, and the Jerome Robbins Dance Division of The New York Public Library for the Performing Arts. At that library I worked most often with Phil Karg, Monica Moseley, Madeleine Nichols, Els Peck, Charles Perrier, and Myron Switzer. Although the great dancer and stager Frederic Franklin, who is in the process of writing his memoirs, asked me not to delve into the 41-transcript oral history that Monica and I conducted with him over the year 2000 for the Dance Division, in a project cosponsored by NYPL and The George Balanchine Foundation, that project is the most useful contribution I ever made to the field of theatrical dancing, and I urge readers to consult the edited transcripts and/or the tapes in the library's archives. In the library, one can also find Roland John Wiley's magnificent collection of nineteenth-century Imperial Theater memoirs and critiques, *A Century of Russian Ballet.* Professor Wiley denied permission to reproduce several of them here; yet his unique book, which he both edited and translated, is a peerless resource in English, and I hope that readers will search for it. In addition, I wish to acknowledge the excellent announcers and the programmers of the radio station WQXR-FM, who continue to home-school me on the subject of classical music.

Some individuals deserve to be showcased for their help:

The dance critic Robert Greskovic made the connection for me with Oxford in the first place. He gave me anecdotes. He vetted the manuscript for historical accuracy. And, at the last minute, he lent me two key volumes. I don't know how to commend his kindness with language commensurate to its depth and wisdom.

A deep révérence to Claude Conyers, who read through the manuscript and made invaluable suggestions and who also took over the daunting task of securing permissions with a skill and good cheer that made it possible to withstand the tension of waiting. He, too, is central to this book's publication.

Barbara Palfy, considered the finest proofreader in dance publishing, took the time to look over some of the manuscript and make impeccable suggestions. She did this at an anxious moment in her own life; she gave me a precious gift of herself. Any proofreading mistakes in this text are entirely my fault.

On Janice Ross, who is the living embodiment of friendship, I bestow a blessing. Janice has believed in me for decades and acted on that belief in material ways. In the 1990s, when I started to sell my belongings, she gave me steady financial assistance. She has provided countless hours of morale by phone and E-mail. And, as if that all weren't enough, she suggested that her student, the delightful and accomplished interviewer Emily Hite, speak to several dancers, as noted in the bibliography.

Dennis Grunes, the magisterial film critic and historian in Portland, Oregon, supported me over decades in ways intellectual, emotional, and material. The section "Dancing and the Movies" is a personal tribute to what he has taught me about the cinema.

Dear Suzanne Sekey, the distinguished interior designer, for over a decade opened to me a room in her office suite in Manhattan with all its resources, along with her oceanic depths of friendship, to work on *Dance Anecdotes*. A model of kindness, understatement, high taste, and twinkling humor, she is the book's godmother. If you like any of the stories, you are in contact with her benevolent influence and aristocratic sensibility.

Suzanne picked up the baton in a relay of individuals who provided work space for this book. In a rare instance of a choreographer going to bat for a critic, Paul Taylor compassionately offered me an office for a year. And, in the early 1990s, *The New Yorker*, where I was a freelance contributor of unsigned weekly pieces with a small child at home, took pity and perched me in a series of unused offices, where I warbled for a time.

The poet and patron of poets, my longstanding friend Ansie Baird, supplied warm, unstinting emotional support, as well as several large gifts of funds for me to survive in the past few years. The poet Elizabeth Macklin provided intellectual and emotional sustenance at monthly breakfasts for almost a decade. For these poets, who helped a friend so much at such difficult moments in their own lives, I included the poems in this collection.

Mildred Goldczer, my witty and wise friend of thirty-six years who can quote half the canon of English poetry by heart, supplied several large gifts of funds. For Millie I included the excerpt from *A Jewish Dancing Master of the Renaissance*.

Gifts, loans, jobs, food, or intense if ineffable morale were generously supplied by other friends, among them Mimi Arsham, Mary and the late Tad Gesek, Jonnie and Roger Greene, Sally Hess, Christopher Howell, Charliss Jennings, Nancy Willard and Eric Lindbloom, Janet Lock, Deirdre McMahon, Diane Pien and Merle Weiss, and Dr. Bernice Schaul. The Dance Critics Association has also been a tremendous friend, and I give special thanks to all its members by naming former president Karyn Collins and current president Steve Sucato as representatives.

Leslie Getz, the dance historian and bibliophile and a ministering spirit beyond belief, arrived from the blue during the last stages of this book to help me move. She also brought delicious food, the only food I ate sometimes, and a dazzling sense of morale and purpose.

A bend of the knee and a tip of the hat are offered to Chip McGrath, who suggested an anecdote from an out-of-print book and lent me his own pristine copy to read. Chip also very kindly studied two versions of the "Note" prior to my handing in the entire manuscript, made exactly the right suggestions concerning structure, and contributed one brief sentence (the best sentence) to it. Dance is not Chip's field, nor even his interest; yet he gave me his full attention in the midst of a thousand distractions for him, and he gave me his time when he had no time to give.

Marty Cohen's devotion to the arts, encyclopedic memory, and support were fundamental to my well-being over many of the years this project occupied.

It is something of a tradition in the writing of book acknowledgments that one reserve thank-yous to one's family for the end. Although I have followed that convention, my stylistic conservatism should in no way suggest that the true first place belongs to anyone but my extraordinary father and late mother, who loved the idea of this book from the beginning and who both worked on it, with my mother setting up my files and my father plumbing such publications as *The Legal Intelligencer* for anecdotes; and to my twenty-year-old daughter, Ariel Nikiya Cohen, the family star and heroine. Dear Ones, I salute you.

—M.A.

Credits

Index